Bio-Inspired Optimization in Fog and Edge Computing Environments

A new era of complexity science is emerging, in which nature- and bio-inspired principles are being applied to provide solutions. At the same time, the complexity of systems is increasing due to models such as the Internet of Things (IoT) and fog computing. Will complexity science, applying the principles of nature, be able to tackle the challenges posed by highly complex networked systems?

Bio-Inspired Optimization in Fog and Edge Computing Environments: Principles, Algorithms, and Systems is an attempt to answer this question. It presents innovative, bio-inspired solutions for fog and edge computing and highlights the role of machine learning (ML) and informatics. Nature- or biologically-inspired techniques are successful tools to understand and analyze collective behavior. As this book demonstrates, algorithms, and mechanisms for the self-organization of complex natural systems have been used to solve optimization problems, particularly in complex systems that are adaptive, ever-evolving, and distributed in nature.

The chapters look at ways to enhance the performance of fog networks in real-world applications using nature-based optimization techniques. They discuss challenges and provide solutions to the concerns of security, privacy, and power consumption in cloud data center nodes and fog computing networks. The book also examines how:

- The existing fog and edge architecture is used to provide solutions to future challenges
- A geographical information system (GIS) can be used with fog computing to help users in urban regions access primary healthcare
- An optimization framework helps in cloud resource management
- Fog computing can improve the quality, quantity, long-term viability, and cost-effectiveness in agricultural production
- Virtualization can support fog computing, increase the resources to be allocated, and be applied to different network layers
- The combination of fog computing and IoT or cloud computing can help healthcare workers predict and analyze diseases in patients

Bio-Inspired Optimization in Fog and Edge Computing Environments

Principles, Algorithms, and Systems

Edited by
Punit Gupta, Dinesh Kumar Saini,
Pradeep Singh Rawat, and Kashif Zia

CRC Press
Taylor & Francis Group
Boca Raton London New York

CRC Press is an imprint of the
Taylor & Francis Group, an **informa** business

AN AUERBACH BOOK

First edition published 2023
by CRC Press
6000 Broken Sound Parkway NW, Suite 300, Boca Raton, FL 33487-2742

and by CRC Press
4 Park Square, Milton Park, Abingdon, Oxon, OX14 4RN

CRC Press is an imprint of Taylor & Francis Group, LLC

ISBN: 9781032262901 (hbk)
ISBN: 9781032345895 (pbk)
ISBN: 9781003322931 (ebk)

DOI: 10.1201/9781003322931

Typeset in Garamond
by Newgen Publishing UK

Contents

Preface

Bio-Inspired Optimization in Fog and Edge Computing Environments covers novel and innovative solutions for fog and edge with machine learning (ML) and informatics-based technological solutions for various applications. Recently, nature- or bio-inspired techniques have emerged as a successful tool to understand and analyze collective behavior. Algorithms and mechanisms for the self-organization of complex natural systems have been used to solve optimization problems, particularly in complex systems that are adaptive, ever-evolving, and distributed in nature. What fits more perfectly into this scenario than the rapidly developing era of fog and edge computing?

A new era of complexity science is emerging, in which the motivation for collective problem solving comes from nature- and bio-inspired principles. At the same time, the complexities of the systems are increasing. A manifestation of how demanding the nature of problems can be is evident from upcoming era of the Internet of thing (IoT) and fog computing. Will complexity science that relies on the principles of nature be able to tackle this challenge?

The chapters in this book include subjects around the enhancement of the performance of fog networks for real-world applications that use nature-based optimization techniques. The chapters deal with the challenges and provide solutions to the major concerns in cloud data center nodes and fog computing networks. In addition, security, privacy, and power consumption will be covered.

Chapter 1 covers a general introduction to the role of fog in the most critical sectors in modern smart cities. Human-friendly and intelligent systems are the need of the hour. Artificial intelligence has made inroads into every aspect of human life. Optimization plays an important role and fog computing is an emerging type of computing infrastructure that is designed to assist in the processing of computation-heavy tasks that now require a lot of bandwidth and latency.

Chapter 2 covers various open issues and challenges that have been identified and disclosed by various studies on fog architecture. This is a generation of high computing where everyone holds a smart machine in their hands and millions of devices are connected to cloud. This number will soon reach trillions. With this huge network of devices, a large number of challenges exist that are related to the handling of data, data analysis, security, and resource management.

Chapter 3 shows how existing fog and edge architectures are used to provide solutions to the future challenges for fog and edge computing. This architecture is an integrated platform that performs various applications.

Chapter 4 shows how a geographical information system (GIS) can be used with fog computing to improve the performance of existing systems. In urban regions the access to primary healthcare is an inspiring task in the policy and research fields across the world. A GIS in the medical field becomes effective when we have a better understanding public health. The purpose of using medicine in geography, public health, and informatics is to understand how user health issues have an impact on populations and trends. The device supports GIS, disease supervision, and various analytical approaches such as the dynamic continuous area space–time analysis, geographical analysis machine, cellular mechanisms, agent-based modeling, special statistics and a self-organizing map system.

Chapter 5 covers information on the role of optimization for resource optimization in fog. In this chapter, various optimization works are discussed that were used for optimization. Resource management covers the storage, computing, and network resource management requirement for resource availability of the end user across the globe. Optimization provides the optimal assignment of tasks on a virtual machine. This chapter covers a detailed study on how an optimization framework could help in cloud resource management.

Chapter 6 refers to a network of interrelated computing devices, such as sensors, which share the ability to exchange data with other communication devices over the internet. The IoT has made devices more powerful and efficient, which makes our lives easier by connecting people and objects to each other.

Chapter 7 covers the agriculture sector, which is one of the largest sectors in India for revenue. A significant increase in the IoT applications is due to an emerging concept, which is known as smart agriculture. This plays an important role in increasing various farming activities, such as crop cultivation, growing, and horticulture. Smart agriculture can be defined as a method that uses modern technology to improve yields in the quantity and quality of agricultural products. Traditional cloud-based systems with IoT models lacked the capacity to handle the traffic and overflow database. At the same time, fog computing works to improve the quality, quantity, long-term viability, and cost-effectiveness of agricultural production.

Chapter 8 covers the role of fog computing for smart traffic control. Currently, different innovative IoT services are optimized that use the implementation of fog and edge computing to reduce the computational cost and latency in the cloud environment. Real-time traffic monitoring and analysis for optimized route suggestions is still a tough task because of the mass estimation of sensor data in real-time.

Chapter 9 covers an introduction to the cloud and how virtualization supports fog in current industry standards. Virtualization is a process that abstracts physical resources and gives them the appearance of logical resources. It can be applied to many different layers, such as compute, storage, and network. Virtualizations enable the allocation of resources as if more were available; therefore, making it possible to use more resources that would otherwise not have been available.

Chapter 10 covers the importance of optimized cloud storage data analysis using an ML model. This chapter discusses handling the data that is stored inside the S3 cloud. The framework focuses on decision-making that is based on a real-time dataset with performance metrics of accuracy and resource availability using SLA (service level agreement) management. The results of the ML model ensure the real-time decision-making process that depends on accuracy level.

Chapter 11 covers performance measurement that uses the performance metrics of energy consumption and execution time. The fog network is integrated with the cloud using an internet service provider level gateway. The chapter also focuses on an optimization model that can enhance the performance metrics and efficiency of a fog computing network that uses an optimal fog computing network.

Chapter 12 covers a combination of fog computing with other methodologies, such as the IoT and cloud computing. Medical and healthcare services can now more easily predict and analyze diseases in patients. Fog computing is defined as a methodology in which wireless network components and cloud-based applications work together to produce results that are specific to the application workflow logic. Fog computing also collaborates with many IoT-based technologies in healthcare systems to track the health of people and provide medical assistance.

Chapter 13 covers a comprehensive review of the existing technologies for the implementation of an effective healthcare system. The ideas presented in this chapter try to pave the way for future work in IoT based smart healthcare.

We hope that the work published in this book will help the concerned communities of ML and healthcare.

Acknowledgments: The editors are thankful to the authors and reviewers of the chapters who contributed to this book with their scientific work and useful comments, respectively.

Editors

Dr. Punit Gupta is currently working as associate professor in the Department of Computer and Communication Engineering, Manipal University, Jaipur, India. He completed his PhD in Computer Science and Engineering at Jaypee University of Information Technology, Solan, India. He is a gold medalist in MTech from Jaypee Institute of Information Technology. He has research experience in the Internet of Things (IoT), cloud computing, and distributed algorithms and has authored more than 80 research papers in reputed journals and international conferences. He is a guest editor for the *Recent Patent in Computer Science* journal and an editorial manager of *Computer Standards & Interfaces* and the *Journal of Network and Computer Applications.*

He currently serves as a member of the Computer Society of India and the IEEE (Institute of Electrical and Electronics Engineers) and is a professional member of ACM (Association for Computing Machinery). He organized a special session on fault tolerant and reliable computing in the cloud, ICIIP (International Conference on Image and Information Processing) 2019, India. He has enthusiastically participated and acted as an organizing committee member for numerous IEEE and other conferences.

Prof. (Dr.) Dinesh Kumar Saini received his PhD (Computer Science, M.E. (Software Systems) and MSc (Technology) from one of the premier universities in India, BITS (Birla Institute of Technology and Science), Pilani, Rajasthan, India. He is a full professor in the department of Computer and Communication Engineering, School of Computing and Information Technology, Manipal University, Jaipur, India. Dr. Dinesh Kumar Saini has vast experience in academia as a professor, researcher, and administrator in Indian universities, such as BITS Pilani and abroad and a proven record of accomplishment in leadership skills in higher education and the tertiary education sector. He served as dean in the

Faculty of Computing and Information Technology, Sohar University, Sultanate of Oman. He has been an associate professor at Sohar University, Oman since 2008, and an adjunct associate and research fellow at the University of Queensland, Brisbane, Australia between 2010 and 2015. In addition, he is the founder and has been program coordinator and head of department for Business Information Technology at Sohar University, Oman for more than 10 years. He won the Emerald Literati Award in 2018 for the article, "Modeling human factors influencing herding during evacuation" that was published in the *International Journal of Pervasive Computing and Communications.* His academic credentials can be measured by different quantifiable metrics (e.g., Research Gate score 36.36, Google citation count 976, H-Index-13, and i10 Index 22). Dinesh believes in the spirit of teamwork; therefore, he has constantly augmented and consolidated research capacity building in the faculty by encouraging and supporting colleagues and junior faculty members to publish in journals and participate in conferences. This is evident in several publications that have been carried out in collaboration with his colleagues in the faculty. He has visited the US, UK, France, Germany, Austria, the United Arab Emirates, Australia, Russia, Bahrain, and the Kingdom of Saudi Arabia for academic purposes and has learned a lot of good practices from the universities of these developed countries.

Dr. Pradeep Singh Rawat joined the Department of Computer Science & Engineering as an assistant professor on January 7, 2010. He received his PhD in Computer Science & Engineering from Uttarakhand Technical University, Dehradun, India. He received his MTech in Information Security & Management from Uttarakhand Technical University, Dehradun, India and a BTech in Computer Science & Engineering from Kumaun University, Nainital, India. Pradeep's interests center on cloud computing and its applications, data communication and networking, data science applications in the cloud, and soft computing. He received the Research Excellence Award 2019–2020 at DITU (Dehradun Institute of Technology University) and was a bronze medalist in his post-graduation (MTech) from Uttarakhand Technical University, Dehradun, India. He has published four papers in SCIE (Science Citation Index Expanded) indexed journals with the highest impact factor (6.72). Dr. Pradeep Singh Rawat has more than 11 years of experience in academia. He has published and presented several research papers in various international journals and conferences of repute. He is an active member of the Universal Association of Computer and Electronics Engineers.

Dr. Kashif Zia is currently working as associate professor in the Faculty of Computing and Information technology, Sohar University, Oman. He obtained his PhD from the Institute for Pervasive Computing, Johannes Kepler University, Linz, Austria. Dr. Zia's research interests revolve around sociotechnical systems, particularly focusing on crowd dynamics and simulation. His PhD work related to large-scale agent-based modeling and analysis of sociotechnical systems that utilize parallel and distributed simulation. He has over 100 research publications, of which 21 publications were in reputed journals.

Contributors

Arnaav Anand
Computer and Communication
Engineering
Manipal University
Jaipur, Rajasthan, India

Ujjwal Bhushan
Dehradun Institute of Technology
(DIT) University
Dehradun, Uttarakhand, India

Vaishali Chourey
Department of Computer Science
Nirma University
Ahmedabad, India

Chhavi Deshlahra
Computer Science
Manipal University
Jaipur, Rajasthan, India

Amit Dua
School of Computing
DIT University
Dehradun, Uttarakhand, India

Gaurav
Computer Science and Engineering,
Manipal University, Jaipur,
Rajasthan, India

Rakesh Jain
Department of Artificial Intelligence
and Machine Learning
Indore Institute of Science and
Technology (IIST)
Indore, Madhya Pradesh, India

Deep Kumar
DIT University
Dehradun
Uttarakhand, India

Narendra Kumar
School of Computing
DIT University
Dehradun, Uttarakhand, India

Srabanti Maji
School of Computing
DIT University
Dehradun, Uttarakhand, India

Ishita Mehta
Computer Science and Engineering
Manipal University
Jaipur, Rajasthan, India

Sathish Penchala
Department of AIML
IIST Indore
Madhya Pradesh, India

Devendra Prasad
Department of Computer Science and
Engineering, School of Computing
DIT University
Dehradun, Uttarakhand, India

Dheeraj Rane
Department of CSE
IIST Indore
Madhya Pradesh, India

Neeraj Rathore
School of Computing (Computer
Science and Engineering)
DIT University
Dehradun, Uttarakhand, India

Devika Sapra
Computer and Communication
Engineering
Manipal University
Jaipur, Rajasthan, India

Akhilesh Kumar Sharma
School of Computing and Information
Technology (IT)
Manipal University
Jaipur, Rajasthan, India

Prakash Chandra Sharma
Department of IT, School of
Computing and Information
Technology (IT)
Manipal University
Jaipur, Rajasthan, India

Vijay Kumar Sharma
Department of Computer and
Communication Engineering
School of Computing and IT
Manipal University
Jaipur, Rajasthan, India

Akruti Sinha
Computer and Communication
Engineering
Manipal University
Jaipur, Rajasthan, India

Devesh Kumar Srivastava
School of Computing and IT
Manipal University
Jaipur, Rajasthan, India

Chapter 1

Introduction to Optimization in Fog Computing

Punit Gupta and Dinesh Kumar Saini

Department of Computer and Communication Engineering,
Manipal University, Jaipur, India

Contents

1.1 Introduction

In this generation of increasing sensors and remote sensing with connected devices, the need for the management of these connected devices plays an important role. Fog computing is a type of computer network architecture that provides low power, low-cost, and low-latency data access. It is decentralized and scalable, which makes it highly suitable for IoT networks. Fog computing is a new type of computing infrastructure that is designed to assist in the processing of computation-heavy tasks that require a lot of bandwidth and latency.

Fog computing allows the connection of all sensing devices and sends the data to the cloud through base stations or gateways. This allows us to collect a huge amount of data in the cloud and analyze the behavior of the system, which might be applied to systems like health care, water or electricity supply grids. The data analysis could significantly improve the systems and make intelligent decisions to achieve better performance.

According to RCR Wireless, >50 billion connected sensing devices will be interconnected by 2020 (1). This increasing number of connected devices and information comes with significant issues relating to managing data flow, storage, and data computing with analysis at the various stations or intermediate points.

This chapter aims to discuss various fog computing systems and the optimization models that are required to improve the performance of fog. This chapter tries to differentiate between the workings of edge and fog and their need in the system (Figure 1.1).

The fog model has three types of devices:

1. Endpoints, which are the smart devices that generate the data to be analyzed
2. Fog nodes, which are the nodes that process the data at the edge
3. Cloud servers, which are centralized locations that store the data

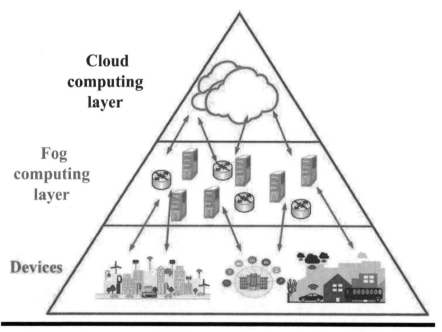

Figure 1.1 Fog computing architecture.

1.2 Fog Computing Versus Cloud Computing

Fog computing has a different type of architecture than cloud computing. Fog networks can be used to process and analyze data at the edge of networks, which makes them more suited for the Internet of Things (IoT). Cloud computing is more centralized and doesn't include edge nodes as fog does. Fog nodes are closer to the endpoints and collect network intelligence. Cloud computing sends data to the cloud as soon as it is created, while fog computing stores data at the edge of networks until it reaches a specific point in time.

1.2.1 Benefits of Fog Computing

Fog computing has a number of benefits. These include lower operational costs, increased efficiency, and better data access. The decentralized nature of the service reduces operational costs by eliminating expensive data transport and storage systems between endpoints and the cloud.

Additionally, fog nodes are low-cost and low-latency, which means they can process data on-site rather than sending it to a centralized location (and waiting for the result). This saves time and money, because it eliminates costly data transport and storage systems. Finally, because of its location at the edge of networks, fog computing provides fast access to data from remote locations with limited internet connections. Fog nodes can store some or all the data locally and provide immediate processing capabilities for those devices. Therefore, it is an excellent service for IoT networks that need to access information quickly without relying on an outside network connection.

1.2.2 Edge Computing

Edge computing is an intelligent computing device that is placed between the fog and cloud layers to reduce the load of computing in the cloud layer. This edge node acts as a base station. These nodes are responsible for various types of optimizations at their end such as optimizing the LAN, power efficiency, fault detection, and many more. This small intermediate node improves the performance of the system significantly, whereas a simple fog system is meant for data transfer from sensor to cloud with fog gateways without intermediate hurdles.

Figure 1.1 shows the roles of the edge layer and fog devices, where edge nodes are intelligent nodes that provide intermediate computing power for improved performance.

1.2.3 Fog Computing Over 5G

The evolvement of highly efficient networks like 4 and 5G, makes it easier to collect data from remote nodes like mobile devices, smart sensors, and many more. These

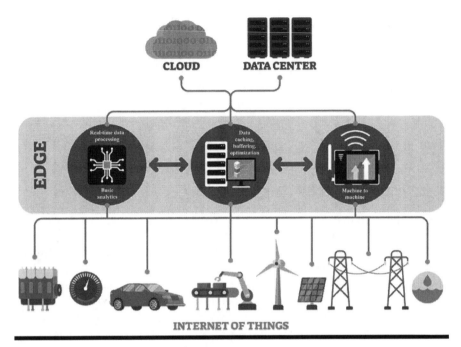

Figure 1.2   Edge computing architecture.

Source: (3)

nodes perform real time processing of the data that they receive, with a millisecond response time. These high-speed networks allow the high-speed transmission of periodical data with a high rate and accuracy to the cloud. This also provides uses for high streaming rate-based sensing devices like ECG signals, heart rate monitors, and many more. The 5G network also provides a reactive response that is possible at a high rate without delays. Systems like fog in health care are only possible due to high-speed networks, because these systems cannot bear any delay or faults in any location.

1.3 Fog Computing System and Examples of Use

Fog computing is found in various systems, some of which are listed below, from health care to smart industries in the digital world.

1. Smart health care
    IoT and cloud computing with smart services have given birth to smart health care. Fog computing allows e-health care services to compute the data in real time and make decisions (4,5).

Smart health care means that the devices or various units are a distance apart but are connected and act like a single unit, for example, a hospital has doctors, patients, a diagnostic unit, and other sensing units that sense live data that are all connected by fog. This system works to diagnose the patient and track the health of all patients in a single window.

This system deals with the optimization of network delay, which reduces the computing time in the cloud, the security of the data, and power consumption of the system when underloaded or overloaded.

2. Smart traffic management

Because of the increase in traffic globally, there is always a need for a global traffic decision management system to make it easy and consume fewer fossil fuels. These systems are meant to connect all the surveillance sensors and traffic lights to the cloud. This could allow the traffic to be routed better

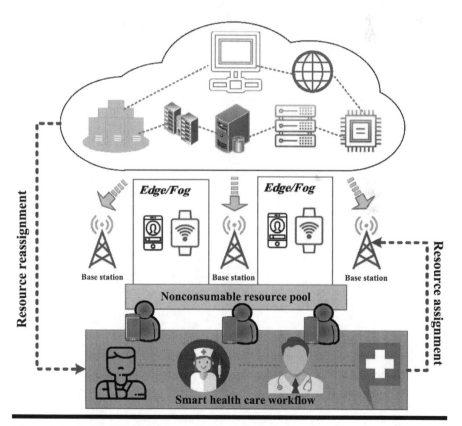

Figure 1.3   Smart health care using fog architecture.

Source: (2)

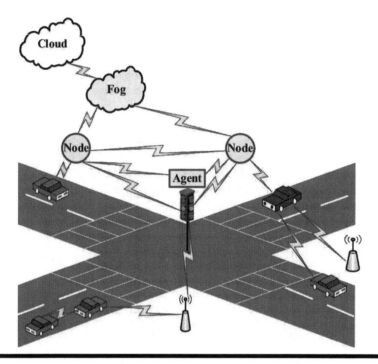

Figure 1.4   Smart traffic management model.

Source: (6)

during underloaded or overloaded conditions without letting it be known to the users automatically.

One similar intelligent traffic light system that used fog was proposed (6), which was meant to analyze and make suitable decisions to route the traffic with the least power consumption and high efficiency. Researchers (7) proposed a fog-based traffic optimization algorithm that used artificial intelligence (AI) to solve the issue under high traffic conditions.

This system optimization places an important role at the edge and cloud to optimize power consumption, and traffic congestion, and reduce network delays.

3. Smart agriculture

In this system, fog is responsible for tracking the growth of the farm and keeping track of the complete growth cycle with complete tracking of soil moisture, soil pH, weeds, and farm health from moment to moment. In such cases, optimization refers to machine learning (ML) models to keep track of multiple sensors in the field and to identify the current situation on the farm remotely. A similar system was proposed (10) to improve the yield of a specific crop that used fog and an optimization model.

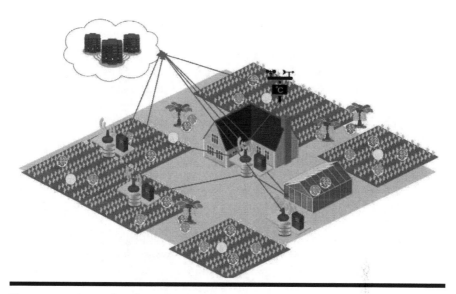

Figure 1.5 Smart farming using Fog.

Source: (10)

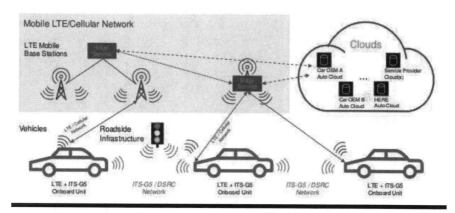

Figure 1.6 V–V communication using fog.

4. Smart vehicles

Vehicle-to-vehicle communication is the next generation in communication that uses long-term evolution (LTE) and 5G. This system allows you to communicate with nearby vehicles in case of an emergency or disaster and sends alerts about the traffic or alerts for nearby areas, speed, and distance for the safety of other vehicles. This also allows the analysis of the system centrally.

5. Smart supply chain system

   In smart cities, it is of great importance that the supply chain system fulfills the daily needs of the users. In smart cities, fog computing plays an important role to improve the performance of conventional systems by connecting all the units into a single chain. This allows each unit to keep track of the speed of the other unit to meet the requirement of the other unit. This helps the system to remain on track without deadlock and failure.

6. Smart transport and logistics

   Similar to supply chain systems, smart cities are largely dependent on smart logistics and transport systems for their needs. Intelligent transportation systems (ITSs) are emerging as an effective means of reducing traffic congestion and enhancing transportation safety. ITS is an integrated system with people, roads, and vehicles, which utilizes a variety of advanced technologies for communication, automation, and computing. An ITS uses the data collected from various sources, such as cameras, sensors, global positioning system receivers, and other vehicles, to optimize the system's performance for traffic flow, safety, delays, and fuel consumption.

   Smart transport means the delivery of the goods from source to destination. It deals with pickup to delivery of the goods using various intermediate delivery providers. Therefore, to safely deliver the goods without delays, the fog environment allows tracking of the user even if it is handled by a different service provider. This also allows you to track the safety of transport carriers, their location and other various safety measures. Figure 1.8 shows a smart transport system where all the units are connected to the cloud for smart logistic tracking and fast delivery. Figure 1.9 shows how various vehicles are connected to the system for further communication through fog and the cloud.

7. Smart water supply

   In smart cities, the water grid is one of the biggest supply grids, in which the chain of water distribution from dams to every household is managed. When this system is connected through fog and the cloud it becomes easier to manage the distribution of the supply and the detection of leaks in the system, which allows wastage of water to be reduced. But such a system with a huge, distributed network requires a lot of analysis and control to manage. In such cases, cloud systems seem to be the best system with fog to provide real-time data to the cloud servers.

   In such a large distributed system, optimization plays an important role to improve the performance of the system for efficient distribution, low power consumption, and high delivery rate.

   A smart water grid management system using clustering techniques was proposed (13). The proposed system keeps track of each unit of water delivered to the endpoint.

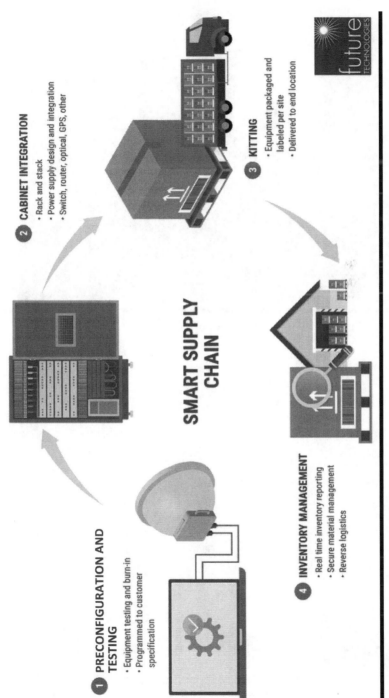

Figure 1.7 Smart supply management system.

Source: (11)

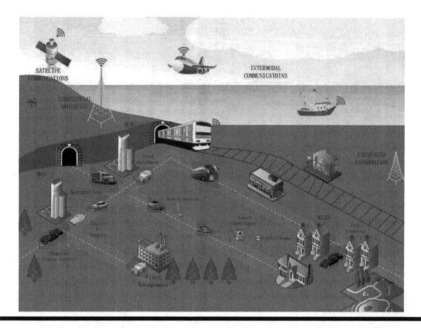

Figure 1.8 Smart city with fog for transport management.

Source: (12)

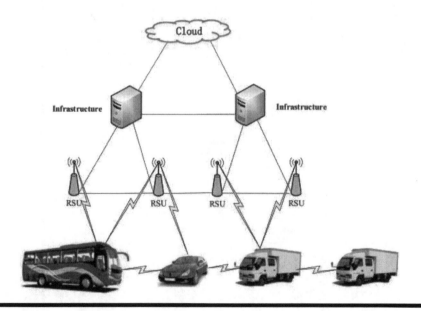

Figure 1.9 Network infrastructure of connected vehicles.

Source: (12)

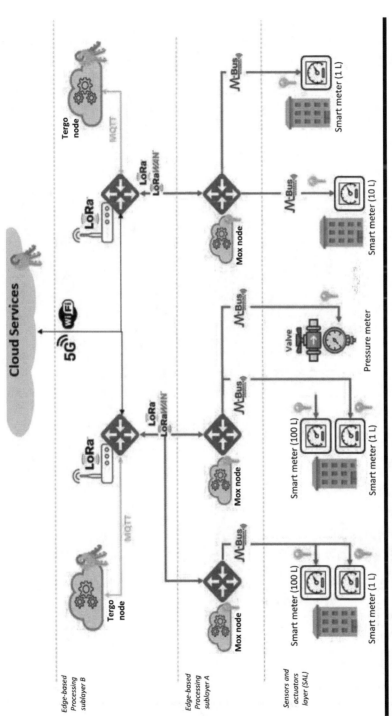

Figure 1.10 Smart water supply grid using fog.

Source: (13)

8. Smart waste management

A smart city comes with issues of a huge waste management system network with various types of component that collect the garbage; however, there are no ideas on how to manage it. In the correct scenario, it is managed with conventional methods. Fog computing has the solution to connect all the devices with the cloud and collect the live data to manage the system with high efficiency. Figure 1.11 shows one system that uses fog where all

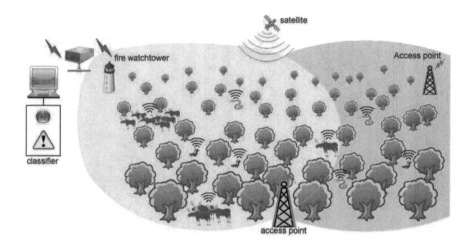

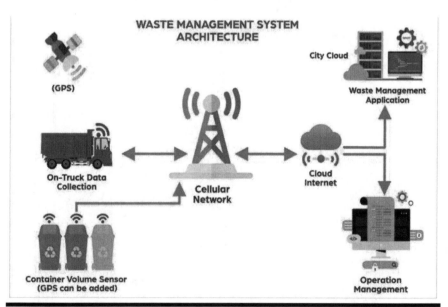

Figure 1.11 Smart waste management and its working.

the nodes or units are connected to the cloud for a live feed and management of the system.

Optimization in such a system plays an important role to provide an intelligent management system for waste management, which is based on the previous behavior of the system. Many algorithms for efficient garbage collection have been proposed by defining efficient routes to collect the garbage with the least fuel and large coverage, which allows the use of ML methods and mathematical models to find an efficient solution.

9. Smart industry for sensing

    Fog computing in Industry 4.0 has played an important role to optimize the performance of industries with high yields. Fog computing in the industry allows various independent units and their production speed to be tracked when working. So, to maintain production at high speeds, the role of sensors is very important; they track the health of the machines and the speed of each unit. Therefore, fog computing plays an important role.

    Industrial units like smart power grids for power generation are dependent on such systems to maintain the production rate in line with the demand from users. A fully automated system is the outcome of a fog computing system with real time tracking and control of the system, which has high accuracy and the lowest probability of failure in the system to achieve high throughput.

10. Smart electricity grid management

    Current grid management, from generation to the distribution of electricity is a very complex system, which requires high-end tracking at the generation and base stations. Complex grid networks are used to keep track of the complete system; however, the involvement of edge computing in the system can be managed remotely with high precision and efficiency.

    Figures 1.13 and 1.14 show how multiple power generation units are connected to the control center for the further distribution and control of power with efficient tracking.

    In such systems, optimization plays an important role. Finding an efficient mechanism to equally distribute power that is based on demand and future requirements is required. Otherwise, the system might collapse. So, intelligent algorithms are required to optimize and find an efficient solution that is based on past performance.

11. Smart forest fire

    Forest fires are a common problem throughout history. Various solutions exist, such as wireless sensor networks and many more; however, they all have various issues such as limited battery life and local network access. A network that uses fog computing allows more sensing capability, such as live streaming and an increased sensing range. This allows for better results due to cloud-based analysis and better analysis.

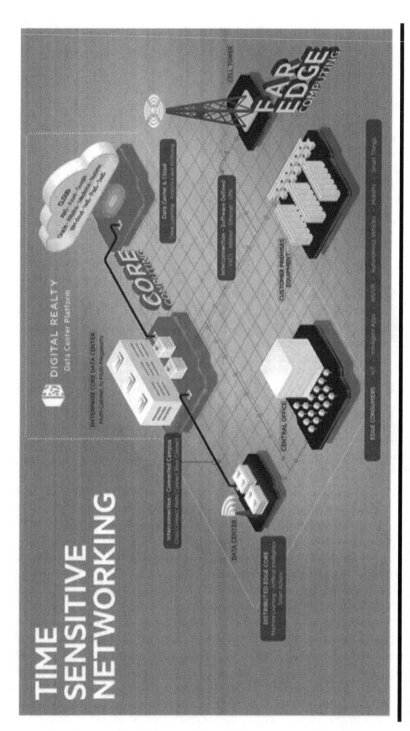

Figure 1.12 Smart industry with fog computing.

Source: (14)

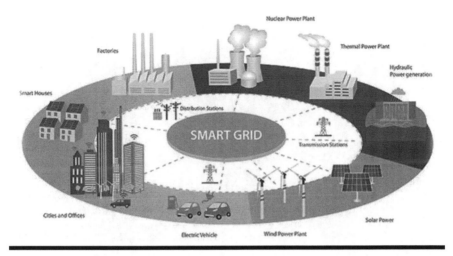

Figure 1.13 Smart electricity grid.

Source: (16)

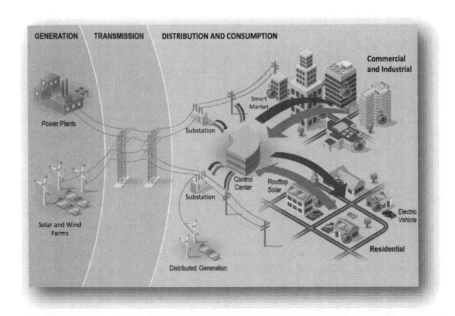

Figure 1.14 Smart electricity grid and distribution architecture.

Source: (15)

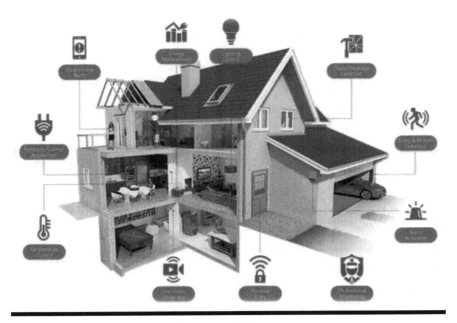

Figure 1.15   Forest fire system for smart cities.

Source: (17)

Similar work has been showcased previously (17), where a fog network was used to collect data and send it to the cloud for detection. This also allowed the detection of false alarms.

A smart fire detection system in smart cities has been proposed to predict forest fires or fires in the city area (20).

12. Smart houses or offices

This system is very popular where offices or multistory structures are connected and controlled by the cloud to improve the power consumption and ventilation systems efficiently and automatically. This system allows you to control your home, analyze daily consumption and reduce the daily energy consumption of offices and houses.

Such systems are efficient and can connect you to your home from anywhere and send alerts about the various events in the house. Some of the smart home systems are used to learn the behavior of the users and adapt to the needs of the user when required. This allows home management in a well-defined manner.

13. Smart crowd management

This is another upcoming system, which is required in upcoming smart cities where there are many hot spots of over-crowded places. In this situation, they need to track such situations in various places in the cities and

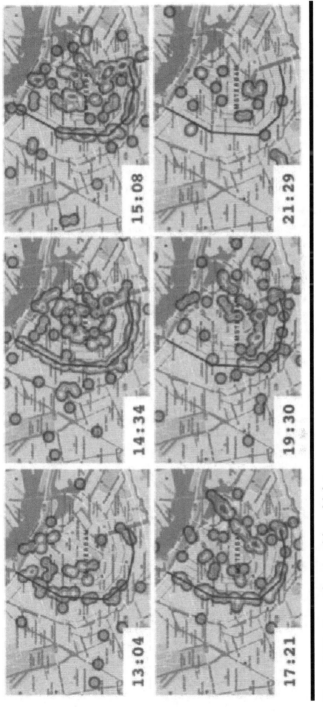

Figure 1.16 Smart house with multiple sensors.

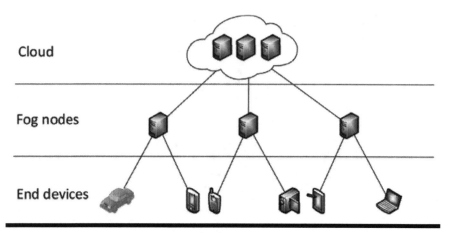

Figure 1.17   Proposed cloud detection system.

Source: (21)

need to send an alert at correct time to avoid any bad situations of an overcrowded nature. These systems are implemented using fog computing (23), which is a collection of many occupancy sensors and cameras that are connected in order to analyze the situation in the cloud.

Some of these systems are already in use in some religious locations, where it has proved to be a great success to manage crowds and easy management of crowds at the right place and time.

1.4 Optimization in Fog

In all the previously discussed systems, the most common components are the end sensor node, intermediate fog node, and cloud server. The previous systems aimed to collect the data at the end node and deliver it to the cloud server. The cloud analyzes and predicts future decisions, which is based on the current behavior of various nodes in order to improve the performance of the system.

So, to improve the performance of the system, optimization models are placed at various locations in the fog architecture. This could improve the efficiency of the system and might be defined by energy efficiency, load bearing capacity and more, which varies from system to system.

As shown in Figure 1.18, the architecture is divided into three layers: (1) edge and end node; (2) fog node: and (3) cloud layer. Each node is responsible for its independent tasks in the architecture, and end nodes sense and decide if it is possible to upload data from the fog gateways to the cloud. These sensors are smart mobile, smart cameras, or low-power systems with CPUs and network connections for data

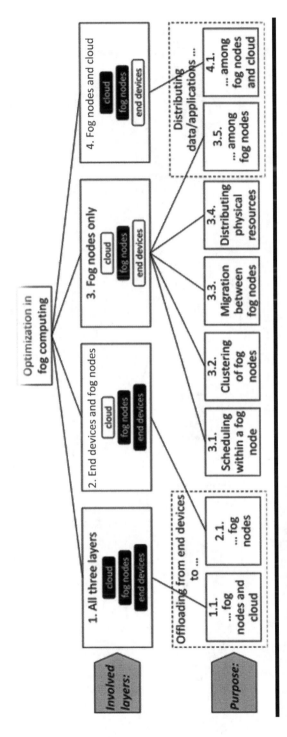

Figure 1.18 Traditional fog architecture.

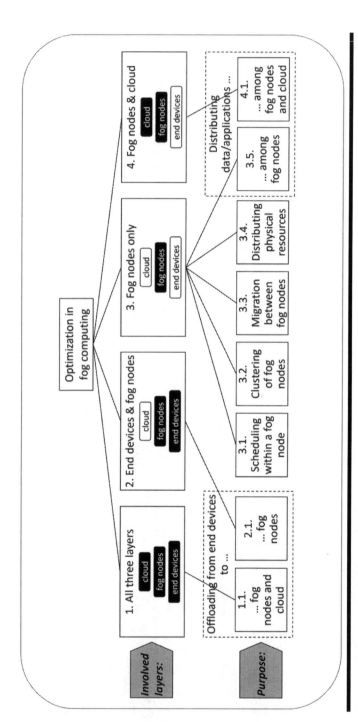

Figure 1.19 Classification of optimization problems in fog computing.

Source: (22)

Table 1.1 Classification of Optimization Type

Category	Subcategory	Decisions Resulting from optimization
Optimization involving all three architectural layers	Offloading computing tasks from end devices to fog nodes and cloud	Problem to offload computing tasks from the end devices to the fog nodes.
		Problem to further offload computing tasks from the fog nodes to the cloud.
Optimization involving end devices and fog nodes	Offloading computing tasks from end devices to fog nodes	Problem to offload computing tasks from the end devices to fog nodes.
		To which fog nodes the tasks should be offloaded.
Optimization involving fog nodes only	Scheduling within a fog node	How to prioritize incoming computing tasks within a fog node.
		How to assign tasks to computing resources within a fog node.
	Clustering of fog nodes	Issues in determining the size of a cluster of fog nodes to handle the relevant requests.
	Migration between fog nodes	Problem to migrate data or applications between fog nodes or to leave them where they are.
	Distributing physical resources (before operation)	Problem to place physical resources in the network.
		With which computing resources should fog nodes be equipped?
	Distributing applications or data between fog nodes	Which fog node should host which applications and which data?
Optimization involving fog nodes and cloud	Distributing applications or data between fog nodes and cloud	Whether to place data or applications on individual fog nodes or in the cloud.

transfer. The optimization problem can be classified into various zones (22): 1. all three layers; 2. between the fog and sensor; 3. at the fog node; or 4. between the fog and cloud. Figure 1.19 shows various types of optimization algorithms that could be designed and placed for optimization in fog such as scheduling and clustering algorithms and resource allocation.

Table 1.1 lists a glimpse of various issues and optimization models that could improve the performance of fog architecture for smart health, electricity grids, or smart vehicles. These optimization models will always be part of any such system. This gives great scope for improvements in future for researchers to identify fog computing and optimization algorithms that could be inspired by nature, metaheuristic algorithms, or mathematical models. In the current generation, data science and ML models are the leading models, which are opening new paths for improvement.

In the following chapters, the need for open issues and various aspects of issues in fog and edge computing are discussed.

1.5 Conclusions

Fog computing is a new type of computing infrastructure that has been designed to assist with the processing of computation-heavy tasks that require a lot of bandwidth and latency.

References

1. RCR Wireless.com [Internet] [cited 2022 Jan 17]. Available from: http://rcrwireless.com/20160628/opinion/reality-check-50b-iot-devices-connected-2020-beyond-hype-reality-tag10.
2. Oueida S, Kotb Y, Aloqaily M, Jararweh Y, Baker T. An edge computing based smart healthcare framework for resource management. Sensors. 2018; 18(12):4307.
3. Innovation Network.com [Internet] [cited 13 January 2022] https://innovationatwork.ieee.org/real-life-edge-computing-use-cases.
4. Aazam M, Zeadally S, Harras KA. Health fog for smart healthcare. IEEE Consum Electron Mag. 2020; 9(2):96–102.
5. Ijaz M, Li G, Wang H, El-Sherbeeny AM, Moro Awelisah Y, Lin L, et al. Intelligent Fog-enabled smart healthcare system for wearable physiological parameter detection. Electr. 2020; 9(12):2015.
6. Qin H, Zhang H. Intelligent traffic light under fog computing platform in data control of real-time traffic flow. J Supercomput. 2020; 77(5):4461–4483.
7. Dhingra S, Madda RB, Patan R, Jiao P, Barri K, Alavi AH. Internet of things-based fog and cloud computing technology for smart traffic monitoring. Internet of Things. 2021; 14:100175.

8. Gia TN, Qingqing L, Queralta JP, Zou Z, Tenhunen H, Westerlund T. Edge AI in smart farming IoT: CNNs at the edge and fog computing with LoRa. 2019 IEEE AFRICON. 2019; pp. 1–6.

9. Nandhini S, Bhrathi S, Goud DD, Krishna KP. Smart agriculture IOT with cloud computing, fog computing and edge computing. Int J Eng Adv Technol. 2019; 9(2):3578–3582.

10. Montoya-Munoz AI, Rendon OMC. An approach based on fog computing for providing reliability in IoT data collection: A case study in a Colombian coffee smart farm. Appl Sci. 2020; 10(24):8904.

11. Smart supply chain, Future Technologies [Internet] www.futuretechllc.com/smart supplychain Accessed: 22 January 2022.

12. Yang Y, Luo X, Chu X, Zhou MT. Fog-enabled intelligent transportation system. Fog-Enabled Intelligent IoT Systems. Springer: Cham, Switzerland; 2020. pp. 163–184.

13. Amaxilatis D, Chatzigiannakis I, Tselios C, Tsironis N, Niakas N Papadogeorgos S. A smart water metering deployment based on the Fog computing paradigm. Appl Sci. 2020; 10(6):1965.

14. Distributed architectures: How fog and edge computing can fit into your cloud and colo strategy, Digital Realty [Internet] www.digitalrealty.com/blog/fog-computing-and-what-it-means-for-the-cloud Accessed: 23 January 2022.

15. Can smart grid transform the Indian power sector? Ecoideaz [Internet] www.ecoid eaz.com/expert-corner/smart-grid-systems-in-india Accessed: 23 January 2022.

16. Flexibility of the smart grid, The Electricity Forum [Internet] www.electricityforum. com/electrical-training/smart-grid-flexibility Accessed: 23 January 2022.

17. Sahin YG. Animals as mobile biological sensors for forest fire detection. Sensors. 2007; 7(12):3084–3099.

18. Aakash RS, Nishanth M, Rajageethan R, Rao R, Ezhilarasie R. Data mining approach to predict forest fire using fog computing. 2018 2nd International Conference on Intelligent Computing and Control Systems; 2018; pp. 1582–1587.

19. Aakash RS et al. Data mining approach to predict forest fire using fog computing. 2018 2nd International Conference on Intelligent Computing and Control Systems; 2018.

20. Sharma A, Singh PK, Kumar Y. An integrated fire detection system using IoT and image processing technique for smart cities. Sustain Cities Soc. 2020; 61:102332.

21. Franke T, Lukowicz P, Blanke U. Smart crowds in smart cities: Real life, city scale deployments of a smartphone based participatory crowd management platform. J Internet Serv Appl. 2015; 6(1):1–19.

22. Bellendorf J, Mann ZA. Classification of optimization problems in fog computing. Future Gener Comp Sy. 2020; 107:158–176.

Chapter 2

Open Issues and Challenges in Fog and Edge

Punit Gupta and Dinesh Kumar Saini

Department of Computer and Communication Engineering,
Manipal University, Jaipur, India

Contents

2.1 Introduction

In this generation of high computing, everybody has a smart machine in their possession and millions of devices are connected to the cloud; this number will soon reach trillions. With this huge network of devices, a large number of challenges exist that are related to the handling of data, data analysis, security, and resource management. This increasing size of the network and interconnected devices gives us a great opportunity to study, analyze, and improve the performance of existing systems to give humans better lives with a better level of data reach and handling.

DOI: 10.1201/9781003322931-2

In this chapter, we will discuss various open issues and challenges that have been disclosed by various studies on fog architecture.

2.2 Issues with Fog

Fog computing architecture and applications come with various optimization, open issues and security concerns, which is due to the huge distributed connected network and scattered resources. So, the issues in fog and edge computing can be broadly categorized into security and resource optimization issues.

2.2.1 Open Issues

1. Optimization issues (1)
   a. Scheduling optimization
   b. Network optimization
   c. Resource allocation
   d. Task scheduling at edge or fog
   e. Load balancing at edge or fog
2. Security issues
   a. Intruder detection
   b. Secure data transfer

2.2.2 Optimization Issues

Optimization and useful resource control issues are commonly divided into scheduling, allocation, load balancing, and provisioning. Optimization issues in fog and edge exist due to the huge network and distributed resources that are edge nodes and cloud servers where the load can be distributed. Figure 2.1 shows the categorization of the optimization techniques in fog computing (2).

Optimization in fog is similar to optimization in the cloud where huge resources are available; however, a task needs to allocate a resource that can complete the task in the lowest simulation time, execution time, execution cost and many more. Some of the parameters for performance evaluation follow.

1. Make span
2. Network delay
3. Cost
4. Waiting time
5. Power consumption
6. Average execution time
7. Scheduling time
8. Number of tasks completed
9. Number of tasks failed
10. Task migration time

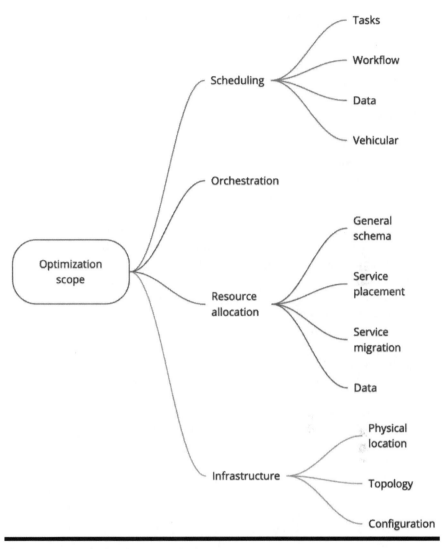

Figure 2.1 Optimization issues in fog.

11. Number of tasks migrated
12. Number of tasks meeting deadline
13. Average load over data center or host
14. Number of hot spots
15. Number of overloaded data centers or hosts
16. Average task execution time
17. Number of underloaded servers

The previous parameters are some of the optimization functions that define the performance of the model and the optimization function in an algorithm.

An optimization algorithm can be implemented in the following form.

1. Resource allocation
   a. Service migration
   b. Data allocation
   c. Service placement
2. Task scheduling
   a. Task scheduling
   b. Workflow scheduling
3. Infrastructure
   a. Network optimization
   b. Network topology design

In the previously defined categorization, data allocation and service migration are next to optimization, which only exist in fog architecture. Because in fog, there are two level processes: 1. collection of data and refining it; and 2. processing of the data in the cloud. Therefore, defining the location of resources that will collect the data and refine it is one type of optimization and the service that will process it is the second category of optimization in fog.

Similarly, some algorithms can be implemented at the fog and edge levels to reduce the load at the cloud level, where the decision can be derived at the fog level where some computation can be implemented. Resource allocation and task scheduling in the cloud can be of various types in fog as follows.

1. Static algorithms
   These algorithms are those which define working behavior at the initial stages of working, such as round robin, FCFS (first come first serve), and many modes.
2. Dynamic algorithms
   These algorithms are derived from the Mathematica model, which makes a decision that is based on the current performance of the system. These algorithms include network load, cost awareness and others listed here.
   a. Cost aware
   b. Load aware
   c. Network aware
   d. Fault aware
   e. Priority based
   f. Task size-based
   g. Based on execution time
   h. Power aware

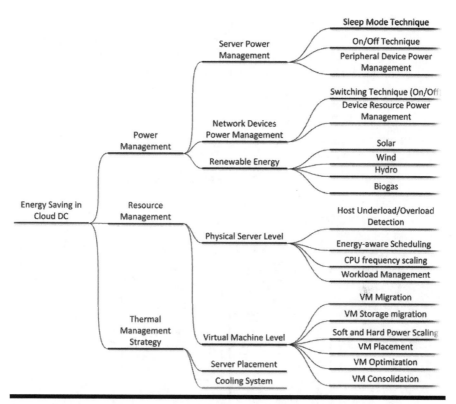

Figure 2.2 Power aware models for resource optimization.

Similarly, various works are proposed in literature based on the objective function where an algorithm can be multiobjective or single objective based algorithms, as shown in Figure 2.2.

3. Learning-based nature-inspired algorithms

These are some of the most advanced algorithms, which are derived from the behavior of nature. Figure 2.3 shows some of the nature-inspired algorithms, which are some of the best optimization models for resource optimization. These models take into consideration the objective function that is derived from the previously defined single variable or multiobjective functions to optimize the functioning of the fog environment.

These algorithms can be at the level of cloud or edge, depending upon the computation capabilities of the system, as shown in Figure 2.3. Some of the algorithms are very complex and computationally intensive algorithms, but few algorithms are best in both time and space complexity.

4. Hybrid machine learning algorithms

These algorithms are some of the best algorithms, which are derived from mathematical models. These algorithms take into consideration the previous behavior of the system to define the future functioning of the system. They include machine learning (ML) and artificial intelligence based algorithms that are derived from learning-based algorithms. These algorithms include clustering-based approaches, neural networks, random forests and many more. Figure 2.4 shows a few of the existing models and their classifications.

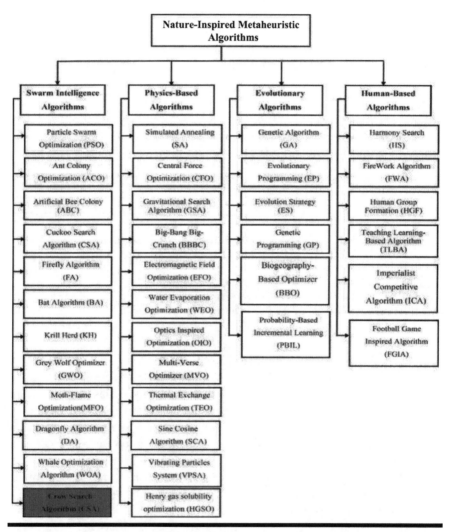

Figure 2.3 Nature-inspired optimization algorithm classification.

Source: (3)

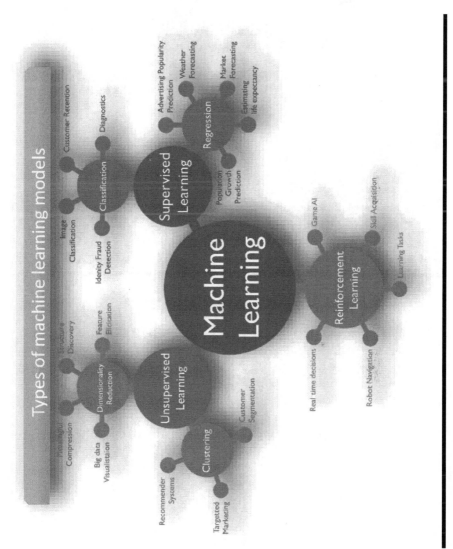

Figure 2.4 Classification of ML algorithms (4).

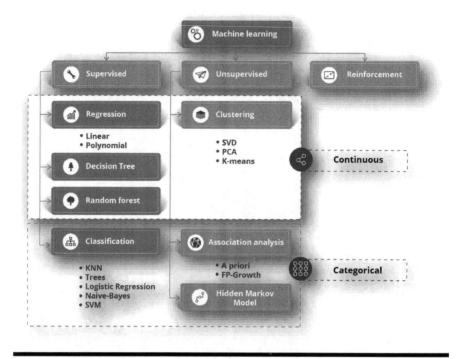

Figure 2.5   Type of ML algorithms (5).

Figure 2.5 shows a list of some of the existing ML algorithms that are used to design hybrid prediction models for the prediction of resources in task scheduling that is based on the previous behavior and work of the task scheduling and resource allocation algorithm.

5. Deep learning algorithms

   These are some of the future generation of models, which will define the future of optimization in distributed systems (2–5). These models define themselves and define their path and work (6).

   Some of the most prominent algorithms in this are.

   a. Convolutional neural networks
   b. Long short-term memory networks
   c. Recurrent neural networks
   d. Generative adversarial networks
   e. Radial basis function networks
   f. Multilayer perceptron
   g. Self-organizing maps
   h. Deep belief networks
   i. Restricted Boltzmann machines
   j. Autoencoders

Some of these models can be mapped in fog architecture in security and scheduling for the prediction of the best resources for the task, which might exist in the edge or cloud layer.

2.3 Optimization in Various Layers of Fog Architecture

So, to improve the performance of the system, optimization models are placed at various locations in fog architecture to improve the efficiency of the system, which might be defined by energy efficiency, load-bearing capacity and many more (which varies from system to system).

Figure 2.6 shows how the architecture is divided into three layers: 1. Edge or end node; 2. fog node; and 3. cloud layer. Each node is responsible for its independent task in the architecture and end nodes are defined to sense and decide if its possible to upload data to the fog gateways and the cloud. These sensors are smart mobile, smart cameras, or low-power systems with CPUs and network connections for data transfer. From the literature (5), optimization can be classified into various zones at all three layers, between fog and the sensor, at the fog node, or between fog and the cloud. Figure 2.7 shows various types of optimization algorithms that can be designed and placed for optimization in fog, such as scheduling and clustering algorithms and resource allocation.

1. All three layers
   At this point, the load balancing of the data and task can be carried out under overloaded conditions.

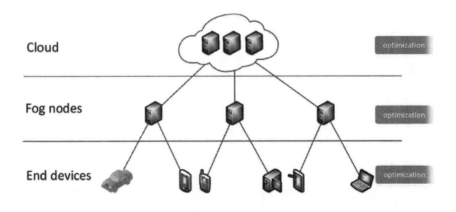

Figure 2.6   Optimization in fog architecture.

2. Cloud layer

This layer is responsible for the optimization of network and computation resources, and storage; however, the main feature is task scheduling. Load balancing clustering in fog nodes and task migration are some of the types of optimizations that can occur here.

3. Edge and fog node

At this point, the decision management and data collection at the edge layer can be carried out. This optimization is also responsible for finding faults in the sensors or faulty nodes.

4. Fog and cloud

This layer defines the placement of data that comes from fog gateways.

Figure 2.8 shows the aggregation of data from sensors that is delivered to the cloud, where the fog gateway defines the destination of the data. Here, the optimization between fog and the cloud has an important role. Figure 2.9 shows the decision-making and optimization at the edge to find the faulty node and optimize the data to reduce the network load.

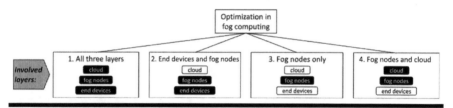

Figure 2.7   Optimization in fog.

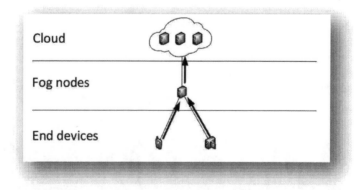

Figure 2.8   Offloading of sensor data.

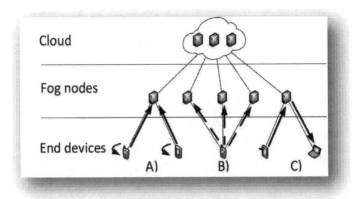

Figure 2.9 Decision-making at edge level.

2.4 Security Issues in Fog

Fog computing architecture is a large, scattered, distributed environment with billions of sensors and mobile sensors. The security of data in such a network is a great concern, which must define the privacy of data from the sensor to the cloud server. So, the security issues lie with all three nodes, for example, at the edge, fog, and cloud levels. Much work has been proposed to study this issue in this network (7–9).

Figure 2.10 shows some of the network protocols that were discussed, which define the working and security in the complete architecture. Some of the most prominent security issues in fog are listed here.

1. Authentication
2. Intrusion detection
3. Access control
4. Malicious fog node problem
5. Data protection
6. Logs-related issues
7. Secure communications in the fog
8. Denial of service attack
9. Encryption
10. Trust
11. Malicious attacks
12. Wireless security issues

Figure 2.11 shows the layered architecture of fog to demonstrate the data flow in the complete system, which allows us to understand where a security breach might occur. Most of the solutions that have been designed are based on lightweight

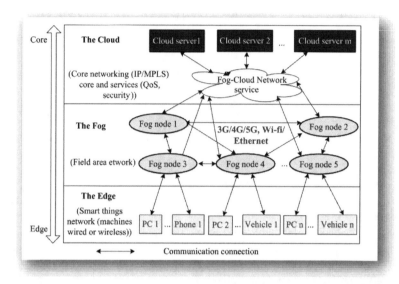

Figure 2.10 Data transfer protocol in fog.

Source: (7)

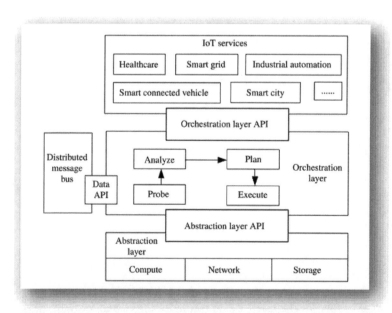

Figure 2.11 Fog layered architecture.

security protocols for edge nodes. Some other solutions are based on lightweight encryption protocols for fog which allow sensor data to be encrypted from the source (10–15).

References

1. Bellendorf J, Mann ZA. Classification of optimization problems in fog computing. Future Gener Comput Syst. 2020; 107:158–176.

2. Guerrero C, Lera I, Juiz C. Genetic-based optimization in Fog Computing: Current trends and research opportunities. arXiv preprint 2021; arXiv:2112.01958.

3. Meraihi Y, Gabis AB, Ramdane-Cherif A, Acheli D. A comprehensive survey of Crow search algorithm and its applications. Artif Intell Rev. 2021; 54(4):2669–2716. Available from: www.edureka.co/blog/machine-learning-algorithms

4. Shahzadi S, Iqbal M, Dagiuklas T, Qayyum ZU. Multi-access edge computing: open issues, challenges and future perspectives. J Cloud Comput. 2017; 6(1):1–13.

5. Lin SY, Du Y, Ko P-C, Wu TJ, Ho PT, Sivakumar V, et al. Fog computing based hybrid deep learning framework in effective inspection system for smart manufacturing. Comput Commun. 2020; 160:636–642.

6. Zhang P, Zhou M, Fortino G. Security and trust issues in Fog computing: A survey. Future Gener Comput Syst. 2018; 88:16–27.

7. Wang Y, Uehara T, Sasaki R. Fog computing: Issues and challenges in security and forensics. IEEE 39th Annual Computer Software and Applications Conference; 2015; 3:53–59. 01-05 July 2015, Taichung, Taiwan.

8. Khan S, Parkinson S, Qin Y. Fog computing security: A review of current applications and security solutions. J Cloud Comput Adv Syst Appl. 2017; 6(19).

9. Mukherjee M, Matam R, Shu L, Maglaras L, Ferrag MA, Choudhury N, et al. Security and privacy in fog computing: challenges. IEEE Access. 2017; 6:19293–19304.

10. Al Hamid HA, Rahman SMM, Hossain MS, Almogren A, Alamri A. A security model for preserving the privacy of medical big data in a healthcare cloud using a fog computing facility with pairing-based cryptography. IEEE Access. 2017; 5:22313–22328.

11. Kang J, Yu R, Huang X, Zhang Y. Privacy-preserved pseudonym scheme for fog computing supported internet of vehicles. IEEE Trans Intell Transp Syst. 2018; 19(8):2627–2637.

12. Dsouza C, Ahn GJ, Taguinod M. Policy-driven security management for fog computing: Preliminary framework and a case study. Proceedings of IEEE 15th Int Conf Info Reuse Integr. 2014; 16–23. 13–15 August 2014, Redwood City, CA, USA.

13. Shi Y, Abhilash S, Hwang K. Cloudlet mesh for securing mobile clouds from intrusion and network attacks. Proceedings of the 3rd IEEE Int Conf Mobile Cloud Comput Servic Eng. 2015; 109–118. 30 March – 05 April 2015, San Francisco, CA, USA.

14. Aazam M, Huh EN. Fog computing and smart gateway based communication for cloud of things. Proceedings of the Int Conf Future IoT Cloud. 2014; 464–470. 27–29 August 2014, Barcelona, Spain.

15. Wang Y, Uehara T, Sasaki R. Fog computing: Issues and challenges in security and forensics. Proceedings of the IEEE 39th Ann Int Comput Software Applic Conf. 2015; 53–59. 01-05 July 2015, Taichung, Taiwan.

Chapter 3

Future Challenges in Fog and Edge Computing Applications

Narendra Kumar

School of Computing, DIT University, Dehradun, Uttarakhand, India

Contents

DOI: 10.1201/9781003322931-3

3.1 Introduction

With the growing interest in the Internet of Things (IoT) development, as well as new opportunities to expand industrial IoT, breakthroughs in technology to address the issue of negotiating with all the sensor data are becoming increasingly abundant, which threatens to overwhelm the present network infrastructure and bring cloud servers to a halt. The huge number of linked devices, such as the IoT, becoming prevalent in everyday lives and surroundings could have been predicted. The IoT is predicted to attach many components and people, which provides us with several benefits. As an outcome of this development, fog computing, and edge computing examples, such as multiaccess edge computing (MEC) and cloudlet are feasible options for the huge volumes of time-sensitive and security-critical data handling that is generated by the IoT (1). The IoT is a platform that supports end-to-end communication, as well as connecting and communicating with real and virtual items. The following are some of the components of a conventional IoT platform: 1. connected objects can be classified as actuators or sensor nodes that can produce the data or operate in response to end-user or cloud-based application commands; 2. sensor nodes and actuators link to local gateways, which are used to enable local networks and communication between the cloud services and server; 3. IoT systems sensor nodes collect data from single or multiple sensors and then send it to a gateway that uses a small range protocol for wireless communication, such as Bluetooth low energy (BLE), Zigbee or Wi-Fi (2). Various methods are used for image enhancement; some methods are based on optimization techniques and computing (3–11). Using enterprise-grade apps, edge computing allows companies and other organizations to handle data more rapidly and efficiently than traditional computing methods. Edge points are utilised to generate significant amounts of data that would otherwise be discarded. Decentralised information technology (IT) architecture offered by the IoT and mobile computing can provide near real-time insights with decreased latency and cheaper cloud server bandwidth demands, all while offering an extra layer of safety for vital data. Edge computing began in the 1990s with the introduction of the first content delivery network (CDN), which placed data collecting nodes closer to end users. This technology, however, was limited to images and movies rather than massive data sets. In the early 2000s, the shift to mobile and early smart devices put extra strain on the present IT infrastructure. Without the IoT or edge devices, clouds can exist. Clouds are not required for IoT and edge computing. Edge computing and edge devices are not required for the IoT to exist. The IoT devices can connect to the cloud or edge. Some edge devices link to a cloud or private data centre, others connect to these central places only occasionally, and others never connect to anything.

Edge computing, however, seldom exists without the IoT, whether employed in manufacturing, mining, processing or transportation processes. Edge devices analyse and activate data without relying on a central location or cloud because the IoT devices (e.g., everyday physical things that collect and convey data or prescribe activities such as manipulating switches, locks, motors or robots) are the sources and destinations (12).

3.2 Related Works

It's a possible new paradigm that, in addition to the advantages and disadvantages that are acquired from cloud computing (CC), offers new opportunities and difficulties. It needs a new hybrid design to increase a network for edge services or computer resources that the end user will find easy to use. This chapter examines current studies on the design architecture, latency, security and energy usage of fog computing at the industrial level and offers a description of the recent characteristics and issues with this unique technology. A complete review of the most recent research that evaluates the architecture, latency, secure system, and power consumption of fog computing at the industrial level was undertaken to describe its challenges and characteristics. Fog computing is an autonomous sector that is dedicated to the advancement of industrial level research and applications that will help to improve and address current difficulties (13).

A basic or atomic security service can be provided by a mobile node. The coordination of numerous atomic security services at distinct nodes yields complex security services. Due to the demanding nature of the environment, the facilities and mobile nodes services at the edge lag in mobile fog situations, and service availability decreases. At the fog and edge levels, complex security requirements need the availability of many atomic services. Therefore, boosting the availability of atomic services is critical, because it improves the security between the edge and fog. A proactive, complicated replication of a security service strategy has been devised to boost fog security service availability. When replicas are requested, the protocol can manage them in advance. Given the edge level challenges of a mobile and cloud environment, such as partitioning behaviour and constant topology changing, a replication protocol that is based on a proactive push that supports many types of complicated security services is required. A proactive push-based replication protocol that enables multiple forms of complicated service of security orchestration has been developed, which considers the edge level problematic elements of a cloud environment for mobile, such as dividing behaviour and changing topology (14). With the expansion of the IoT applications, integrated CC has several risks, which include performance, security, latency, and network failure. These challenges have been solved by bringing CC closer to the IoT with the discovery of fog computing. Fog's primary task is to provide data that is generated by IoT devices at the edge. Rather than transmitting the data to a cloud server, the fog node processes and stores it locally. Compared with the cloud, fog computing provides high-quality services with rapid response times. As a result, fog computing might be a better solution that allows the IoT to provide an efficient and secure service to many IoT customers. Fog computing is a component of CC, not a substitute. It enables data processing at the edge while maintaining the ability to connect to the cloud's data centre. The various computing paradigms and components are available in the reference architecture. The features of fog computing, various fog system algorithms, and a detailed analysis of fog with the IoT are available as a middle layer between devices or the IoT sensors and cloud data centres (15). Fog computing was created as a bridge between the IoT and the cloud, which allows for the collection, aggregation and processing of data from the IoT devices. Because fog computing resources are closer to the edge, the combination of fog with the cloud might minimise communication bottlenecks and data transfers, and contribute to lower latencies. Cloud and fog computing have been discussed in-depth on several occasions (16). Fog computing employs network equipment (e.g., a router, switch or hub) to process gathered data in a latency-aware manner. Then, the most important activity in the fog computing system data security is to identify malicious edge devices. This is because they have specifically permitted privileges to process and use data, and defence against strong attacks from rogue edge devices in a fog environment is a big challenge. In a virtual environment built with Openstack and Microsoft Azure, real-world threats are utilised to test the proposed cybersecurity architecture. The proposed cybersecurity architecture has proved to be effective in detecting malicious devices and reducing the number of erroneous IDS (intrusion detection system) alerts (17). Fog computing improves efficiency, robustness and cloud infrastructure performance; therefore, addressing the limitations of the cloud system. Intriguing designs are created due to the requirement to handle some of the data created at the network's periphery by employing sharp approaches in fog–cloud ecosystems. These designs open new business prospects by allowing IoT devices to respond to customer requests. An exhaustive overview of fog–edge computing is presented in this chapter to offer a basis for solutions presented in studies that involved IoT fog–cloud ecosystems by giving insights into new research topics that cover state of the art fog computing architecture, tools, standards and applications. In a fog–cloud of things, future development patterns and the resolution of unresolved concerns are anticipated (18). The traditional CC paradigm has failed to solve issues, such as excessive latency, bandwidth and resource constraints. As a result, novel computational paradigms, such as fog and edge computing have been developed to address the former concerns at or near the device. Both paradigms provide computational and memory storage alternatives that are near to the device. Regardless of their benefits, no system is flawless. They outline the many security and privacy issues that exist in each of the three computing paradigms, as well as the solutions that have been presented. Many privacy and security issues that exist in all three computing paradigms, as well as their solutions, have been discussed (19). Mobile CC, mobile clouds, cloudlet computing, IoT CC, mobile IoT computing, fog computing, edge computing, multi-access edge computing (MEC), the Web of Things (WoT), the Wisdom WoT, the semantic WoT, opportunistic sensing, mobile crowdsensing, mobile crowdsourcing and participatory sensing are a few of the emerging computing paradigms. This study discusses IoT technologies that included pervasive and ubiquitous computing, the Internet of Underwater Things and the Internet of Nano Things (20). Novel design has been used to build and deliver a flexible framework that includes all the needed components for monitoring, managing and deploying related services while ensuring high availability and simple component distribution across the architecture. The architecture was tested as an alternative to a real-world cloud deployment in a tunnel, which demonstrated the advantages of using an edge, fog, or cloud hierarchy (21).

3.3 CC, Fog and Edge Computing

Cloud, fog and edge computing infrastructures enable businesses to tap into a large range of computational and data storage resources. Despite their similarities, these computing resources represent various levels of IT; each one builds on the preceding layer's capabilities.

CC is currently the gold standard in most sectors; therefore, most firms are familiar with it. Simply explained, CC refers to the process of storing and accessing data and applications over the internet rather than on a hard drive. To be classified as CC, you must be able to access your data or applications over the internet, or have that data synchronised with other data via the internet. CC enables businesses to dramatically expand their storage capacity without needing to add more servers on-site. Data might also be gathered from numerous sites and devices, and it can be accessed at any time and from any location. Data and intelligence are pushed to analytical platforms through fog and edge computing, which are located on or near the data source. This lowers the cost of delays and improves the user experience. There are, nevertheless, significant distinctions between both.

Fog computing (a Cisco idea) extends CC to the edge of an enterprise's network. It sends the intelligence to the LAN, where data is processed by a fog node or an IoT gateway. Simply explained, it entails bringing your computers closer to the sensors that they communicate with. Trains are a good illustration of fog computing. Trains

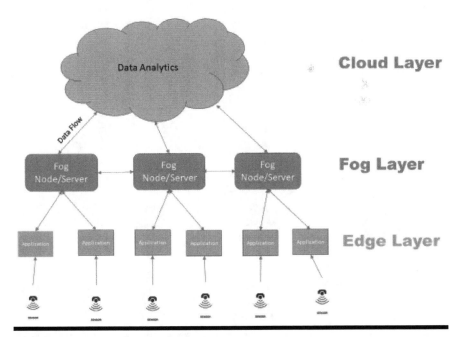

Figure 3.1   Fog computing architecture.

and tracks are being fitted with a new generation of devices and sensors as part of the advent of the Industrial IoT, with trains functioning as the primary hub for all data that is acquired from these sensors. The problem is that trains move so quickly that maintaining a connection to the cloud is challenging. This problem could be avoided by placing fog computing nodes in the locomotive. The architecture of fog computing; however, is based on many communication channels. To move data from the assets' physical world into the digital domain of information technology, fog computing's design relies on multiple links in a communication chain. Each of these connections has the potential to fail.

Edge computing is sensor data processing away from centralised nodes and near to the network's logical edge, towards individual data sources. It effectively moves computing functions to the network's edge. In other words, rather than sending a huge amount of data back to the cloud for analysis and action, this process occurs significantly closer to the data source. Edge computing triages data on the fly, which reduces the quantity of data that needs to be transmitted back to the central repository. It streamlines the fog's communication network and eliminates possible failure spots. Routers, switches and even the IoT sensors that gather the data are examples of edge devices that have significant processing capacity and capabilities (Figure 3.1).

3.3.1 Fog Computing and Related Computing Paradigms

By providing computer, networking, storage and data management on network nodes near the IoT devices, fog computing integrates the cloud and the IoT nodes. Storage, computation, decision-making, networking and data management takes place in the cloud and along the IoT to cloud path as data is sent from the transmitter to the cloud. A horizontal level system architecture with a cloud-to-object continuum

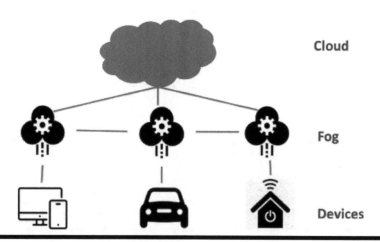

Figure 3.2   IoT data processing in fog.

primarily distributes processing, control, storage and essential networking capabilities closer to the various users. In fog computing, a horizontal platform allows computing jobs to be dispersed across sectors and platforms; however, a vertical platform supports segregated applications, according to the Open Fog Consortium. A vertical platform might be ideal for a certain sort of application. Fog computing provides a flexible platform to fulfil the data-driven needs of operators and customers, in addition to providing a horizontal architecture. Fog computing is intended to offer a solid basis for the IoT, as show in Figure 3.2.

3.3.1.1 Differences Between Fog Computing and CC

The ideas behind the fog and cloud are very similar, as show in Figure 3.3. On some parameters; however, there are some differences between fog and CC.

Table 3.1 Fog Computing Issues and Challanges

Parameter	Fog Computing	CC
Information	Data is received in real-time from IoT devices utilising any protocol in fog computing	Data from several fog nodes is received and summarised through CC
Structure	The fog is built on a decentralised architecture, with information distributed across several nodes at the user's nearest source	Because the cloud contains so many centralised data centres, it's difficult for consumers to get information from their nearest source across the network
Security	Fog is a more secure system since it uses a variety of protocols and standards, lowering the risk of it collapsing while networking	Because the cloud is based on the internet, the risk of it collapsing is considerable in the event of undetected network connections
Components	Other than the benefits offered by the cloud's components, the fog includes certain extra characteristics that improve storage and performance at the end gateways	The cloud consists of several components, including a front-end platform (i.e., a mobile device), back-end platforms (e.g., storage device and server), cloud delivery, and network (e.g., internet, intercloud, and intranet)

(continued)

Table 3.1 (Continued)

Parameter	Fog Computing	CC
Responsiveness	The system's response time is somewhat longer than that of the cloud since fogging separates the data before sending it to the cloud	When transferring data at the service gate, the cloud does not provide any data segregation, raising the load and making the system less responsive
Application	Smart city traffic management, smart building automation, visual surveillance, self-maintaining trains, wireless sensor networks, and other applications can all benefit from edge computing	E-commerce software, word processing software, online file storage, web apps, image albums, and a variety of other applications can all benefit from CC

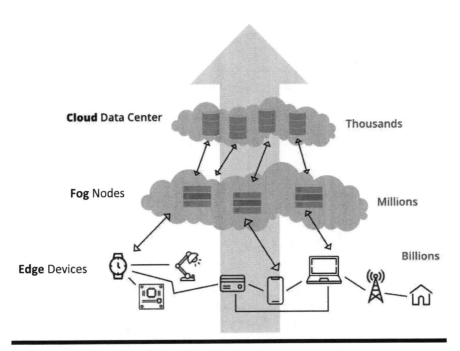

Figure 3.3 Edge and fog computing.

3.3.1.2 Differences Between Fog and Edge Computing

Table 3.2 Comparison Between Fog and Edge Computing

Number	Fog Computing	Edge Computing
1	Highly scalable when compared with edge computing	Less scalable than fog computing
2	Millions of nodes are present	Billions of nodes are present
3	Nodes in this system are installed closer to the cloud (remote database where data is stored)	Nodes are installed far away from the cloud
4	Fog computing is a subdivision of CC	Edge computing is a subdivision of fog computing
5	The bandwidth requirement is high. Data originating from edge nodes is transferred to the cloud	The bandwidth requirement is very low because data comes from the edge nodes themselves
6	Operational cost is comparatively lower	Operational cost is higher
7	The probability of data attacks is higher	High privacy. The probability of attacks on data is very low
8	Fog is an extended layer of cloud	Edge devices are the inclusion of the IoT devices or client's network
9	The fog nodes filter massive amounts of data collected from the device and this requires high power consumption	The power consumption of nodes is low
10	Fog computing helps in filtering important information from the massive amount of data collected from the device and saves it in the cloud by sending the filtered data	Edge computing helps devices to get faster results by processing the data received from the devices simultaneously

3.4 System Architecture

As shown in Figure 3.4, the fog architecture especially for the IoT applications might be categorised into three categories. The first tier (Tier 1) corresponds to the network's endpoints and consists of raw data that is supplied by data sources, such as sensors. As a result, this tier might be regarded as the one that houses the IoT device terminal nodes.

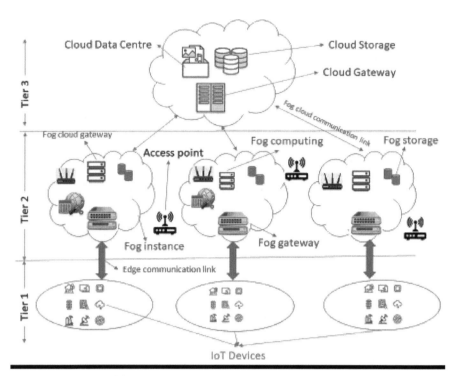

Figure 3.4   Fog architecture.

The fog computing layer, which is known as fog–edge intelligence, is the following tier (Tier 2). This category includes routers, gateways, switches and other gadgets that can process data, and compute and temporarily store the captured data. These devices in the fog are linked to a framework in the cloud and provide data to it regularly.

The CC layer (Tier 3) is related to the cloud intelligence idea and can process and store massive quantities of data; nevertheless, it is entirely dependent on the data centre's capabilities. Not every data packet is transmitted to the cloud in a fog computing system. All latency-sensitive applications and real-time analysis must run on the fog layer. Fog devices have enough computing power to operate a virtual machine. The top layer is the cloud, the middle layer is the fog, and the bottom or granular level is the terminal nodes, which contain the IoT devices and sensors.

As shown in Figure 3.5, the internet is made up of several en-route networking devices that connect the IoT devices or sensors to cloud applications. However, the gateways in the fog that link the IoT devices or sensors to the internet are the gadgets that are of most interest in fog computing architecture.

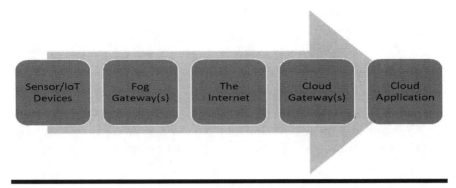

Figure 3.5   Fog architecture level.

3.5 Challenges and Solutions for Edge and Fog Computing

Fog computing is a type of CC that interacts with the IoT. The fog nodes, as they are known, can be used in any setting that has a network connection. To process needs, fog computing includes additional storage resources at the edges. As a result, the fog server must change its services, which results in increased administration and maintenance costs. In addition, the operator must deal with the following challenges.

3.5.1 Scale

Edge computing entails an increase in scale across all areas of IT, and licensing, which includes computing, storage, management, network and security. As businesses deploy applications to the network edge, they must understand the following: edge computing has an impact on everything IT touches, not just extra gear at a remote place.

3.5.2 Control and Management

The physical location of the edge can be variable, such as within a business, or a public or private cloud; however, administration and control must adhere to similar processes. Regardless of the actual location, some requirements must be met. Enterprises will, in theory, employ modern orchestration technologies to assist, manage and control applications reliably across several locations.

3.5.3 Data Accumulation

Data is a valuable organisational resource and obtaining it through the edge can provide extra challenges and hazards if it is not effectively handled. Data access and storage are critical aspects of the data lifecycle, and both require network connectivity.

3.5.4 Backup

The notion of edge computing is generally driven by the location where the data is created. Businesses require a high level of data protection. Because network backup might not be feasible; when selecting how to preserve these assets, network bandwidth constraints will be as important as storage media issues.

3.5.5 Security and Accessibility

Enterprises can be focused on technological and physical security by centralising computing and applications in a data centre, where the virtual wall around the resource forms. To mirror location and traffic patterns, edge computing requires that the network and physical security models for distant servers should be the same as those for the local servers. Edge computing might need users to have access privileges across a greater number of devices.

3.5.6 Latency

Application latency and decision-making latency are lowered by placing computing near the edge, where it is much closer to the data that is being gathered. Back and forth movement from the periphery to the centre results in faster responses and activity. With computation at the core and the edge, application data travels the network in both directions, exchanging data and dealing with access rights.

3.5.7 Distributed Computing

The edge location will need to be considered as an extra part of the computing type used by businesses. Due to increased east–west traffic, consolidated computing models are fading, and networking is a crucial computing element.

3.5.8 Network Bandwidth

As companies transfer computing and data to the edge, the network bandwidth moves. Enterprises have traditionally allocated more bandwidth to data centres and less bandwidth to endpoints. The demand for greater bandwidth throughout the network is being driven by edge computing.

Edge computing, it should be recognised, necessitates multilevel modifications in the technological structures and processes. It needs competent resources to efficiently handle the hardware and software during expansion and development. As a result, companies that are interested in using this technology must identify appropriate use examples and develop a comprehensive plan that addresses all the essential areas, such as devices, prices, security, scale, monitoring and governance. Businesses must analyse and choose between the options that are available on the market based on their specific needs. The following solution might address the various problems in edge computing.

1. Reduce the time it takes for applications and cloud services to respond. Low latency is required by increasing reliance on edge computing and IoT applications, which requires closing the data loop to assure faster connections for end users.
2. Protect sensitive information at locations other than the primary data centre. Application software integrates with systems that are used to improve monitoring and detect and mitigate power issues before they arise.
3. Reduce capital and operational costs. All the solutions interact with current hardware and software and are scalable, which allows expenses to be controlled and future expansion only planned for as needed.
4. Edge computing sites provide real-time data and notifications. Advanced data analysis identifies, prevents and corrects issues before they become more serious, which means the operator is in command and risk is reduced.

3.6 Conclusions

The ever-increasing number of networked IoT devices, as well as the strict needs of emerging IoT applications, have posed serious difficulties to CC's existing state-of-the-art design, such as data privacy and network congestion. As a result, academics have proposed a novel approach to address these issues, which involves bringing some computing resources nearer to the user. The technique used in this solution increases the efficiency of the cloud by increasing its processing capacity at the network's end; therefore, resolving its problems. As this approach was improved, various paradigms emerged, all with the same underlying objective of putting additional resources at the network's edge. Aside from their shared goal, several paradigms were affected by the use they were designed for, such as the MEC paradigm, which allows resource-constrained devices to offload sections of their programmes to conserve resources. Both paradigms, like the fog and cloud, were created to allow the processing of the IoT applications at network endpoints, and they have more in common than others. Apart from the naming convention, the distinction between the two was indicated at the start by the site where computations were conducted, for example, edge computing places the application on the edge devices and fog computing extends the cloud to form a cloud to things continuum. Because there have been enormous developments in edge computing in the last few years, the distinction between the two has vanished, with fog and edge attempting to put applications as near to the network's edge as possible.

References

1. Yousefpour A, Fung C, Nguyen T, Kadiyala K, Jalali F, Niakanlahiji A, et al. All one needs to know about fog computing and related edge computing paradigms: A complete survey. J of Syst Archit. 2019; 98: 289–330. doi: 10.1016/j.sysarc.2019.02.009.

2. Nguyen Gia T, Queralta JP, Westerlund T. 16 – Exploiting LoRa, edge, and fog computing for traffic monitoring in smart cities. Chaudhari BS, Zennaro M, eds. LPWAN Technologies for IoT and M2M Applications. Amsterdam, Netherlands: Academic Press. 2020. pp. 347–371. doi.10.1016/B978-0-12-818880-4.00017-X.

3. Shukla HS, Tripathi RP. Image restoration using modified binary particle Swarm Optimization Richardson-Lucy (MBSO-RL) algorithm. Int J Appl Eng Res. 2015; 10(22):43077–43081.

4. Kumar N, Dahiya AK, Kumar K, Tanwar S. Application of IoT in agriculture. 9th International Conference on Reliability, Infocom Technologies and Optimization (Trends and Future Directions) (ICRITO). 2021; 1–4. 03–04 September 2021, Noida, India.

5. Kumar N, Dahiya AK, Kumar K. Image restoration using a fuzzy-based median filter and modified firefly optimization algorithm. Int J Adv Sci Technol. 2020; 29(4):1471–1477.

6. Shukla HS, Kumar N, Tripathi RP. Gaussian noise filtering techniques using new median filter. Int J Adv Sci Technol. 2014; 95(12):975–8887.

7. Kumar N, Tiwari A, Dahiya AK. A dual ascent-based median filter for image restoration. Proceedings of 2nd International Conference on Advanced Computing and Software Engineering (ICACSE 2019). 2019; 2:432–435. 08–09 February 2019, Sultanpur, Uttar Pradesh, India.

8. Pandey H, Mishra AK, Kumar DN. Various aspects of sentiment analysis: A Review. Proceedings of 2nd International Conference on Advanced Computing and Software Engineering (ICACSE 2019). 2019. 08–09 February 2019, Sultanpur, Uttar Pradesh, India.

9. Kumar N, Dahiya AK, Kumar K. Modified median filter for image denoising. Int J Adv Sci and Technol. 2020; 29(4S):1495–1502.

10. Shukla HS, Kumar N, Tripathi RP. Median filter-based wavelet transforms for multilevel noise. Int J Comput Appl. 2014; 107(14):975–8887.

11. Kumar N, Shukla HS, Tripathi RP. Image restoration in noisy free images using fuzzy-based median filtering and adaptive particle swarm optimization – Richardson-Lucy algorithm. Int J Intell Eng Syst. 2017; 10(4):50–59.

12. Kumar N, Kumar K, Shah R. Role of IoT to avoid spreading of COVID-19. Int J Intell Net. 2020; 1:32-35. doi.10.1016/j.ijin.2020.05.002.

13. Caiza G, Saeteros M, Onate W, Garcia MV. Fog computing at industrial level, architecture, latency, energy, and security: A review. Heliyon. 2020; 6(4). doi.10.1016/j.heliyon.2020.e03706.

14. Hamdy M, Abbas S, Hegazy D. Enabling fog complex security services in mobile cloud environments. Alex Eng J. 2020; 60(4): 3709-3719 doi.10.1016/j.aej.2021.02.039.

15. Sabireen H, Neelanarayanan V. A review on fog computing: Architecture, fog with IoT, algorithms and research challenges. ICT Express. 2021; 7(2): 162-176. doi.10.1016/j.icte.2021.05.004.

16. Bittencourt L, Immich R, Sakellariou R, Fonseca N, Madeira E, Curado M, et al. The Internet of Things, fog and cloud continuum: Integration and challenges. Internet of Things. 2018; 3–4:134–155. doi.10.1016/j.iot.2018.09.005.

17. Sohal AS, Sandhu R, Sood SK, Chang V. A cybersecurity framework to identify malicious edge devices in fog computing and cloud-of-things environments. Computers and Security. 2018; 74:340–354. doi.10.1016/j.cose.2017.08.016.

18. Alli AA, Alam MM. The fog cloud of things: A survey on concepts, architecture, standards, tools, and applications. Internet of Things. 2020; 9. doi.10.1016/j.iot.2020.100177.

19. Parikli S, Dave D, Patel R, Doshi N. Security and privacy issues in the cloud, fog, and edge computing. Procedia Comput Sci. 2019; 160:734–739. doi.10.1016/j.procs.2019.11.018.

20. Elazhary H. IoT (Internet of Things), mobile cloud, cloudlet, mobile IoT, IoT cloud, fog, mobile edge, and edge emerging computing paradigms: Disambiguation and research directions J Netw Comput Appl. 2019; 128:105–140. doi.10.1016/j.jnca.2018.10.021.

21. Martín C, Garrido D, Llopis L, Rubio B, Díaz M. Facilitating the monitoring and management of structural health in civil infrastructures with an Edge/Fog/Cloud architecture. Comput Stan Inter. 2022; 81. doi.10.1016/j.csi.2021.103600.

Chapter 4

Geographic Information Systems-Based Modeling of Health Care Data and its Optimization Using Various Approaches

Srabanti Maji, Pradeep Singh Rawat, and Amit Dua

School of Computing, DIT University, Dehradun, Uttarakhand, India

Contents

DOI: 10.1201/9781003322931-4

4.1 Introduction

The study of earth sciences and medical research are interlinked; this combined field could be termed "On Air, Water, and Places" (1). In the future, it will be necessary to utilize mapping and geographical information to better understand the process of diseases, for their treatment along with research (2). In 1984, the physician John Snow described a milestone toward this. This research created the foundation of cartographic as well as geographic techniques as tools in medicine. Today, there have been rapid improvements in technologies that have resulted in the development of new disciplines that combine medical research and medicine (3). Currently, a variety of health care transports are being developed, and costly health care sectors have concerns about quality, access, and effectiveness. Geographic information systems (GISs) provide numerous tools to recognize the need for health care in remote locations and its improvement. In GISs, new techniques have grown rapidly, and new techniques have been utilized in health care applications. GISs can generate a variety of satellite images to provide soil types, temperature, land-related information, and to recognize the occurrence of diseases. This chapter focuses on GISs as a technology and their applications in medicine and health care. In addition, how GIS could perform as a decision maker and contribute to healthiness-related policies.

4.2 Various Material and Their Methodologies

This chapter studies the evolution of remote sensing parameters to monitor health care service environment-related information. Useful databases include HEAL-Link, PubMed, and Google Scholar (4). The Texas Medical Center (TMC), Houston, Texas, USA is where a large number of medical professionals and experts work. The TMC Library contains a large collection of GISs on health care related data. It can be a very powerful resource for displaying health data and can be utilized to create predictive models.

4.2.1 Benefits of GIS

GIS has several benefits, and can be utilized to collect a large amount of data from diverse sectors, sources, systematic collection, and data analysis tasks. It can eliminate the cost of data distribution across the organization. It provides a conjoined podium for disease surveillance. All information must be standardized using geo-referencing of epidemiological information for data management. Here structure can be transformed for another disease, by a disease data replacement process.

GIS can be utilized as a global positioning system (GPS) to identify single features in a map (4). Satellite and aerial images are utilized to obtain accurate maps of various regions. It might identify the origin an infectious diseases, like the Disney and measles outbreak in 2014. GIS mapping can be used as a public health apparatus in diseases from cancer to cholera. It could guide the restructuring of the health care system, and it is considered to support health care managers and policymakers. The analysis provides a way to expand the productivity of health care service delivery for the increasing human population (5).

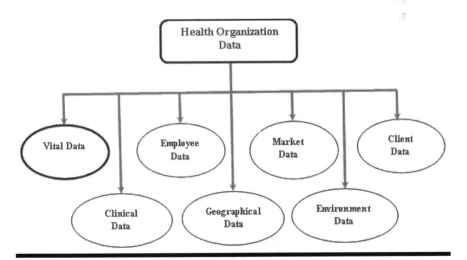

Figure 4.1   Data classification of health data.

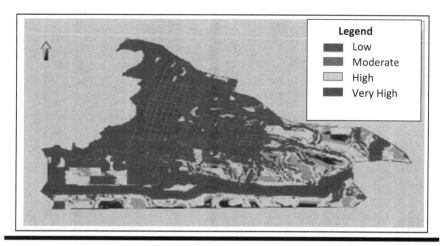

Figure 4.2 Surroundings and its health hazards.

Source: (6)

4.2.2 *Various Classification of Health Data in GIS*

In health organizations, GIS can be utilized to identify the unobserved data in spreadsheets, charts, and reports to provide accurate information faster. By integrating database operations, we can predict, plan, and recommend several strategies. The categorization of GIS data is shown in Figure 4.1.

4.2.3 *Visualization*

GIS has developed various tools for predictive modeling. It controls the variation in diseases and geographic distribution (6). To symbolize the strength of an illness, it produces thematic maps as shown in Figure 4.2. A map that is developed using GIS is a more effective resource for general users and it is easier for policymakers to understand the technique. It produces a dynamic link between the maps and databases to reflect the updated data.

4.3 Overlay and Analysis in GIS

This technique superimposes diverse facts, and executes medical research using a multicriteria technique, for example relating similarities between specific diseases with some geographic features.

4.3.1 *Buffer Zone Analysis in GIS*

GIS can construct buffer zones around certain structures. For example, a radius of approximately 12 km near a clinic to portray a catchment area, or 5 m for sewerage, or 1 km in a pollution region to specify the growth of pollutants. The worker notes the size of the buffer by combining some proofs from the disease prevalence facts to identify the number of cases inside the buffer. These analyses are utilized for mapping the impact zones in vector breeding sites.

4.3.2 GIS-Based Network Analysis

GIS supplies the facilities to access the geoanalysis dynamics of an administration's service area (7), discovers areas of hospitals and new health facilities in an accurate and timely manner for the health service locations, and maps to reach them.

4.3.3 Statistical Analysis in GIS

GIS perform various calculations on distance to observe wellbeing centers and areas that are covered by specific health-related programs, along with percentages of areas at risk (7).

4.3.4 Query in GIS

SQL (Structured Query Language) is used to define the query layer. The GIS projects within ArcMap are united with query layers to identify the necessary facts present

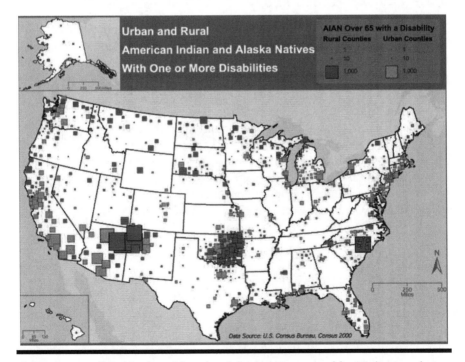

Figure 4.3   Earliest plotting of functional detriment among older Native Americans.
Source: (7)

in the graph, table, or map. For example, utilizing the GIS in the earliest plotting of functional detriment among older Native Americans is shown in Figure 4.3. It can also be used for extrapolation techniques to map unsampled areas.

4.3.5 Web-Based GIS

The latest advances in GIS are for the storage of health data in a central server, which can be accessed through the internet or intranet. Therefore, some increase in statistical and epidemiological techniques is required to maintain confidentiality when accessing data. The dynamic map facility will help patients to uncover convenient services at their doorstep.

4.4 GIS and Its Applications in Health Sciences

GIS has started uniting various applications in the health sciences, these include the analytic techniques of epidemiology, statistics, and geographic information science to bring exciting progress in the systems.

4.4.1 GIS and Epidemiology

Recognizing various infectious diseases has become increasingly global (8). GIS techniques have been utilized to improve the performance of epidemiological surveillance information management and analysis. Large public diseases can be mapped to their neighboring environment and health and social infrastructures. This function is an influential tool to monitor and manage diseases and public health as shown in Figure 4.4.

Various factors are responsible for the growth of certain illnesses, such as social, economic, and environmental conditions. If the root causes are known, health agencies can respond effectively. Software packages can help medical practitioners to visualize clinical data, which is interlinked with the human body in graphical form and the geographical location by linking unique codes to the patient (8). Such coordination is valuable when assessing environmental risks.

4.4.2 Routes to Provide Services

Providing health care facilities in patient homes can be scheduled using transportation, routes, and street patterns. For example, ArcLogistics Route software provides a dynamic solution for the existing schedule and routing processes, which is joined to the admission discharge transfer system (8).

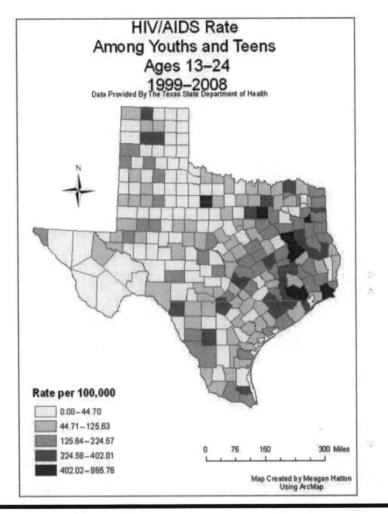

Figure 4.4   Percentage of HIV/AIDS between teenagers and youths.

Source: (8)

4.4.3 Health Systems in Hospitals

Various health care professionals can analyze the data and organize graphical presentations for reports and maps when planning and analyzing stocks. This system is based on different units including E Population Health, E Market Planning, E Research and Evaluation, Emergency Response & E Preparedness, E Location Services, and E point of Service GeoCoding.

4.4.4 Social Services

To provide better analysis of studied interactions and phenomena, GIS is utilized in social sciences as well as humanities research. In the present scenario, GIS has been increasingly utilized to have a better facility for social services via government agencies (7). It acts as the dynamic link between databases and maps. This precise social service field has various units including E Planning of Service, E GeoCoding Point of Service, E Case Management, E Tracking of Client E Service Location, and E Data Management, as shown in Figure 4.5.

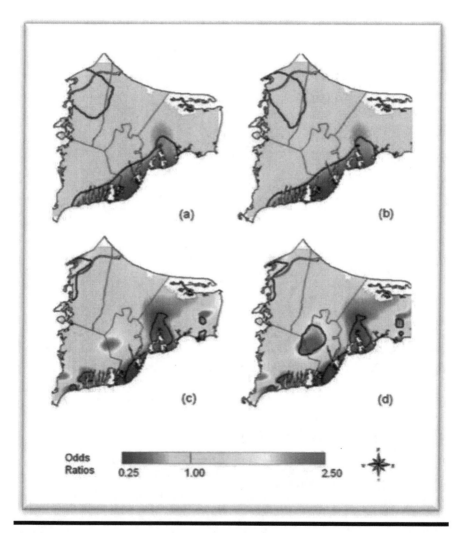

Figure 4.5 Mapping population-based case control.

Source: (9)

4.4.5 Customer Service

GIS can be used to provide accurate service location information and maps that help to provide better facilities for the customer. The dynamic maps, along with the internet, allow patients to avail themselves of convenient services from home. MapObjects is the Internet Map Server that is used to publish information regarding site and travel guidelines at the caller's location (9).

4.4.6 Site Selection

There are numerous facilities to access the geodemographic dynamics to fulfill the request for services, which needs a flexible and deep analytical system. These include Business Analyst in ArcView, GIS in ArcView, Atlas that uses GIS, and MAP PRO Business mapping software (9).

4.4.7 Managed Health Care

We pay for health care; therefore, to provide better services, health organizations are using GIS. It classifies a large number of administrative, medical, and social services for patients and clients. It is composed of E Data Management, Network Management, and Population Health, along with Disease Management.

4.4.8 Resource Management

Medical equipment supplies and location have a great impact on capability; they must be linked or distributed over a medical campus to be a powerful tool. ArcView GIS has this facility (10). It is an effective technology to build, access, incorporate, and broadcast relevant information in the geographical field.

4.5 Requirements for Health Care Services

Global populations diverge in various aspects, such as gender, culture, age, economic status, and the requirement for health care. GIS has been used in small areas. The community's environmental health profile designates the economic, lifestyle, and demographics of the population to expose possible environmental risks (7). The data collected from the calculation survey was coded and mapped to provide an improved understanding of health-related risk factors, and sensitivities in spatial variation (10,11). Various techniques have been mentioned to improve needs assessment in GIS data (12).

Recently, there has been a large increase in digitized health service data, and utilization reflects service, need and affordability, and practice patterns (14). Therefore, large rates of hospitalization for asthma and diabetes indicate the requirement for primary care (15). Cluster analysis was used for geographical service areas, where mapping and statistical analysis revealed that high rates of ACSC (ambulatory care sensitive conditions) were strongly related to poverty and social status. Current research is using analytic skills to determine data sets to produce meaningful service zones (16).

4.5.1 Analysis of Health Care Facilities

Accessibility to health care plays a vital role in nations. Some users face immense difficulties when obtaining health care-related policies. E-healthcare services define the capability to use health services at the time of need. GIS places emphasis on the geographical dimension. It depends on the type and quality of services available, distance, time, and expenditure (16). The medical conditions require systematic interaction with the facilitator for the duration of travel (17, 18).

4.5.2 Access Measurement

There are two types of geographical access measures in health care: 1. area-based measures that illustrate the towns, counties, states, rate of population requirement to services (19). This is used to geocode the dedicated sites and link populations with service data sets. Area-based measures have certain limitations (12); and 2. distance-based measures or hospital referral regions, which is the approach in which larger regions have to be covered to detect actual travel patterns. Euclidean distances are calculated along with hospital-based geriatric services with frequency distribution to form precise measures of geographical separation that combines spatial, transportation, and population-related data (20). It also calculates network distances and travel times (21, 17, 22).

There are different types of health care providers, who provide better services and can travel long distances (12, 22). These techniques analyze and explore general practitioner services (22); they should be sensitive to the geographical context and health care. Today, people are interested in health care facility services in their workspaces for personal care (23, 24). GIS models incorporate space–time activity patterns to assure health services research (25).

With the help of variations in access, policies, and research, GIS tools can explore the differences in health care access. (15). A study on the Canadian population showed that improved GIS techniques were needed to integrate transport as well as population data to scrutinize access inequities. A study showed that there were certain connections with social disadvantages and the quality and quantity of GP services (25, 26). In addition, people that live in remote locations might have some drawbacks when obtaining appointments. To overcome access to health care facilities for children and minorities there is now increased surveillance in the US (15), which can help to pinpoint vulnerable populations to help facilitate services and treatments (26).

4.5.3 Geographic Variations in Health Care

In the US, research revealed huge inconsistencies between area utilization and costs for elective and nonelective treatments and procedures (14). To manage spatial data sets and display maps, GIS always runs in the background. It was applied to geographic variation research, such as hospital service areas, and compared their rates, which had multiple limits. It can be used to inspect the sensitivity of findings, and research that is based on geographical assumptions. Multiple methods can function together with data that belongs to small geographical areas and have an influence on health care workers (27). Gradually, researchers are utilizing these multilevel modeling techniques to learn to identify the correlation between infection and health status (28). In England, this technique observed that the likelihood of acceptance always depended on infants and their family's member's characteristics.

4.5.4 Health Care Delivery and GIS

Novel GIS-based research in Missouri observed that the status of public health centers was improving (29). The gap between actual areas served with the area targeted in GIS was measured in real time (30). The technique permitted analysts to portray maps of response times using maps and graphs, shown in Figure 4.6.

Effective health care depends on structural and technological improvements in the medical field, and its changes are different in various places (31). In GIS, the impact of health factors plays a crucial role (18). The variety of services might differ based on the decisions made by the decision maker, spatial organization, and providers performance, and could help integrate spatial and model spatial databases (17, 32).

4.5.5 Health Services Locations

Medical practitioners and analysts deal with locations to choose new service resource locations, which are close to the existing facilities, and techniques to improve their services. There are models for location-allocation, optimization methods, and various other tools (33). GIS-based spatial data and location-allocation models are increasing in popularity.

The objective function is the crucial factor of a location-allocation model, which can achieve the objectives by service locations selection. They initially select simple objective functions, average distance minimization, or population coverage maximization for the countries where health services differ according to location (34). In Greece, they developed an ambulance deployment system, which has ambulances with GPS receivers, automated geocoding of the incident location, and a shortest path algorithm for ambulance route detection (27). To implement such a system, broad testing is necessary, and human decision-making plays a crucial role in deployment systems. It is used to focus on certain health facilities and has a multiobjective model for ambulance service facilities (35). It was developed to locate aeromedical

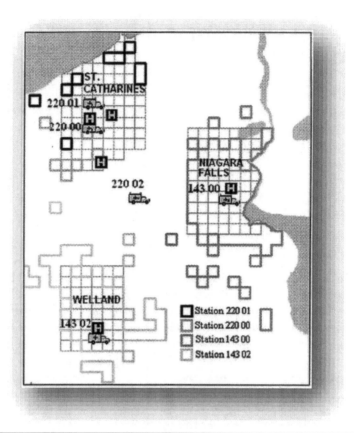

Figure 4.6 Ambulance catchment areas.

Source: (30)

depots and hospital-based trauma centers for optimizing coverage by ground and air-based ambulance facilities for trauma centers (36). In Maryland, US, the model demonstrated that the significant improvements could result in larger coverage of patients. This technique can also be utilized to fulfill health outcome criteria, for instance, the development of systems for coronary care (32, 33).

Currently, GIS is used to give precise and comprehensive representations for services in location-allocation models. Numerous investigations of EMS services integrated information for vehicle collisions were used to estimate ambulance locations along with the best localities (37). To report specific health-related complications, it can geocode the pertinent data from surveillance systems along with health reviews to identify the best location (36). It can be utilized to measure network travel times (36, 37, 38). Using various tools that are available in this field, analysts can utilize this facility to identify the best health care facility provider locations (34).

4.6 Spatial Decision Support System

Spatial decision support systems (SDSS) read spatial data, combine spatial with nonspatial characteristics, and perform visualization and analysis in GIS. It evaluates solution alternatives as well as assessments. SDSS was invented by Hopkins and Armstrong (38) and became widely popular (37) in research compendium science in 1991 (38). It is popular in decision support functions as well as spatial data (40) and plays a vital role in SDSS applications. The decision support system (DSS) is related to the domain of the decision maker (40). The latest development is the involvement of volunteered geospatial information using ad hoc crowdsourcing initiatives and using the public through Open Street Map (41).

In rural regions, there is a facility to reduce health service allocation using SDSS. A web-based graphical user interface (GUI) facility (WebGUI) has been developed. It is used to identify the best area for health care facilities, along with the number of individuals to whom services must be provided (42). SDSS has been deployed for response planning in the US–Mexico border area and for tuberculosis control in South Africa (43). Researchers select the tools and data for SDSS, then provide user input to test and change the systems (44). In another approach during development, the decision makers and stakeholders are involved (45). In the design, input was collected from the user during interviews conducted with managers and care services planners. Internet-based SDSS is utilized in health care fields, where systems have limited capabilities and they are not certified as SDSS (46). It is a web-based system, has many limitations, and provides small area coverage.

4.6.1 GIS in Homeland Security

Recently, various agencies are using support from GIS technology for security purposes. On October 8, 2001, the White House Office of Homeland Security and Executive Order was signed, which was aimed at homeland security; >50 agencies share or coordinate their information during an emergency. This map can display a variety of buildings, churches, daycare centers, malls, tunnels, airports, and highways. A specific user can be tracked to specific addresses, homes, or businesses. The managers are required to develop operational techniques to accumulate, analyze, and share area-specific information. GIS maps play a very important role in defense management and terrorist attacks (i.e., the World Trade Center) to estimate vital infrastructure systems, coordinate emergency response, and verify populations with businesses (47).

4.6.2 GIS in Indian Health Care

The Danida-assisted National Leprosy Eradication Program is the prime group that uses GIS in India to provide health care services. It plotted drug deliveries to patient locations in Madhya Pradesh and was used in TB control, HIV/AIDS, and maintaining equipment for polio. The health research in India is quite limited, however, the use of more techniques is increasing daily. The areas under the high requirement class were 46.62% and 7.55%, respectively, and 3.39% and 42.63% of the total areas came under low and moderate requirement classes in the Varanasi district of Uttar Pradesh, India. Initial information was collected from 800 respondents in 16 villages: 25.38% were happy with the available health care facilities or primary health centers (PHCs), and 60% were marginally content (48).

GIS in combination with DSS has been implemented in several areas. It has several advantages: 1. incorporates diverse approaches; 2. strengthens the precision of the result to decrease the drawbacks; 3. availability to health care facilities has been confirmed; and 4. streamlining the complex connection between various criteria. The government must find enormous spaces for isolation services to gain protection from the novel coronavirus. In India, 13,495 definite cases are known. It was presumed that Murshidabad in West Bengal, India, was more susceptible due to the deficiency in the elementary infrastructures (49).

4.7 Conclusions

The amazing perspective of GIS will provide benefits for the health care services. It could create a foundation in the society, which might be in the private and public sectors or a hybrid model approach. The advanced techniques are used to combine data integration with the spatial visualization power of GIS systems. It creates improved health mapping and analysis. In addition, health professionals have rapid access to large volumes of data. It has various dynamic analysis tools and visual techniques to manage and monitor pandemics. The possibilities are limitless. To handle this new GIS technology efficiently, health care professionals and researchers need proper training and user support. GIS technology optimizes the increase in applications of GIS systems in health care services. It also includes GIS-based modeling of health care services.

4.8 Future Directions

The GIS-based modeling of the health care system provides a unique direction to explore the health care requirements for small geographical regions for health facilities, and unique approaches to analyze and plan service locations. Many researchers consider GIS a mapping tool.

Research into health services needs spatial data based on health resources, population, utilization, treatments, and outcomes. Data that is used for these GIS applications, along with treatments, is often controlled by health insurance companies. Therefore, there might be occurrences of complications when sharing information with them.

In the public field, health-related geographical databases have been developed, which allow users to define geographical areas. It will assist GIS-based health care research and innovations. However, the human dimension in GIS is limited. It is often used for mapping; however, maps can be misrepresented. Some researchers propose that health planners might have reduced knowledge of spatial concepts and spatial analytic techniques. Users will be able to collect health care information easily at diverse locations and for types of health problems. With the rapid progress in the health care system combined with the new direction in ambulatory services, telemedicine is fundamentally modifying health care delivery systems with the association between spatial organizations. These new spatial behaviors in GIS could be a high priority for upcoming research.

References

1. Jankowski P. Spatial decision support systems. In Kemp KK ed., Encyclopedia of Geographic Information Science. Thousand Oaks, CA, USA: SAGE Publications. 2008; pp. 407–409.
2. McLeod KS. Our sense of snow: the myth of John Snow in medical geography. Soc Sci Med. 2000; 50(7–8):923–935.
3. Fortney J, Rost K, Zhang M, Warren J. The impact of geographic accessibility on the intensity and quality of depression treatment. Medical Care. 1999; 37(9):884–893.
4. Salehi F, Ahmadian L. The application of geographic information systems (GIS) in identifying the priority areas for maternal care and services. BMC Health Ser Res. 2017; 17(1):482.
5. Musa GJ, Chiang P-H, Sylk T, Bavley R, Keating W, Lakew B, et al. Use of GIS mapping as a public health tool – from cholera to cancer. Health Serv Insights. 2013; 6:111–116.
6. Calovi M, Seghieri C. Using a GIS to support the spatial reorganization of outpatient care services delivery in Italy. BMC Health Serv Res. 2018; 18(1):883.
7. Bell N, Schuurman N, Hayes MV. Using GIS-based methods of multicriteria analysis to construct socio-economic deprivation indices. Int J Health Geogr. 2007; 6(1):17.
8. Ezatti M, Utzinger J, Cairncross S, Cohen AJ, Singer BH. Environmental risks in the developing world: Exposure indicators for evaluating interventions, programs and policies. J Epidemiol Community Health. 2005; 59(1):15–22.
9. Kamadjeu R, Tolentino H. Web-based public health GIS for resources-constrained environment using scalable vector graphics technology: a proof of concept applied to the expanded program on immunization data. Int J Health Geogr. 2006; 5(1):24.

10. Peters J, Hall GB. Assessment of ambulance response performance using a geographic information system. Soc Sci Med. 1999; 49(11):1551–1556.

11. Phillips R, Kinman E, Schnitzer P, Lindblom E, Ewigman B. Using geographic information systems to understand health care access. Arch Fam Med. 2000; 9:971–978.

12. Gibson A, Asthana S, Brigham P, Moon G, Dicker J. Geographies of need and the new NHS: methodological issues in the definition and measurement of the health needs of local populations. Health Place. 2002; 8:47–60.

13. Cromley E, McLafferty S. GIS and Public Health (Second Edition). New York, NY, USA: Guilford Press, 2011.

14. Wennberg JE, Fisher E, Skinner J. Geography and the debate over Medicare reform. Health Affairs. 2002; 21:10–22.

15. Ricketts T, Randolph R, Howard H, Pathman D, Carey T. Hospitalization rates as indicators of access to primary care. Health Place. 2001; 7(1):27–38.

16. Goodman DC, Mick SS, Bott D, Stukel T, Chang CH, Marth N, et al. Primary care service areas: a new tool for the evaluation of primary care services. Health Ser Res. 2003; 38(1):287–309.

17. Fortney J, Rost K, Zhang M, Warren J. The impact of geographic accessibility on the intensity and quality of depression treatment. Med Care. 1999; 37(9):884–893.

18. Haynes R, Gale S, Mugford M, Davies P. Cataract surgery in a community hospital outreach clinic: Patient costs and satisfaction. Soc Sci Med. 2001; 53(12):1631–1640.

19. Susi L, Mascarenhas AK. Using a geographical information system to map the distribution of dentists in Ohio. J Am Den Assoc. 2002; 133(5):636–642.

20. Perry B, Gesler W. Physical access to primary health care in Andean Bolivia. Soc Sci Med. 2000; 50(9):1177–1188.

21. Lovett A, Haynes R, Bentham G, Gale S, Brainard J, Suennenberg G. Improving health needs assessment using patient register information in a GIS. In: Gatrell A, Loytonen M, editors. GIS and Health. London, UK: Taylor & Francis, 1998; pp.191–204.

22. Goodman D, Wennberg J. Maps and health: the challenges of interpretation J Public Health Manag Pract. 1999; 5(4):xii–xvii.

23. Nathens AB, Jurkovich GJ, Maier RV, Grossman DC, MacKenzie EJ, Moore M, et al. Relationship between trauma center volume and outcomes J Am Med Assoc (JAMA). 2001; 285(9):1164–1171.

24. Nemet GF, Bailey AJ. Distance and health care utilization among the rural elderly. Soc Sci Med. 2000; 50(9):1197–1208.

25. Miller HJ, Wu YH. GIS software for measuring space-time accessibility in transportation planning and analysis. GeoInformatica. 2000; 4:141–159.

26. Hyndman JCG, Holman CDJ. Accessibility and spatial distribution of general practice services in an Australian city by levels of social disadvantage. Soc Sci Med. 2001; 53(12):1599–1609.

27. Rushton G. Spatial decision support systems. International Encyclopedia of Social Science. 2001; 14785–14788.

28. Subramanian SV, Kawachi I, Kennedy BP. Does the state you live in make a difference? Multilevel analysis of self-rated health in the US. Soc Sci Med. 2001; 53(1):9–19.

29. Phillips R, Kinman E, Schnitzer P, Lindblom E, Ewigman B. Using geographic information systems to understand health care access. Arch Fam Med. 2000; 9(10):971–978.

30. Peters G, Hall GB. Assessment of ambulance response performance using a geographic information system. Soc Sci Med. 1999; 49(11):1551–1566.

31. Kronick R, Goodman D, Wennberg J, Wagner E. The marketplace in health care reform: The demographic limitations of managed competition. New Engl J Med. 1993; 328(2):148–152.

32. Nathens AB, Jurkovich GJ, Maier RV, Grossman DC, MacKenzie EJ, Moore, M, et al. Relationship between trauma center volume and outcomes. JAMA. 2001; 285(9):1164–1171.

33. Cromley EK, McLafferty SL. GIS and Public Health, 2nd edition. New York, USA: Guilford Press; 2002.

34. Møller-Jensen L, Kofie RY. Exploiting available data sources: location/allocation modeling for health service planning in rural Ghana. Danish J Geog. 2001; 101(1):145–153.

35. Harewood S. Emergency ambulance deployment in Barbados: A multi-objective approach J Oper Res Soc. 2002; 53(2):185–192.

36. Branas CC, MacKenzie EJ, Revelle CS. A trauma resource allocation model for ambulances and hospitals. Health Serv Res. 2000; 35(2):489–507.

37. Cromley E, Wei X. Locating facilities for EMS response to motor vehicle collisions. Proceedings of Health GIS Conf. 2001; 06 November 2001, Washington DC, USA.

38. Hopkins LD, Armstrong MP. Analytic and cartographic data storage: a two tiered approach to spatial decision support systems. Proceedings of 7th International Symposium on Computer-assisted Cartography; American Congress on Surveying and Mapping. 1985; Washington DC, USA.

39. Maguire DJ, Goodchild MF, Rhind DW. Geographical Information Systems: Principles, Techniques, Management and Applications, 2nd edition, Abridged edition. New York, USA: Wiley, 1999.

40. Sugumaran R, Degroote J. Spatial decision support systems: principles and practices. Int J Geogr Inf Sci. 2011; 25:1–2.

41. Haklay M. How good is volunteered geographical information? A comparative study of OpenStreetMap and Ordnance Survey datasets. Environ Plan B: Plann Des. 2010; 37(4):682–703.

42. Schuurman N, Randall E, Berube M. A spatial decision support tool for estimating population catchments to aid rural and remote health service allocation planning. Health Inform J. 2011; 17(4):277–293.

43. Tanser F, Wilkinson D. Spatial implications of the tuberculosis DOTS strategy in rural South Africa: A novel application of geographical information system and global positioning system technologies. Trop Med Int Health. 1999; 4(10):634–638.

44. Gorr W, Johnson M, Roehrig S. Spatial decision support systems for home delivered services. J Geograph Syst. 2001; 3(2):181–197.

45. Foley R. Assessing the applicability of GIS in a health and social care setting: planning services for informal carers in East Sussex, England. Soc Sci Med. 2002; 55(1):79–96.

46. Goodman DC, Mick SS, Bott D, Stukel T, Chang CH, Marth N, et al. Primary care service areas: a new tool for the evaluation of primary care services. Health Serv Res. 2003; 38(1):287–309.

47. Kataoka M. GIS for Homeland Security. Redlands, CA, USA: ESRI Press, White Paper, 2007.

48. Rai PK, Nathawat MS. GIS in healthcare planning: A Case study of Varanasi, India. Forum Geografic. 2013; 12(2).

49. Parvin F, Ali SA, Hashmi S, Khatoon A. Accessibility and site suitability for healthcare services using GIS-based hybrid decision-making approach: a study in Murshidabad, India. Spat Inf Res. 2021; 29(1):1–18.

Chapter 5

Application of Optimization Techniques in Cloud Resource Management

Pradeep Singh Rawat

School of Computing, DIT University, Dehradun, Uttarakhand, India

Punit Gupta

Department of Computer Science and Engineering, Manipal University, Jaipur, India

Contents

DOI: 10.1201/9781003322931-5

5.1 Introduction

Computing, communication, and storage resources play important roles in a technology evolution paradigm. The technology evolution paradigm includes a service-oriented computing paradigm, for instance, a cloud computing paradigm (1, 2). Resource management is the primary focus of the user class across the globe. The cloud provides unlimited storage for data management anywhere at any time (1). The resources can be useful in various applications. Health and education departments and any businesses require a service-oriented computing paradigm for smooth functioning of the system with minimum management and operational costs of the resources (3). The storage, computing, and network resources can be accessed using service level agreements (SLAs) with the service providers. The quality of service from the resources at the infrastructure and platform levels can be improved using a wide application of optimization techniques. The resource provides the users with service delivery models. The service delivery models include Infrastructure as a Service (IaaS), Software as a Service (SaaS), Platform as a Service (PaaS), and Data as a Service (DaaS). The resource management policy can be implemented at the level of the host node and virtual machine (VM) level. The policy implementation depends on the performance focus of the users, which includes developers, end users, and business people. Hence, resource management is one of the challenging concerns across the globe in a distributed environment (4). The optimization techniques assure the quality of service that uses time, cost, and reliable resource allocation. It can be analyzed using effective provisioning and management (5). In this chapter, the primary focus is a detailed study of the optimization techniques and the application of optimization techniques in resource management. The results section will cover performance evaluation and analysis using an optimization approach. Section 5.2 covers the related works on cloud resource management that use optimization techniques.

Section 5.3 covers the motivation of the work, Section 5.4 covers optimization techniques, Section 5.5 covers the optimization techniques in cloud resource management, Section 5.6 covers the analysis and evaluation of the performance, and Section 5.7 covers the conclusions, which includes a subsection on future directions.

5.2 Related Works

The optimization techniques have wide applications in the service-oriented computing paradigm. Cloud computing provides unlimited resources at the infrastructure level, platform and application, and storage. Researchers have focused on static, dynamic, and metaheuristic approaches for resource management in the service-oriented computing paradigm. Researchers have presented the taxonomy for the profiling of SaaS and focused on tools (6). The focus of the profiling includes effective resource management. Research (7) is focused on the management of hardware resources with a primary focus on consolidation, discovery, monitoring, and allocation of the resources with a high level of reliability. In addition, some work is focused on a thorough review of the resource management methodologies. The novel approach was presented with an in-depth review of the existing work (8). A focused resource management approach that was based on processed data collection was the focus of the cloud environment (9). It also presented recommendations and issues in cloud computing scenarios. A cost and time aware resource management for SaaS was presented (10). In addition, (11) presented an intelligent resource management technique for cloud resource management that used a reinforcement deep learning mechanism. Guzek et al. (12) encompassed a detailed survey on cloud resource management and a key aspect of cloud computing in industry that reshaped and had environmental impact solutions. Chaudhrani et al. (13) presented a particle swarm optimization (PSO)-based VM placement that used performance metric energy consumption. It supported operational cost management, which mandates data center life management with robustness and green computing environment support. Rawat et al. (14) presented an astronomy-based optimization technique that contributed to resource management in a scalable cloud computing environment. The big bang big crunch cost-aware technique performed better than the existing static and dynamic approaches. Rawat et al. (15) proposed a power-efficient neural bioinspired approach. It also focused on VM placement to the end user requests that were mapped from different geographical regions. Performance metrics include power saving and time. Rawat et al. (16) presented an efficient resource management technique that was based on a hybrid model, for instance a genetic approach and a human brain-inspired model. The hybrid model follows the learning methodology for the training of the model and test results are obtained using a varying number of cloud resources at the level of infrastructure and platform. Rawat et al. (16) focused on performance evaluation and the analysis of virtual cloud resources using cost and time aware bioinspired techniques, which are used for the validation of the presented astronomy-based model. Therefore, researchers have focused on detailed review and management policies with resource availability. The service-oriented computing technology creates environmental pollution and power consumption challenges. Computing, communication, and technology are key aspects during the COVID-19 pandemic; however, we need to consider the environment with integrated environmental support. The detailed review will be helpful for the advances in new hybrid computing techniques for better resource utilization accessibility.

5.3 Motivations for the Work

Organizations need to provide resources to their employees to perform their work on time. The resources can be provided to the end users as an in-house computing resource or higher resources on a rental basis. Resource hiring is the choice of every individual. The motivation comes when providing the resources to the users with no in-house operational costs. The in-house operational costs can be minimized using data center resources across the globe in a scalable manner, which uses a pay-as-you-go-based pricing model. The objective is to provide the facilities to the end users with a major focus on innovations. The innovations in computing, communication, and technical aspects support people with a conducive platform and network facilities. Researchers still need to focus on data center architecture that will support minimum power consumption and maximum resource utilization. The objective of resource availability with minimum downtime can be achieved using resource optimization techniques in cloud computing. The motivations also come with unlimited data storage and processing power in cloud computing, which provides better resource management in the aggregated computing environment. The traditional computing paradigm provides limited storage, bandwidth, and computing resources. The cloud computing paradigm provides the solution to this resource limitation problem.

5.4 Optimization Techniques

Cloud computing provides SaaS, PaaS, and IaaS to the end-user in an on-demand fashion. Resource availability is primarily required to provide quality service to the end users. The service availability and objective of cloud resources can be improved using static dynamic and metaheuristic techniques. The optimization can be achieved using soft computing nature-inspired techniques. It includes ant colony optimization (17), PSO (18), Elephant Herd Optimization (EHO) (19), Pigeon-Inspired Optimization (PIO) (20), BAT (21), and WOA (Whale Optimization Algorithm) (22). The primary focus is the optimal assignment of cloud resources in a cloud environment. Qiu and Duan focused on PIO techniques for multiobjective problem-solving. This technique can also be used for cloud resource management (23). The efficient fitness function estimation was based on this technique, which might be helpful in a cloud computing virtual resource management and resource optimization (24). The optimization computing paradigm provides better results when integrating with the neural network classifier and machine learning-based models. The neural-optimization model provides better outcomes in complex problems for data management and resource allocation.

5.4.1 Classifications of Resource Management Techniques in Cloud Computing

1. Resource identification
   First, the service providers take responsibility for identifying the requests that come from various time zones across the globe. The data center broker takes responsibility for graphing the requests and forwarding them to the data center node.

2. Resource gathering
   This is performed by listing out the idle resources for on-demand allocation. The gathered resources can be allocated to the identified requests in Step 1.

3. Resource brokering
   This process ensures the accessibility of cloud resources for the consumers according to the pricing model, for example, subscription-based or pay-as-you-go model.

4. Resource discovery
   This covers the resource discovery for optimal assignment. The resource discovery provides a piece of useful information about the host and VM nodes. Resource discovery includes the identity of the VM and host machines for effective mapping.

5. Resource selection
   This process selects the optimal fit resource for mapping the cloud computing consumer requests. The cloud computing consumer puts the demand according to the requirements and uses a standard pricing plan.

6. Resource mapping
   This process performs the one-to-one, many-to-one, and many-to-many mapping of user requests on VMs using the appropriate assignment and mapping management. The resource mapping management depends on the configuration parameters of resources and their availability for user requirements.

7. Resource allocation
   The principal objective is to fulfill cloud consumer needs and income generation of the user requests for cloud computing service providers. The allocation process depends on the optimization technique and resource provisioning scheme of tasks on a VM in a scalable cloud computing environment. The process of efficient resource management is shown in Figure 5.1.

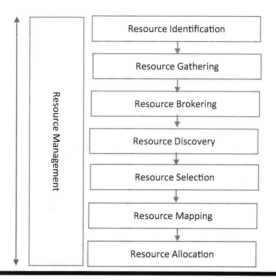

Figure 5.1 Taxonomy of cloud resource management process in cloud environment.

All phases of the taxonomy support the optimal allocation of the VMs. The real cloud scenario and simulated cloud scenario support the accessibility of the resources in a scalable manner. The seven layers cover the service delivery model and cloud computing deployment model in a scalable fashion. The VM allocation and utilization can be improved using VM consolidation, which supports the minimization of power consumption and maximization of security level. The resource management policy ensures the quality of service with minimum operational costs. The process shown in Figure 5.1 is the resource assignment at the initial level. Apart from the initial level, optimization of resources is required periodically. The periodic manner of resource optimization includes the following:

1. Provisioning of virtualized resources globally
   Data centers are located across the globe in different geographical regions. The provisioning techniques are required for the management of the VM on an appropriate host machine that uses scalable simulation and real cloud deployment. The provisioning technique balances the user requests on available VMs and tasks using scalability and reliability.
2. Cloud resource assignment
   The service-oriented computing paradigm provides services to a different class of users via this utility-based computing paradigm. The productivity of the cloud resources is improved using on-demand assignment with zero downtime in the data center node.

3. Estimation of resource utilization

   Resource utilization is also a primary concern for service providers. The utilization percentage depends on the input load that comes from the cloud computing consumers. The cloud computing consumer puts the demand for resources in a multitenant environment. A multitenant environment includes the node that has physical and virtual resources powerful allocation, and assignment of the data center IaaS, PaaS, and SaaS services.

4. Virtualized resources scheduling locally

   The maximization of resource utilization and minimization of faults at the host level and the VM is the primary concern of the cloud service provider and cloud computing consumer. The load is shared equally between the nodes using scalability and reliability.

5. SaaS level scaling and provisioning SaaS node

   The scaling provisioning of the cloud SaaS modeler depends on the availability of the user's access and data center node management that has a high level of node reliability.

6. Dynamic provisioning charges

   The end users need to pay per use of the resources across the globe. The dynamic provisioning depends on the dynamic allocation policy for which

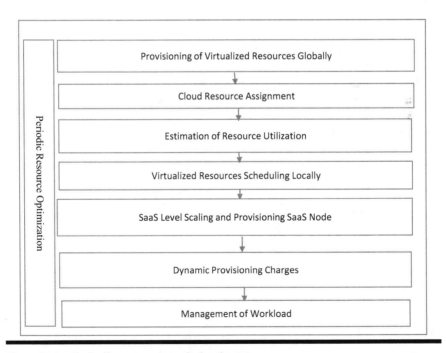

Figure 5.2 Periodic resource optimization process.

the primary focus includes the implementation of optimization techniques for provisioning and processing.

7. Management of workload

The input workload is shared among the nodes, for instance, the part of workload management in a cloud computing environment. Proper resource utilization is performed using various approaches (25). The flow of the periodic manner of resource optimization is shown in Figure 5.2. The periodic resource optimization plays an important role in cloud resource optimization using scalable simulation and modeling processes.

5.5 Resource Management Using Optimization Techniques

The service-oriented computing paradigm provides the infrastructure and platform to the end users in an on-demand fashion. The resource requirement increases exponentially. Users cannot manage the resources with manual and static approaches. The optimization techniques place the foundations of resource management with the proper utilization of computing, communication, and network resources across the globe. The optimization techniques place the foundations for the efficient utilization of cloud resources using the optimization criteria of time and the cost of the storage, computing, and network resources.

The following architecture has been proposed for resource management and the availability of resources.

Figure 5.3 shows the cloud resource management system that includes a data center, service model, and techniques for optimal resource management using scalability and reliability. The primary focus is the optimizer for the resource allocation using the service-oriented computing paradigm. The cloud resource management components are implemented using an integrated environment CloudSim 4.0 and NetBeans IDE 8.0.1 (26). The resource configuration parameters are initialized

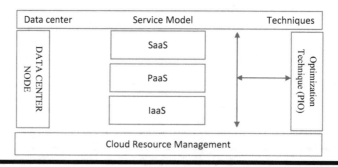

Figure 5.3   Cloud resource management system.

and tested using various optimization techniques and metrics (e.g., fitness value of virtual resources at platform level and average execution time at the level of application or user requests execution). The data center utilization can be improved using an optimization technique with availability and reliability. The application of cloud resources can be used with various computing paradigms. The cloud resources include storage, computing, and network resources that can be assigned to the developers, end users, and business class users according to their requirements. The cloud resource management layer shown in Figure 5.3 provides on-demand access to the resources that use the optimization layer, which is implemented at the data center broker level. The data center broker node takes responsibility for allocating an appropriate VM to requesting users. The broker layer provides the interface to report the information on the status of all the nodes that work in a cloud environment.

5.5.1 Resource Management Techniques Taxonomy Using Performance Metrics

The resource management techniques based on optimization methods can be broadly classified into the following categories.

5.5.1.1 Energy Aware Resource Management

The energy aware optimization techniques use the objective function based on power consumption measured in kWh. The power consumption relies on the host and network communication nodes.

5.5.1.2 SLA-based Resource Management

The SLA aware resource management technique depends on the availability of the cloud resources and the availability depends on the downtime and uptime parameters as shown in the following equation. The optimization is performed using performance metrics SLA violations level.

$$\% \text{ Availablity} = \left(1 - \text{Down Time}\middle/\text{Up Time}\right) \times 100 \tag{5.1}$$

where:
% availability = status of SLA level (violated/ not violated).

In real-time applications, for instance in a banking automation system, the service providers ensure that there should not be any violation of the SLA. If there is any outage time in the cloud resources then the service providers carry out legal compliance with the cloud computing consumer. In a multitenant environment, cloud service providers and consumers need to follow the SLA management policy for better utilization of the resources at the infrastructure and platform levels. In a multitenant environment, the resource management policy can be evaluated for VM migration and consolidation. The host level resource management is challenging in static management techniques using Min–Min, Max–Min, and suffrage techniques. The nature-inspired optimization approach provides the optimal solution with minimum cost and time.

5.5.1.3 Fitness Value Aware Resource Management

The fitness value aware resource management technique uses optimization with a fitness function, which depends on the computing power of the VM and MI (machine instruction) length of the user requests. Hence, in this chapter, the focus was on the execution time and fitness function aware optimization techniques.

5.5.1.4 Time Aware Resource Management

Time aware resource management includes the optimization method that is based on the execution time of the user requests on a VM, which uses the most efficient VM with minimum execution time and maximum utilization of VM that uses the processing element MIPS (millions of instruction per second) rating.

5.5.2 Network Parameters Aware Resource Management

This includes an optimization of the bandwidth and latency using an optimization method with a high quality of service, which uses a high bandwidth utilization with a low latency period. Network usage improvement is also a primary concern to enhance performance. The usages in megabytes provide resource utilization and performance enhancement.

5.5.3 Integration of Cloud Deployment Model With Service Model Using Optimization Mechanism

Figure 5.4 shows the integrated cloud model that includes the deployment model and service model. The resource management is performed using the appropriate availability and optimization techniques. There are three layers: 1. Layer 1 which corresponds to the deployment model; 2. Layer 2 which corresponds to the service model; and 3. Layer 3 which corresponds to the SLA management and optimization. The model is simulated and implemented using real cloud and virtual cloud scenarios. The complete layered architecture of the service-oriented computing paradigm is embedded inside the CloudSim 4.0 tool. It supports the modeling and simulation of the presented architecture using a scalable simulation.

5.5.3.1 Layer 1: Deployment Model

Cloud computing consumers have a degree of freedom to select the deployment model of their choice. The choice of the deployment model depends on the requirement of the services. Figure 5.4 contains a short description. The deployment model includes public, private, hybrid, and community cloud environments with high resource availability. The public cloud resource management is the responsibility of the service providers only. All the services, for instance XaaS, are available for all the users anywhere at any time without any interruptions and delays.

5.5.3.2 Layer 2: Service Model

All the resources in a cloud computing environment are provided as a service. The most important service model includes SaaS, PaaS, and IaaS. The resource management policy is implemented inside the previously mentioned service layers. The order of the layers includes IaaS, PaaS, and SaaS respectively. The position of the Layer 2 service model is shown in Figure 5.4.

5.5.3.3 Layer 3: SLA Management Policy Implementation

This includes the complete information on the resource availability at the host and VM levels. The SLA is violated or does not decide the resource demand and outage

Figure 5.4 Integration of cloud deployment model with service model using optimization.

time of the resources from the user end. Service providers have some legal compliance with the consumer for the system with high availability and reliability.

5.5.3.4 Cloud Computing Model for Resource Management

The outer layer shows the cloud computing model for resource management, which includes all the sublayers. It helps the user to provide the resources on-demand with an optimization management policy. The policy implementation of the cloud resource provides node management with evaluation and analysis that use Base-PSO, BA, ABC, EHO, WOA, and MSA approaches. The service-oriented computing paradigm extension with the fog computing paradigm provides a new avenue for data analysis and the onsite computing and storage process. A cloud only system has various pros and cons in different areas. The aggregated computing paradigm is the solution to the future of computing and real-time application management. Real-time application management, specifically in health care and real-time natural disaster management, places the demand on aggregated computing systems. The cloud computing paradigm with fog computing and Internet of Things-based computing provides the solution for future generations of computing.

5.5.3.5 Implementation Procedure of Resource Management Policy Using Simulation Process

The resource management policy implementation follows a procedure that uses an integrated environment with CloudSim 4.0 and Java supported IDE (Eclipse/NetBeans IDE 8.0.1).

1. Initialization of cloud entities
2. Define the VM configuration parameters
3. Define user requests parameters
4. Define host configuration parameters
5. Implement the resource management policy at the data center broker level
6. Start the simulation process
7. Stop the simulation process and print the simulation results for the performance metrics
8. Decide to switch to a real cloud environment

5.6 Performance Evaluation and Analysis

This section covers the quality of service and analysis of scenarios that use cloud resource management systems implemented as shown in Figure 5.5. The quality of service for optimal resource management techniques included Base-PSO, BA, ABC, EHO, WOA, and MSA. The fitness values of the virtual resources are evaluated using 10 different scenarios. The 10 different scenarios include variations in population size

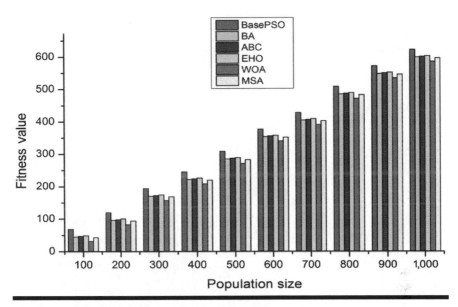

Figure 5.5   Population size versus fitness value.

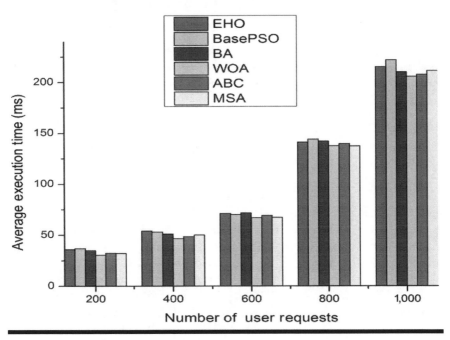

Figure 5.6   Number of user requests versus average execution (ms).

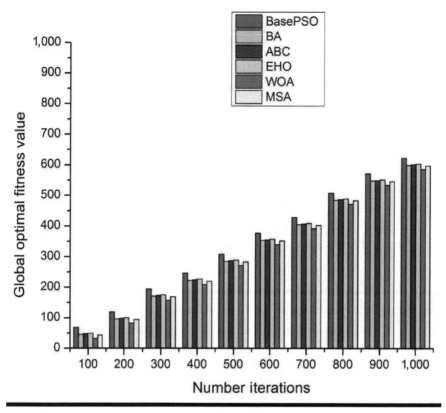

Figure 5.7   Iterations versus global optimal fitness value.

(e.g., solution space or search space size). The whale optimizer provides an optimal solution in 10 different scenarios including the size of the search space (e.g., 100–1,000). The optimizer shown in the results section provides scalable computing, communication, and storage resources. The optimizers are implemented inside the data center broker. The data center broker acts as the mediator between the cloud service provider and cloud computing consumers.

Figure 5.6 shows the quality of the service parameter [i.e., average execution time (ms)]. The average execution time varies with user requests modeled as the SaaS delivery model. The average execution time varies between 29 and 215 ms.

Figure 5.7 shows the performance metric global fitness function values, which vary with several iterations (100–1000) with steps of 100. The six nature-inspired optimization techniques were compared with WOA and provided an optimal solution in all 10 scenarios. The optimizers EHO, Base-PSO, BA, WOA, ABC, and MSA are used for resource management in cloud computing scalable scenarios and compared against the global fitness values of the schedules of the user requests on VMs using dynamic provisioning and scalable infrastructure.

The optimizers EHO, Base-PSO, BA, WOA, ABC, and MSA are used for resource management in cloud computing scalable scenarios. The optimizer has wide applications in the service-oriented computing paradigm, including resource scheduling at the host and VM levels. In this chapter, the focus was to test the performance of the resource optimizer in the cloud infrastructure, platform and networks, and application management. The results were compared and explained using six techniques. Apart from these six techniques, a hybrid approach that includes intelligent computing and optimization techniques with fitness function parameters based on the data center and VM configuration parameters could be used.

5.7 Conclusions

The optimization techniques were used to evaluate the performance of cloud resources across the globe. The computing and communication resource availability and management were enhanced using six optimizer methods, the optimizer techniques. The results section showed that the whale optimization outperformed the existing nature-inspired metaheuristic optimizer. This chapter's primary focus covered the implementation of optimizers inside the resource management system. The performance was evaluated using fitness value and average execution time (ms). This chapter covered the performance metrics aware resource management and periodic resource optimization techniques. The performance evaluation and analysis section covered the performance metrics fitness values of VMs and the execution time for the variations in population size, the number of iterations and the number of user requests mapped on VMs. In all the scenarios the whale optimization algorithm outperformed the other optimization techniques. Therefore, the optimizers were evaluated and analyzed in a virtual cloud environment.

5.7.1 Future Directions

In the future, the presented approaches will be implemented in real cloud scenarios that use real cloud IaaS, the PaaS service models. The optimizer will be tested in a four deployment model, for example, public, private, community, and hybrid cloud computing scenarios. Apart from the average execution time and fitness values of the cloud resources (VMs) other performance metrics, for example SLAs and security and privacy concerns, will be covered in simulated and real cloud scenarios. In the future, the simulated optimization techniques for cloud resource management will be implemented using the real cloud scenario of Amazon's Elastic Compute Cloud services, the Microsoft Azure platform that will provide infinite resources of IaaS (infrastructure as a service) and PaaS (platform as a service) levels. The performance of the nature-inspired optimization technique will be tested using similar configuration parameters. The cloud resource management system shown in Figure 5.1 will be embedded inside the real cloud environment and extended into the cloud computing paradigm, for instance, fog computing with onsite computing power. In the future, the energy, network, and SLA aware resource optimization techniques will be implemented to provide a high quality of service and resource availability with minimum outage time. Aggregated computing will be the optimal choice for real-time applications that use a sensor node at the data source. Cloud computing unlimited storage will be used for pan tilt zoom captured data or information analysis that uses a cloud or Edwards computing system, which includes a cloud layer at the root level and a fog layer at the leaf and internal levels.

References

1. Sangeetha KS, Prakash P. Big data and cloud: A survey. Adv Int Syst Comput. 2015; 325:773–778.
2. Shiva Jegan RD, Vasudevan SK, Abarna K, Prakash P, Srivathsan S, Gangothri V. Cloud computing: A technical gawk. Int J Appl Eng Res. 2014; 9(14):2539–2554.
3. Vignesh V, Sendhil Kumar KS, Jaisankar N. Resource management and scheduling in cloud environment. Int J Sci Res Pub. 2013; 3(6):1–6.
4. Mishra M, Das C, Kulkarni P, Sahoo A. Dynamic resource management using virtual machine migrations. IEEE Comms. 2012: 50(9):34–40.
5. Lin W, Wang JZ, Liang C, Qi D. A threshold based dynamic resource allocation scheme for cloud computing. Procedia Engineering. 2011: 695–703, 1877–7058. doi:10.1016/j.proeng.2011.11.2568
6. Weingartner R, Brascher GB, Westphall CB. Cloud resource management: A survey on forecasting and profiling models. J Netw Comput Appl. 2015; 47:99–106.
7. Nzanywayingoma F, Yang Y. Efficient resource management techniques in cloud computing environment: A review and discussion. Int J Comput Appl. 2019; 41(3):165–182.
8. Mustafa S, Nazir B, Hayat A, Madani SA. Resource management in cloud computing: Taxonomy, prospects, and challenges. Comput Electr Eng. 2015; 47:86–203.
9. Aslam S, ul Islam S, Khan A, Ahmed M, Akhundzada A, Khan MK. Information collection centric techniques for cloud resource management: Taxonomy, analysis, and challenges. J Netw Comput App. 2017; 100:80–94.
10. Coutinho RDC, Drummond LM, Frota Y. Optimization of a cloud resource management problem from a consumer perspective. European Conference on Parallel Processing. Berlin, Germany: Springer; 2013; pp. 218–227.
11. Zhang Y, Yao J, Guan H. Intelligent cloud resource management with deep reinforcement learning. IEEE Cloud Comput. 2017; 4(6):60–69.
12. Guzek M, Bouvry P, Talbi EG. A survey of evolutionary computation for resource management of processing in cloud computing. IEEE Comput Intell. 2015; 10(2):53–67.
13. Chaudhrani V, Acharya P, Chudasama V. Energy aware computing resource allocation using PSO in cloud. Information and Communication Technology for Intelligent Systems. Singapore: Springer; 2019; pp. 511–519.
14. Rawat PS, Dimri P, Kanrar S, Saroha GP. Optimize task allocation in cloud environment based on big-bang big-crunch. Wirel Pers Commun. 2020; 115(2):1711–1754.

15. Rawat PS, Gupta P, Dimri P, Saroha GP. Power efficient resource provisioning for cloud infrastructure using bio-inspired artificial neural network model. Sustain Comput: Infor Syst. 2020; 28:100431.

16. Rawat PS, Dimri P, Gupta P, Saroha GP. Resource provisioning in scalable cloud using bio-inspired artificial neural network model. Appl Soft Comput. 2021; 99: 106876.

17. Senthil Kumar AM, Venkatesan M. Multi-objective task scheduling using hybrid genetic-ant colony optimization algorithm in cloud environment. Wirel Pers Commun. 2019; 107(4):1835–1848. doi.10.1007/s11277-019-06360-8.

18. Masdari M, Salehi F, Jalali M, Bidaki M. A survey of PSO-based scheduling algorithms in cloud computing. J Netw Syst Manag. 2017; 25(1):122–158.

19. Almufti S, Asaad R, Salim B. Review on elephant herding optimization algorithm performance in solving optimization problems. Int J Eng Tech. 2018; 7:6109–6114.

20. Cui Z, et al. A pigeon-inspired optimization algorithm for many-objective optimization problems. Sci China Info Sci. 2019; 62(7):1–3.

21. Yang XS. A new metaheuristic bat-inspired algorithm. Stud Comput Intell. 2010; 284:65–74.

22. Mirjalili S, Lewis A. The whale optimization algorithm. Adv Eng Software. 2016; 95:51–67.

23. Qiu HX, Duan HB. Multi-objective pigeon-inspired optimization for brushless direct current motor parameter design. Sci China Technol Sci. 2015; 58:1915–1923.

24. Lin Q, Liu S, Zhu Q, Tang C, Song R, Chen J, et al. Particle swarm optimization with a balanceable fitness estimation for many-objective optimization problems. IEEE Trans Evol Comput. 2018; 22:32–46.

25. Boukerche A, Cheng X, Linus J. A performance evaluation of a novel energy-aware data-centric routing algorithmic wireless sensory networks. Wirel Netw. 2005; 11(5):619–636.

26. Calheiros RN, Ranjan R, Beloglazov A, De Rose CA, Buyya R. CloudSim: A toolkit for modeling and simulation of cloud computing environments and evaluation of resource provisioning algorithms. Software Pract Exp. 2011; 41(1):23–50.

Chapter 6

Use of Fog Computing in Health Care

Ishita Mehta
Computer Science and Engineering, Manipal University, Jaipur, Rajasthan, India

Arnaav Anand
Computer and Communication Engineering, Manipal University, Jaipur, Rajasthan, India

Contents

DOI: 10.1201/9781003322931-6

6.1 Introduction

The Internet of Things (IoT) refers to a network of interrelated computing devices, such as sensors, that share the ability to exchange data with other communication devices over the internet (1). The IoT has made devices more powerful and efficient, which makes our lives easier by connecting people and objects to one another.

The IoT has numerous implementations in various fields, such as smart cities, automation, traffic management, and medical and health care services. These are the most significant areas for IoT growth. Because health is an important issue for humans, reducing treatment costs when maintaining high-quality patient care is an important area of concern. With the increase in life expectancy, real-time results and error-free investigations have become a necessity, and thus, our medical and health care services need to prosper in an innovative environment to retain prominence in this industry.

Various technological trends, such as artificial intelligence (AI) for systematic data analytics and NLP (natural language processing) for voice-enabled devices have contributed to the escalation of the health care industry over the years. The evolution of the IoT in health care has improved the quality of life by tracking users' everyday lives like sleep cycles, eating habits, and exercise routines in a cost-effective manner (2). Extensive information is analysed and processed by these IoT devices and sensors. Big data and machine learning (ML) can be applied to sensory data to gain insights into the effectiveness of treatments, identify patients at risk, and personalise care.

Since many patients need to be monitored, the sensors must be small and convenient so that they can be worn without any obstruction. In addition, these devices need to store large volumes of data due to memory and battery limitations. Their infrastructures require high maintenance and are expensive, and therefore, need a common infrastructure to forward their data to more comprehensive applications.

Cloud computing can help in overcoming these obstacles by offering an unlimited storage capacity and ample processing capabilities. Cloud computing could free the sensors from battery-draining tasks and serve as a platform for aggregating different sensors. Patient information is tracked and analysed in a much more effective manner through cloud services because it offers a major reduction in medical expenses along with a healthy patient environment.

However, the basic sensor-to-cloud architecture is not feasible in many health care applications, because cloud-based systems fail to fulfil real-time requirements due to intermittent delays, high bandwidth requirements, and security issues.

Moreover, relying entirely on remote data sensors is unacceptable as network issues or data centre failures can result in inappropriate results, which puts patient safety at risk.

To address these challenges, an extension of cloud computing (fog computing) has been developed. Rather than continuously transmitting data from sensor to cloud, fog computing carries out a variety of tasks close to the customers that include network administration, storage, and processing. Hence, it is a magnificent, virtualised register that provides numerous advantages between the end user and gadgets.

Fog computing incorporates the following:

1. Context awareness
   Devices and hubs on the earth possess information about nature.
2. Remote access organising
   Highly suitable for remote detecting devices that require time-to-time examination.
3. Heterogeneity
   As the fog hubs are portrayed in dispersed scenarios and contain differing structure factors.
4. Better help for versatility
   Given a more direct correlation between fog applications and the cell phones.
5. Backing for a wide assortment of mechanical applications
   Through continuous investigation.

Examples of some popular creations based on fog computing are Google Glass, Microsoft HoloLens, and Sony Smart Eyeglass. Fog computing offers improved capacities for processing large amounts of information, which can conduct information acquisition, preprocessing, empowering gathering, transport of information, and alter registering power along these lines. Numerous benefits of fog computing are derived from the IoT.

6.2 Evolution of the Industry to Healthcare 4.0

The medical industry has grown over hundreds of years and has been through various revolutions to reach the current state where most tasks are automated, and the use of technology is as important as having a doctor in a hospital. All of this has been possible because of the various industrial revolutions that occurred, which led to manifold changes in the equipment, design aspects, production, and personalisation (3–7). Four major changes that paved the way for modern-day Healthcare 4.0 are:

1. Industry 1.0

   The invention of the steam engine by James Watt and the consequent development of the railways as a mode of transport gave birth to this first revolution in the industrial sector. This was the revolution that led to the development of mechanical systems and devices that extracted power from water and steam sources to work properly.

2. Industry 2.0

   This revolution gave birth to the processes for the mass production of various goods and commodities with the help of assembly lines that worked on the power that was generated by electricity instead of steam and water. This was the era when production increased to such an extent that it could cater to a much larger audience and their needs.

3. Industry 3.0

   This was the revolution that brought automation into play. The inventions and development that took place in sectors like information technology (IT) and microelectronics made this revolution a possibility. This revolution further led to a huge change in the system; for example, PCs, main frame devices, and robotics became a topic of interest among people with more time and investment going into their further development.

4. Industry 4.0

   This revolution that is taking place in the twenty-first century is the one that has led to the evolution of various modern-day technologies like remote sensing, autonomous systems, smart devices, analysis, networking, AI, the IoT, smart factories, and digital manufacturing. These technologies are interrelated to each other, because the use of technologies like ML, three-dimensional printing, and cyber systems was quite important in the further development of subsequent technologies.

The development of the industries from the first industrial revolution to the current form has created the best platform for the development of the health care sector from Healthcare 1.0 when this sector was still a work in progress (4). The focus was on cost-cutting techniques and to reach a stage where automation could be achieved to some extent and the use of resources like paper could be decreased as much as possible. However, the biggest hurdle in achieving this was the lack of available resources and the stand-alone systems with limited usage. This challenge was one of the first challenges that was overcome when the industry moved from Healthcare 1.0 to 2.0. Starting in 2000, the health care sector began to use technologies like clinical imaging to generate health reports for patients. There was a surge in the use of networking in the IT systems used in health care to provide easier access to anyone. Healthcare 2.0 was crucial in increasing networking; however, 6 years down the line, Healthcare 3.0 brought with it lifesaving inventions like wearable and implantable devices that have since been crucial in saving millions of lives across the

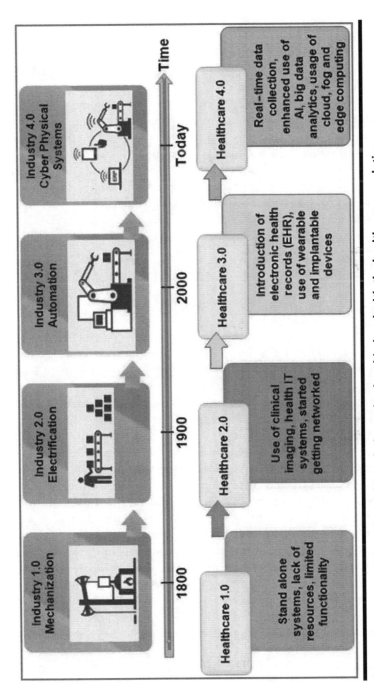

Figure 6.1 Stages of the Industrial Revolution going hand in hand with the health care revolution.

world. Another important invention of this period was the electronic health records (EHRs) which worked as the perfect solution to the problem of storage of the genomic sequences of people online.

The development of modern health care led to Healthcare 4.0. In Healthcare 4.0, there has been increased use of technologies like AI, ML, the IoT, and cloud and fog computing (8). There has also been an increase in real-time data collection. With this, there have been improvements in the accuracy of the information collected and it is easily accessible for any medical professional anywhere in the world. The data is easily portable, which allows the doctors as well as patients to get second opinions from medical experts from anywhere in the world. The advances in ML, AI, data science and analytics have helped in the creation of better prediction models. These have helped significantly in the creation of prediction models that have enabled the early diagnosis of irregularities in an individual's habits and in finding the correct treatment for their condition before it becomes terminal or fatal. This stage has improved the decision-making and the quality of health care services that are provided to people all over the world (Figure 6.1).

6.3 Fog Computing in Healthcare 4.0

The industrial revolution has brought about changes in the industrial sector and much-needed acceleration in the IT industry. Therefore, the technology, as well as the devices produced, have improved in every way, shape, or form. When talking about fog computing, IoT devices are important in the successful deployment in any such environment. Due to the industrial revolution, the storage capacity, processing power, and computational speeds have improved in the IoT devices that are used currently. In addition, the sensors are improving with every passing day, their size is decreasing to enable easy handling, and their numbers are increasing to aid better processing. They need to be working continuously without any stoppages, because data collection must never stop. Today, these sensors are fitted in devices like fitness bands, smart glasses, or even things as small as contact lenses to trace certain biometric characteristics of the user (6, 7). The data that is collected from these sensors can be classified with the help of various ML and data analytics models to extract information that would not normally be discovered by humans any other way. With the emergence of big data analytics models, the accuracy of these predictions has been impeccable recently. This has helped save the lives of many people, because the early detection and treatment of people with irregularities have prevented their condition from becoming terminal. In addition, it has helped many others to find the right lifestyle for them to live their lives with a lower risk of diseases than before.

The use of such devices has been a major asset in the health care sector; however, a few challenges remain, which is why fog computing has become even more important in some situations, as shown in Figure 6.2. Since the sensors on wearable

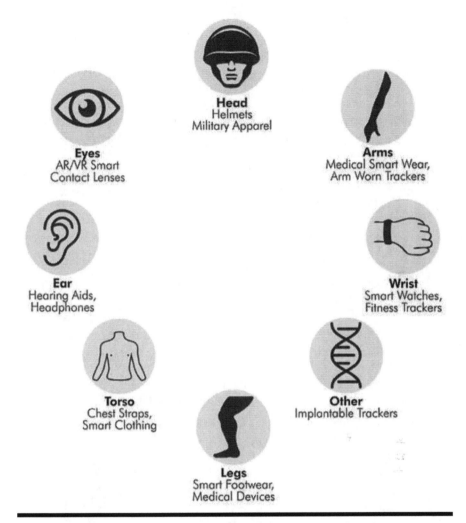

Figure 6.2 Various places in human body where sensors can be used.

devices must work 24/7, a large amount of information is collected and processed, and this information needs to be stored at a safe location for monitoring. This creates the situation where there is a lack of storage space to physically store this data. Thus, this data is collected and sent directly to be processed and stored. This step requires a good internet connection, because the data is transferred via the cloud, and therefore, having a faultless connection goes a long way towards the completion of the process and storage of the obtained results. Cloud computing can carry out the entire process; however, there are quite a few situations that require a better form of storage of this data, and these situations require fog computing. These situations include:

1. Risk in security

   When it comes to the matter of security, cloud networks have a framework in place to deal with any breaches in the security of a network; however, some flaws exist that could easily be exploited by people with bad intentions, which has been proved from time-to-time with various breaches and leaks of personal data that have occurred. This becomes an even more important issue when it comes to the health care sector, because most of the data is related to the medical history of an individual, and therefore, is a very sensitive topic.

2. Issues regarding proper implementation

   The tasks that occur simultaneously in a cloud environment always need a system that is reliable and efficient at the same time. If the implementation is not perfect, which is a possibility when it comes to cloud computing, there are issues, such as incomplete upload of data, unnecessary leaks of data to scammers, and the shutdown of business services.

3. Availability and control issues

   As we saw in the implementation issues in the cloud, there are quite a few times when cloud platforms crash and the data cannot be accessed. One of the biggest benefits of EHR devices is that the data is available at any point in time. Therefore, there needs to be a solution that ensures that patient data can be accessed by medical professionals when the cloud service is down.

4. Compliance with Health Insurance Portability and Accountability Act (HIPAA)

   Any company that provides cloud solutions for medical purposes must comply with the rules and regulations set by HIPAA. Most companies try

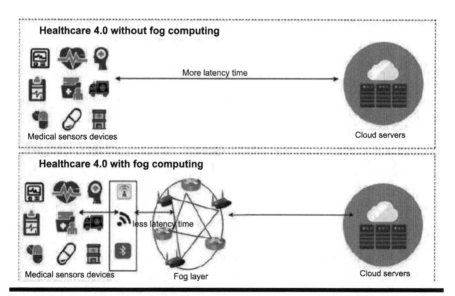

Figure 6.3   How fog computing aids cloud systems.

their best to comply with the laws including patient privacy, security threats and breaches, compliance with cyber laws, and providing notification about any type of harmful activity taking place. However, there are still some providers that find loopholes and risk endangering the data of the patients and risk their organisation in doing so, as shown in Figure 6.3.

To create a solution for these issues, the new paradigm of fog computing was announced, which solved the issues faced by cloud computing and created a safer and much more feasible way to store, handle, and process data that was collected from sensors.

6.4 Benefits of Fog Computing in Health Care

1. Flexibility of computation locus
   Fog computing provides computational resources based on the requirement and provides the user with flexibility for the execution of computation. The location of the computing devices can be dynamic and depend on the current environment and application requirements.
2. Integration
   The introduction of sensor devices makes the requirement of a reliable support infrastructure mandatory. With fog computing, new sensors can be mounted onto the existing architecture.
3. Patient mobility
   Application-specific services limit the regions where a patient can be monitored, which can prolong patient stays in hospitals. Fog computing allows efficient environment transitions without affecting the quality of service.
4. Bandwidth
   The fog layer filters, analyses and preprocesses raw data, which means that the volume of data that needs to be sent to the cloud is reduced. At times, fog nodes can address requests from gadgets through cached information, and thus, communication with the cloud might not be compulsory.
5. Energy efficiency
   The sleep cycle duration of sensors can be increased using gateways, such as communication proxies, thus improving energy efficiency within sensor devices. The gateway monitors incoming updates and is acted upon once the sensor is awake.
6. Real-time computation
   It is simpler to achieve real-time results due to the lack of distance between the fog nodes and the edge devices. Simple computations can be carried out on these nodes and quick real-time results can be provided.

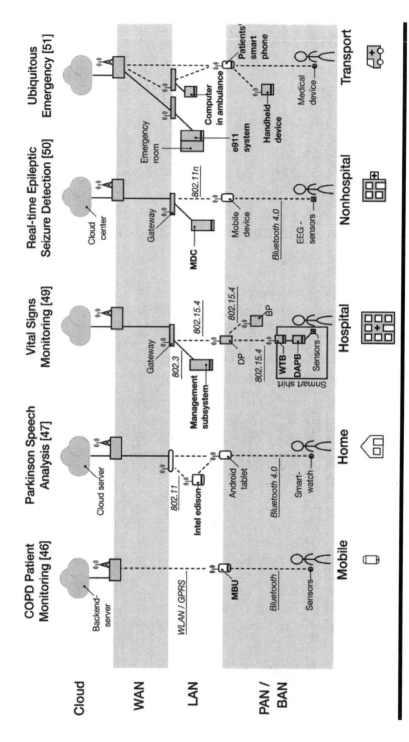

Figure 6.4 Actual deployment of fog computing.

7. Security

   Due to the severe consequences of tampering with devices, and the need to maintain the confidentiality of patient data, security provisions in health care are quite high. Fog computing minimises the quantity of data being transferred back and forth to the cloud; therefore, minimising security risks.

These features are a necessity in the health care industry and the fog layer in fog computing addresses most of the challenges that are associated with cloud computing. Single or multiple nodes can be combined to perform various fog computing tasks like filtering, analysing, aggregating, and temporarily storing data. More fog nodes can be added when there is an increase in the requirement for computing power, as shown in Figure 6.4. The ease of accessibility of patient-related information and the ability to maintain the confidentiality of data allow doctors to make smarter choices and improve the lives of the disabled population.

6.5 Challenges in Fog Computing

Despite the numerous advantages of fog computing in health care, some factors need to be taken into consideration before deploying it in any environment, these include:

1. Authentication

   Fog-based systems provide access to front nodes for many users, and thus, authentication becomes one of the primary security concerns of fog computing at different fog nodes. However, a variety of secure and cost-friendly solutions have been proposed to overcome this problem, which involves physical contact for pre-authentication such as fingerprints or touch-based and face authentication.

2. Dodgy fog node

   A fog node that appears to be permissible and persistently persuades users to establish a connection to it is referred to as a dodgy fog node. Connecting to the dodgy node makes all incoming and outgoing requests from the cloud to the end-user and vice versa prone to manipulation, and tampers with user data, which makes it vulnerable to further attacks. The presence of such a node becomes an important threat to the user's data privacy. It is inconvenient to deal with such problems for the following reasons:

   a. Since every trust situation is dissimilar, each situation requires different trust management schemes.

   b. It becomes tedious to keep a record of rogue nodes due to the dynamic creation and deletion of VM instances.

3. Invasion of privacy

Since fog nodes are near the users, tampering with private information such as saved passwords, user data, and current location is a possibility. When a fog client uses multiple fog facilities at different locations, there is a possibility of disclosure and tracking the path to the fog nodes, if the fog nodes connive. The location privacy of the patient will remain at risk if a fog client is attached to a person or an object.

4. Exponential growth in health care

Currently, the amount of research and development going on in the world is greater than it has ever been in the past. This is not different when we talk about medicine. The constant growth leads to manifold changes in technology as well. This is another challenge that needs to be overcome to ensure that the technology and health care sector develop together.

5. Dealing with complicated datasets

The current datasets in the health care sector are more diverse and complicated compared with other fields. With this complexity and the constant arrival of new datasets, which could contain some new data points that might never have been discovered before, it becomes a huge task to manage and process the amount of data received every time.

6.6 Differences Between Cloud, Fog, and Edge Computing

Before we learn more about fog computing, we must understand how it is different from the cloud and edge computing. The meaning and definition might seem very similar; however, the differences between their infrastructures are easily visible. All these technologies provide on-demand services to the user; the amount of storage and computational speeds divide them into different layers of IIOT (industry internet of things). The in-depth meaning for all three follows.

1. Cloud computing

The most easily available of the three, cloud computing is something that most users are well versed with due to its vast use in various industries and for individual purposes. The cloud networks formed by this architecture have fog and edge computing as their important assets, which go on to create a set of servers. This gives organisations higher capacity when it comes to storage and processing; therefore, enabling them to cross their incomes and making them independent from setting things up at their servers. The fact that data can be stored at any location for cloud structures makes them a very useful asset today.

2. Fog computing

We know that fog computing is different from cloud in many ways; however, there is little knowledge when it comes to differentiating between fog and edge computing. The main difference between them is the location where things like process control and intelligence are located. Fog has all its data in the LAN (local area network), which enables data to travel through gateways and is then sent to bases for the use and return of the data that is transmitted, and edge uses the processing power and intelligence of the devices for data transfer.

3. Edge computing

The IoT is another up-and-coming technology, which has led to unlimited usage of beneficial network devices. This increase in usage of the IoT has led to higher use of a combination of data and the processing of information at a single data centre. The transaction takes place at the edge of the network; therefore, this type of computing has been named edge computing.

6.7 Applications of Fog Computing

A few applications of fog computing in the health care sector are discussed in the following sections.

6.7.1 Fog Computing-Based IoT for Health Monitoring Systems

In this chapter, the authors have proposed fog computing techniques to efficiently monitor patients that suffer from chronic diseases, where the primary challenge is to sort context-sensitive information that has relevance to the health of the patient.

The authors have implemented a context-sensitive fog computing environment, with improved security due to the limited exposure of data, because it does not have to communicate back and forth in the network, as shown in Figure 6.5.

A three-tier architecture for context and latency-sensitive health monitoring has been implemented, where the three layers are composed of cloud computing, fog computing, and sensors that function in concurrence with each other. Sensors include attachable or nonattachable devices that are mounted onto patients as smartwatches and glasses. The edge devices are handled by the cloud and fog layers. In context-sensitive health monitoring, context can be categorised as intrinsic and extrinsic. Extrinsic is composed of external factors like a patient's surrounding environment. Environmental sensors are used to obtain the extrinsic parameters, and the intrinsic parameters of the user can be obtained by biosensors, as shown in Figure 6.6. The

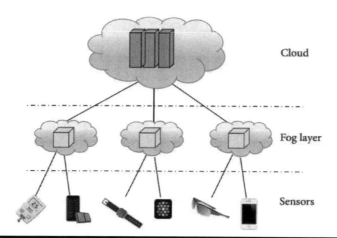

Figure 6.5   Layers of IoT.

relevance of the data is defined by the condition or disease of the patient, due to which context-sensitive data needs to be processed in the fog layer:

The description of the three tiers is as follows:

1. Sensor tier
   The sensors gather intrinsic and extrinsic information from the patients. Extrinsic data is composed of temperature and location and intrinsic data refers to blood pressure and heartbeat.
2. Fog computing tier
   This layer is responsible for the analysis and aggregation of the data. This layer behaves as the server, where all the data that is acquired by the edge devices is processed. An efficient task scheduling algorithm must be implemented to conduct the processing work distribution.
   a. Work distribution
      Tasks are distributed using a task scheduling mechanism that uses two graphs, the task and process graphs.
      Let G = V, and E represent the task graph, where G is a directed acyclic graph; V is the set of vertices; and E is the set of edges where each edge (e_{ij}) ∈ E implies that the task (v_i) has a corresponding workload (w_i) that signifies the amount of work to be processed at a particular resource. Every e_{ij} has a corresponding weight (c_{ij}), which represents the amount of data that is transferred from v_i to $v + i$. Let H = R, L be a DAG (directed acyclic graph) that represents the processor graph, where R denotes the set of vertices P1, P2, Pn where each Pi ∈ R is a processor at the cloud or fog. The edge (l_{ij}) ∈ L denotes a link between processor Pi and Pj. Now, R = Ncloud U Nfog, as shown in Figure 6.7.

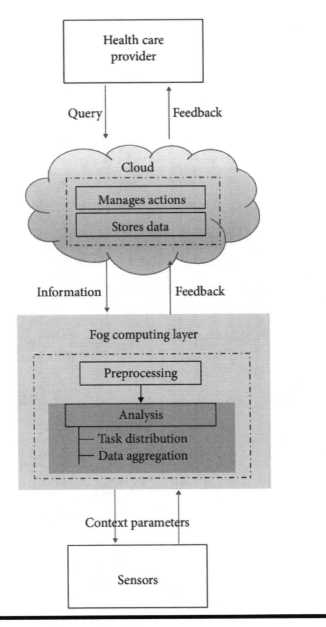

Figure 6.6 Diagram of proposed architecture.

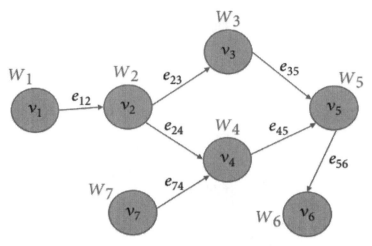

Task graph, $G = (V, E)$,
where $v = \{v_1, v_2,..., v_7\}$ and $E = \{e_{12}, e_{23}, e_{24}, e_{35}, e_{45}, e_{56}, e_{74}\}$

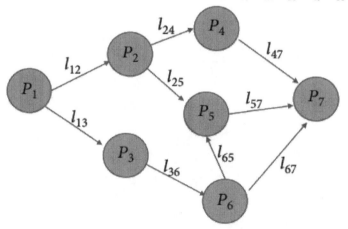

Processor graph, $H = (R, L)$,
where $R = \{P_1, P_2,..., P_7\}$ and $L = \{l_{12}, l_{13}, l_{24}, l_{25}, l_{36}, l_{47}, l_{57}, l_{65}, l_{67}\}$

Figure 6.7   Graphs created.

b. Data aggregation

This is composed of three components: duplicated detection, schema mapping, and data fusion. Duplicated detection removes redundancy from the data. Schema mapping ensures data flow, and that the aggregation of data takes place rationally. The fog device is secured by restricting false data injection and is executed by an additional local filter arranged in the fog device. In the final stage, the final information is combined as one entity as a part of the data fusion process.

3. Cloud computing tier
   This layer is mainly responsible for supervising the health monitoring system.

6.7.1.1 Experimental Analysis

1. Latency
   The amount of data and time transferred from tier to tier differs, and hence the latency differs too.

   $Lf = ts + tr + ef$

   $Le = ts + ef + ee$

   where:
   Lf = latency when the evaluated data must be returned to the IoT devices
   Le = latency when the data is forwarded to the cloud
   ts = time taken from the sensors to the fog layer
   tr = time taken for the data to return from the fog layer to the IoT devices
   ef = evaluation time taken by edge devices
   ee = evaluation time taken at the cloud

2. Computation
   Various techniques have been adopted to reduce the complexity of computations, because they must be real-time and latency-sensitive.

3. Security analysis
   The presence of a fog layer in the given architecture reduces the security risk of patient information getting lost due to network and system failures. Patient data is secured by encrypting their data with a secret key.

After multiple evaluations, it was deduced that despite its potential, fog computing still has not reached its full potential and can only be partially implemented. Many factors have hindered the implementation process of fog computing, such as software that is not readily available, and a lack of a unified view, which is required in the grander vision of fog computing for health care.

The authors state that their future work will focus on deploying this architecture to various edge devices and judging the behaviour of the system.

6.7.2 Data Processing and Analytics in Fog Computing for Healthcare 4.0

In this chapter, the authors aimed to shed light on data processing and analysis in the proposed three-tier architecture that provides real-time results and uses fog and cloud computing.

6.7.2.1 Need for Data Processing and Analysis

The IoT devices gather data and possess a lot of information that needs to be extracted. The data that is collected from different sources, which contains different formats and is unstructured and unintelligible, makes the processing of data mandatory. Analysing patient behaviour, clinical data, and pharmaceuticals can help improve patient care and carry out operations smoothly and effectively, which lowers the overall costs. Data analysis plays a core function in day-to-day operations and upgrades performance by offering data-based quality services, which shortens patient waiting times and lowers readmission rates to isolate patients at risk.

6.7.2.2 Case Study

1. Fog-assisted IoT-enabled health monitoring systems

   A fog-assisted IoT-enabled health monitoring system has been proposed for patients, where data from 67 patients were simultaneously generated for 30 days. In an intelligent communication mechanism, the health history of a patient can be accessed from the cloud layer. However, in regular communication, updates regarding fog nodes are sent to the cloud along with patient information for future references. This model is a three-layered architecture that incorporates the data acquisition, fog, and cloud layers.

   a. Data acquisition layer

      IoT devices handle the responsibility for retrieving patient data in this layer. These devices acquire environmental and psychological parameters and send them to the fog layer.

   b. Fog layer

      In this layer, the raw data generated from the IoT devices is converted into an appropriate format before sending it to the cloud. Here, data is classified as normal or abnormal. When health parameters are higher than usual, for instance high blood pressure, it is classified as an abnormal state.

   c. Cloud layer

      This layer primarily focuses on extracting meaningful data from the fog layer. Continuous data that is generated by the source is used to run training algorithms on this layer. The classification of parameters is done as a safe state (SS) or unsafe state (US) for the patients. The US alerts an emergency signal from the fog layer to the source of data generation.

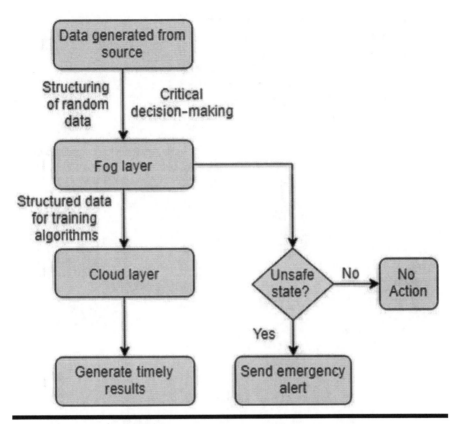

Figure 6.8   Decision-making in three-layered architectures.

Otherwise, the data is transmitted to the cloud, to generate timely results, as shown in Figure 6.8.

2. Pima Indians Diabetes Set

The Pima Indians diabetes dataset was used to predict if a person was suffering from diabetes or not by observing parameters, such as age, blood pressure, and glucose levels that were generated from numerous IoT devices. Various ML algorithms such as K-Nearest Neighbour (KNN), Random Forest (RF) and Linear Regression (LR) were applied to obtain the results. The KNN model gave an accuracy of 65% with an F1 score of 0.72. The LR model gave an accuracy of 67% at a learning rate of 0.3 and 800 epochs. The RF algorithm gave an accuracy of ≤75.32% when applied with 100 estimators. It proved that the result of the analysis mainly depended on the algorithm used.

3. BodyEdge architecture

BodyEdge is an architecture that concatenates the IoT devices network with edge computing to overcome challenges such as response time, scalability, privacy, etc. The following system is intended to be implemented by factory workers, athletes, or even for monitoring the health of patients at the hospital. The architecture comprises two components:

a. BodyEdge mobile body client (BE-MBC)

   Phones with the installed software and IoT devices undergo communication through BE-MBC. It also imparts data to the next component from these devices.

b. BodyEdge gateway (BE-GTW)

   BE-GTW communicates with different edge gateways and public or private clouds along with managing data to achieve interoperability.

Comparisons were carried out between compute engines based on the prediction of high-stress conditions on the following users.

1. Factory workers
2. Athlete's during training

The results were computed on three platforms.

1. Raspberry Pi 3
2. Nano PC
3. Azure cloud

On evaluation, it was noted that Raspberry Pi 3 took 1,600 ms for 100 factory workers and 3,200 ms for 100 athletes, and Nano PC and Azure cloud produced similar results.

6.7.3 Fog-IoT Environment in Smart Health Care: A Case Study for Student Stress Monitoring

In this chapter, a novel IoT-aware student-centred stress observing system that used a two-stage Temporal Dynamic Bayesian Network (TDBN) to predict a student stress index was proposed.

6.7.3.1 Proposed Methodology: A Case Study of Fog Computing in Student Stress Monitoring

The Bayesian Belief Network (BBN) was used to categorize tension as natural or unusual and used physiological attributes from therapeutic sensors. A TDBN model analysed stress based on confirmations of the leaf core, workload, background, and student health characteristics. Decisions for generating warnings were made by releasing time-sensitive data once the stress record was processed.

1. Obtaining data

   To obtain stress-related data, physiological, visual and conduct sensors installed in the IoT could be embedded. The IoT gadgets gathered physiological information, which was grouped using BBN for usual and abnormal stress situations.

2. Fog layer

   Data acquired from the procurement layer was sent to the fog layer to order the stress information into various classes. Three datasets were considered to assess stress parameters: physiological, behavioural, and visual datasets.

Table 6.1   Categorisation of Datasets

Activity Set	IoT Technology Used	Attributes
Visual dataset	Shrewd camera gadgets (e.g., wide edge and slender point)	Pupil diameter, mouth openness, squinting recurrence, normal eye conclusion speed, head development, and eyebrow development
Physiological dataset	Savvy wearables, heart sensors, body sensors, EEG screen gadgets	Pulse fluctuation, skin temperature, EEG (stress-related mind waves), expanding perspiration, cool skin, cold hands and feet, the feeling of queasiness, tense muscles, and so forth
Behavioural dataset	Kinect SD sensor	Student body posture

Table 6.2   Dataset Found from SWELL-KW

Features	Preprocessed Sensor Data	Features Taken Under Consideration (number of features)
Physiological	Information from restorative sensors (records with headings per 1 min time allotment)	Pulse changeability (2), skin conductance (1)
Facial signs	FaceReader yield (txt logs and records with facial and time-stamped data)	Head direction (3), facial developments (10), feelings (8), eye discovery and following (30 s time swap window)
Body postures	Joint directions and chest area edges (txt records, also time-stepped area)	Distance (1), joint angles (10)

Algorithm 1: Stress-Based Dataset Generation

# **Input:** 25 students associated SWELL-KW dataset for stress displaying in student sphere and eye assortment and tracking dataset for **BF** (blinking frequency) and **AECF** (average eye closing speed) calculation	
# **Output:** Prognostic stress index	
1.	Let **n** be the required number of stress records for each leaf node value initialised with one do
2.	Extract a record from the SWELL dataset and a record from the eye detection and tracking dataset to generate all leaf node values in a particular context
3.	Create a new dataset by combining all leaf nodes symptoms for each student during a definite time interval
4.	Assign a new identification number **S_ID** to the stress database
5.	If **S_ID** already exists in the database, then discard the record
6.	Else
7.	Add the record to the database
8.	End if
9.	End do

3. Information mining layer

   This is the layer that uses various datasets to recover data from a cloud environment. In the model discussed previously, there is a need to set up time and the method of temporal mining was used to create a list that studied and understood the pressure slowly and precisely. With the use of the occasion activation mode in this layer, the important processed information was stored in places known as the fog hubs.

4. Prediction layer

   To measure an element's stress index, different resources were used. The biggest example of this was the use of various techniques to treat mental disorders like PTSD, autism, depression, and anxiety. The TDBM model was used to treat patients in these cases by first analysing and then reporting the points that could be vulnerable in some situations. The process was divided into two stages where the first one involved marking out the points that caused a change in the understudy stress file, and in the second stage, the rest of the processing was carried out to make the right prediction for the situation mentioned.

5. Decision-making

   With the help of the results that were obtained at the predictive stage; the stage was reached where decisions that were controlled by stress reaching a certain threshold level could be made.

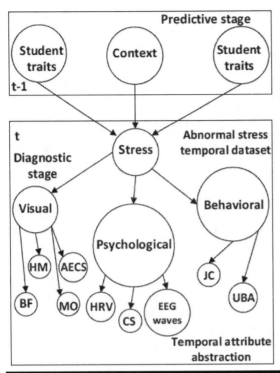

BF: Blinking frequency
AECS: Average eye closing speed
HM: Head movement
MO: Mouth openness
HRV: Heart rate variability
EEG: Electroencephalography
ST: Skin temperature
CS: Cool skin
JC: Joint coordination
UBA: Upper body angle

Figure 6.9   Working of mining layer.

6.8 Future of Fog Computing in the Health Care Sector

With fog computing being an up-and-coming technology, there will be some changes and improvements in every sector it is currently being used in. This is the case in the health care sector, which has its fair share of areas where significant improvements can be expected in the near future. The following is a list of a few of the changes that could happen in this sector.

1. Data migration and applications

   The situations that arise in fog computing scenarios mostly consist of users who have high movement rates and agility as an important characteristic. This leads to the need for services that match the mobility of these users through data and software services that need to be transported with the help of fog. These services, although still prevalent, require major upgrades that could help with the growth of fog and match the needs and uses of the users in the future. Fog architecture has some very advantageous and practical uses, because it helps with the immediate storage of small data packets at the network's edge; however, it requires the help of a well-established cloud infrastructure to be able to process, store, and use large data units.

2. Building smart cities

With the advances in AI technologies and automation taking over in various fields, there is room for its introduction in hospitals and medical centres. Things like diffusion pumps in hospitals can be automated to administer prescribed drugs to patients, which could be automated with feedback and notifications for the medical professionals to help with the mixing of drugs and chemicals. With these developments, companies must determine the number of times and the work that needs to be carried out to get fog computing architecture in place to build the cities and ensure that user feedback is considered. This must occur before building something and releasing it for use by the public. With constant involvement and investment by the authorities and continuous user feedback, this technology could unlock major development opportunities in the future.

3. Use in nanotech

Nanotechnology means devices and structures <100 nm. With its current use in fields like neuroscience, biotechnology, and IT, nanotechnology could play an important role in the future due to its properties, such as improved strength and durability, and ease of movement, combined with its molecular size in nm. This technology could flourish in the near future. In the medical sector, nanoparticles [(titanium dioxide (TiO_2)] have generally been utilised to prepare dietary products and day-to-day products like sunscreen and lotions. With these products playing an important role in modern medicinal products, fog computing and nanotech go hand-in-hand.

4. Digital medicine

Currently, the apps being used display the ongoing medical records and history of the patient and are based mostly on traditional methods that have been used for a long time. This process is comparatively slower and inefficient when it comes to maintaining the right standards. With the help of digital medicine, a clearer image of the type of medical issue a patient is facing, analysis of the treatment process, its effectiveness and connections with people suffering from similar issues could be achieved. The advances made could help in making the use more prevalent among the public and help in gaining the trust of the public. The discussion about the use of technologies like NLP, computer-generated reality, and profound learning could help to ensure a higher use of this system when providing health care services to the public.

6.9 Conclusions

As we move towards a generation of technology that is based more on the use of IoT devices and online storage applications, we are also moving towards a future where technologies like fog and edge computing come to the forefront. More effort and time will be spent on research, development and subsequent uses in various fields like storage, management, defence services, and data scraping. This is similar in health care. There is still a long way to go before the proper development and heavy use of fog computing in health care industries; however, the basic structure and the architectural design to build for the future are well in place. As discussed previously, fog computing has huge potential to be an important part of the health care sector in the future. With good financial support and proper scrutiny and testing, millions of lives could be saved, and living standards could be increased as we work towards a better future. In addition, the frameworks currently in place could be improved with the help of various testing techniques, and therefore, result in the better deployment of fog computing in the current environment. Multiple benefits such as high mobility of data transfer, the minimum response time of various orders, higher reliability, scalability, decreased usage of power, efficient use of resources and energy, and high performance are required. Therefore, the upcoming fog computing models have their work cut out for them because these factors make up the biggest opportunities. In addition, the biggest challenges must be addressed for any health care application to produce optimum results and build a stronger network.

References

1. Tanwar S. Fog Computing for Healthcare 4.0 Environments: Technical, Societal, and Future Implications. New York, USA: Springer International Publishing; 2021.
2. Paul A, Pinjari H, Hong WH, Seo HC, Rho S. Fog computing-based IoT for health monitoring system. Journal of Sensors. 2018.
3. Surati S, Patel S, Surati K. Background and research challenges for FC for Healthcare 4.0. In Tanwar S (Ed.), Fog Computing for Healthcare 4.0 Environments: Technical, Societal, and Future Implications. New York, USA: Springer International Publishing; 2021; pp. 37–53.
4. Shah K, Modi P, Bhatia J. Data processing and analytics in FC for Healthcare 4.0. In Tanwar S (Ed.), Fog Computing for Healthcare 4.0 Environments: Technical, Societal, and Future Implications. New York, USA: Springer International Publishing; 2021; pp. 131–154.
5. Nair A, Tanwar S. Fog computing architectures and frameworks for Healthcare 4.0. In Tanwar S (Ed.), Fog Computing for Healthcare 4.0 Environments: Technical, Societal, and Future Implications. New York, USA: Springer International Publishing; 2021; pp. 55–78.
6. Shaikh T, Ali R. Fog-IoT environment in smart healthcare: a case study for student stress monitoring. In Tanwar S (Ed.), Fog Computing for Healthcare 4.0 Environments: Technical, Societal, and Future Implications. New York, USA: Springer International Publishing; 2021; pp. 211–250.
7. Litoriya R, Gulati A, Yadav M, Ghosh R, Pandey P. Social, ethical, and regulatory issues of fog computing in Healthcare 4.0 applications. In Tanwar S (Ed.), Fog Computing

for Healthcare 4.0 Environments: Technical, Societal, and Future Implications. New York, USA: Springer International Publishing; 2021; pp. 593–609.

8. Thapliyal S, Lisa G, Bagla P, Kumar K. Cloud, edge, and fog computing. In V Bali, V Bhatnagar, D Aggarwal, S Bali, MJ Diván (Eds.), Cyber-Physical, IoT, and Autonomous Systems in Industry 4.0. Boca Raton, USA: CRC Press, 2021; pp. 103–115.

Chapter 7

Fog Computing for Agriculture Applications and its Issues

Akruti Sinha, Gaurav Srivastava, Devika Sapra, and Chhavi Deshlahra

Computer and Communication Engineering, Manipal University, Jaipur, Rajasthan, India

Contents

DOI: 10.1201/9781003322931-7

7.1 Introduction

Technology integration and long-term land management are critical for agricultural productivity. Agriculture is essential for a country's development. It is the primary source of income, and the level of agricultural development in a country determines the future path. Food production should be increased at a faster rate than the rate of population expansion. Agricultural businesses should seek assistance from the automation industry to combat population increases. To satisfy the demands, farmers, agronomists, and agricultural companies have begun to employ technology, such as cloud computing, the Internet of things (IoT), big data, and artificial intelligence (AI).

When gathering data from farms, a vast volume of data is produced and should be secured. Cloud computing (CC) allows for the necessary accessibility to analyze data from any location; however, it raises privacy and security problems. Fog and edge computing, which are extensions of cloud computing, have come into play to improve data security. Their approach is to keep and analyze data as close to its source as possible, which is the farm. Fog computing is a distributed network that connects gadgets and the cloud. It's more efficient, has less latency, and has a quicker response time. Fog computing is helping the agricultural sector to advance. Farmers deal with issues such as under irrigation regularly, which can lead to a loss of production and increased waste. The IoT, data analytics, and cloud technology could be used to overcome such problems. Fog computing comes into play for precision agriculture (PA) and natural resource conservation to improve irrigation techniques and examine data for minimum water usage.

Fog computing has improved a variety of industries in a number of ways, which affected profit development. The contribution of this chapter is to analyze the issues and use of fog computing in agriculture and provide a comparative and comprehensive analysis. A comparative study aids in the concise summary and conclusion of previous efforts, as well as a thorough investigation of the accuracy of all fog computing methodologies. The remainder of the chapter is devoted to a discussion of the use of fog computing and the IoT to tackle agricultural production difficulties, as well as the findings from previous studies and some diagrammatic overviews. The final section highlights the findings and discusses future research opportunities.

7.2 Literature Review

Recent breakthroughs and the increase in fog computing in the digital era have provided a new perspective on today's computing equipment, as well as new ways to access computational platforms via fog computing. As a result, a slew of recent studies on fog computing for smart agriculture has been published.

The authors of (1) conducted a review of all previous publications in the cloud, fog, and edge computing from 2015 to date. Based on the findings of this survey, the author proposed a new three-layered architecture model that combined cloud, fog, and edge, with the fog layer on top of the edge layer and the cloud layer on top of the fog layer. The cloud layer is primarily in charge of large-scale data storage and analytics, as well as the installation of algorithms and data analytics tools on the fog nodes. The proposed approach necessitates the installation of a fog layer in local fields, which is responsible for real-time data analytics, such as pest and disease prediction, yield prediction, weather forecasting, and agricultural monitoring automation. The edge layer is made up of end devices, tractors, sensors, and actuators. The primary goal of this layer is to collect data and send it to the fog layer.

Current systems based on standard cloud models, according to previous research (2), are insufficient to handle the vast volumes and variety of data that is generated by linked IoT devices. Moving data processing closer to the source of its generation is critical to reducing latency when supporting real-time decisions based on the data provided. The adoption of fog-based models could aid in this endeavor. As a result, the researchers presented AgriFog, an IoT-fog-based farm management system. It is more competent in terms of efficient bandwidth use and reduced latency for real-time decision-making, according to the research. The AgriFog application was modeled and simulated using iFogSim.

Researchers (3) created a modern agricultural system architecture based on the IoT and fog computing, which used fog rather than CC to reduce service latency. It also improved performance using fog–CC instead of fog computing. Combining fog computing and IoT is better for wireless sensor and actuator networks (WSANs), as evidenced by the results, because fog computing reduces latency.

Cloud computing and the IoT enable the creation of a linked network of smart things, research (4) showed that both paradigms did not allow computing issues to be solved. As a result, a fog-based IoT framework was proposed that employed a two-tier fog and associated resources to reduce data transmission to the cloud, improve computational load balancing, and reduce wait times. The proposed fog computing concept was applied to the rapidly developing field of PA, which included all agricultural land management approaches. Furthermore, the author simulated and demonstrated how the two-tier fog computing strategy can significantly reduce the amount of data transported to the cloud when using this architecture. Based on the previous framework, a prototype application was created and explained to manage and monitor farms, which had a significant impact on commercial and environmental performance.

Researchers (5) proposed a toolset that included sensors, UAVs (unmanned aerial vehicles), and fog locations that aimed at creating a comprehensive farming ecology. The toolkit allowed users to simulate custom farming scenarios, such as sensor placement, coverage area, line of sight deployment, data gathering via relay mechanisms or airborne systems, mobile node mobility models, energy models for on-ground sensors and airborne vehicles, and backend computing support that used the fog computing paradigm. The researchers stated that because most previous studies ignored network factors that could affect the overall performance of any deployed system, their proposed framework also served as a benchmark for transmission latency, packet delivery ratio, energy consumption, and system resource utilization.

According to some research (6), global food security is a difficult task to manage. Several regions, including Southeast Asia, have seen significant reductions in undernourishment rates as agricultural areas have expanded and new agricultural practices have been implemented. Malnutrition rates, on the other hand, have begun to rise, and the region continues to house a sizable portion of the world's undernourished population. As a result, researchers (6) presented a WSAN system architecture with smart IoT-based stations that were based on the fog computing paradigm. The method was created with the needs of Southeast Asian rural farmers in mind. The proposed system architecture could contribute to remote monitoring in inaccessible farming locales with minimal current information technology (IT) infrastructure.

The research in (7) proposed a novel service method based on the IoT CC platform, which could be used to improve the integration of current cloud-to-physical networking and the processing speed of the IoT. Through experimental simulation, the revolutionary IoT platform presented unique status indicators, which included the use of decentralized computations to speed up the verification of real-time computing results. Simultaneously, decentralized calculations were used to analyze data in this study (7). The analysis findings were then disseminated via the internet. By validating the experimental results, the cost of network transmission could be reduced. All data was analyzed using precalculations, and the final analysis findings were used for data transfer.

Researchers (8) proposed a multitier complex event processing strategy (e.g., sensor node, fog, and cloud) that promoted rapid decision-making and was based on 98% accurate data. During testing, the average time to send messages in the network was reduced by 77%. Furthermore, data traffic was reduced by 82%t. The studies produced positive results, with accuracy, precision, recall, and an F1-score routinely exceeding 99%. As a result, the data collected using the proposed method was reliable and consistent with the reality of the monitored environment.

7.3 Smart Agriculture

Farmers have traditionally been under a lot of pressure to increase yields when using fewer natural resources, such as water and energy. As a result, the smart farming management concept, which is known as precision farming, was implemented. This makes the agricultural process more efficient, qualitative, and quantitative. Smart farming is controlled and monitored by software and sensors, respectively (1). So, in general, smart agriculture is a developing concept that employs modern technologies, such as the IoT, robotics, drones, and AI to increase productivity, reduce waste, and, to some extent, save on human labor.

The most common technologies that are used in smart agriculture are.

1. Sensors for the soil, water, light, and moisture, as well as temperature control.
2. Telecommunications, such as GPS (global positioning system) and sophisticated networking technologies are two examples of this technology. Hardware and software for specific applications, IoT-based solutions, robotics, and automation, and enabling IoT-based solutions are all available (9).
3. Data analytics including data pipelines for downstream solutions as well as standalone analytics solutions.
4. Satellites and drones.

Smart farming uses these technologies to assist farmers in monitoring the needs of individual plants and animals. The following are the steps in smart agriculture.

1. Observation, where sensors collect and transmit observational data about crops, livestock, soil, and the atmosphere.
2. Diagnostics, where the observational data is fed into a cloud-hosted IoT platform, where it is analyzed and inferences about the observations are made. As a result, problems are identified (9).
3. Decision: Since the problems have been identified, the software platform or the user decides how to deal with them.
4. Action, where following the creation of the plan, putting it into action begins. Then, the cycles start again.

As a result, smart agriculture holds the promise of delivering more productive and sustainable agricultural production through a more accurate and resource-efficient method.

7.4 Cloud Computing (CC)

Historically, computer power was a scarce and expensive resource. CC has made it abundant and affordable, which has resulted in a significant paradigm shift; a shift from scarcity to abundance computing. This computer revolution accelerated the commoditization of products, services, and business models when disrupting the existing ICT (information and communications technology) industry. CC is a new computing paradigm that aims to provide secure, personalized, and quality of service-assured (QoS) dynamic computing environments to end users. The term cloud computing refers to the on-demand availability of computer system resources, such as cloud storage and processing power, without user direct active supervision. CC allows us to obtain software as utilities over the internet. It refers to the process of modifying, configuring, and accessing this software via the internet. CC enables us to develop, configure, and personalize commercial applications by utilizing the internet. Distributed computing, parallel computing, and grid computing are all subsets of CC.

The term cloud refers to a collection of computers for CC architecture. A cloud is an IT infrastructure that allows remote access to measured and scalable resources. It has evolved into a modern model of information exchange and internet service delivery. Consumers will benefit from services that are more secure, adaptable, and scalable. It's a service-oriented design that reduces end user data overheads.

There are three types of CC: 1. infrastructure as a service; 2. platform as a service; and 3. software as a service. Each type of CC provides varying levels of freedom, control, and administration, which allows you to select the best set of services for your needs. This is a CC stack because it grows on top of itself.

7.5 Fog Computing

7.5.1 Features of Fog Computing

Fog computing is a subset of CC that focuses on objects that interact with the IoT data. Fog computing serves as a bridge between output devices and CC, bringing storage, networking, and compute capabilities closer to the edge nodes. The end units are fog nodes, which can be placed anywhere there is a communication link. A fog node is a device that can process, compute, network, and store data. Fog nodes include switches, servers, surveillance cameras, and routers (10, 11). One of the structure blocks of CC is discussed: fog computing. The following are the primary components of fog computing (12).

1. Cognitive processing
    The ability to respond to client-centered goals is referred to as a cognitive process. Fog-based data processing and analysis provide a better alert about consumer requirements, as well as the best positional handling for transmitting,

storing, and controlling functions over the cloud to the IoT spectrum. End node applications provide a more sensitive and reactive user requirements relationship due to their proximity (13).

2. Variability

   Fog computing is a virtualized architecture that provides computing, storage, and communications services between the central server and the end devices. Its servers are made up of modular building components that are scattered over the network. Edge devices, also known as fog nodes, are created by a variety of companies, and hence, come in a variety of configurations. They must be hosted according to their intended use. As a result, fog can adapt to a variety of platforms.

3. Geographic coverage

   To offer the QoS for cell phones and immobile edge devices, the fog computing ecosystem has been widely deployed (14). In the situation of varied phase environments, such as temperature monitoring, weather forecasting sensors, and patient monitoring systems, the fog network distributes its hubs and sensor systems regionally.

4. Reduced latency in edge location

   The new smart services and applications are insufficient due to a lack of support at the edge of the core network for devices with enabled QoS. Streaming content in traditional TV equipment, tracking devices, gaming and entertainment applications, and several other applications require low latency services in their vicinity (15).

5. Instantaneous communication

   Fog applications that require real-time interactions include tracking a crucial operation on an oilfield with fog edge devices, such as sensors; real-time communication for transportation; video surveillance; and power transmission tracking application programs, among others. Instead of batch processing, fog apps provide real-time processing capacity for QoS.

6. Accessibility assistance

   Mobile support is an important fog computing benefit since it allows clear interaction between portable devices using SDN (software defined network) interfaces (e.g., CISCO Locator/ID Separation Protocol), which disengages hosting identity from position identity using a distributed referencing system (16).

7. Sensor network at a massive scale

   When an environmental tracking system, such as one used in microgrids, intrinsically expands its monitoring equipment due to hierarchical computation and storage material requirements, fog offers a capability that can be employed.

8. Wireless access is available across the platform

   Wireless access protocols and mobile cellular terminals are classic instances of fog node accessibility to end customers in this scenario.

9. Technology that is versatile

To build support for a broad array of services, such as streaming data and real-time computing for the finest data analyses and predictive judgments, fog elements must be eligible to function in an interoperable atmosphere.

These highlighted qualities enable new technologies and business structures that can help the industry increase income, reduce costs, and expedite widespread implementation, as well as entice new investment in the fog architecture installation space.

7.5.2 Architecture of Fog Computing

Fog computing is a method of relocating a few data center processes to the network edge. Fog computing, also known as edge computing, is the next-generation computing that brings the cloud closer to the sources of data. The primary goal of fog computing is to address the issues that CC faces, such as delivering less and more predictable latency for timely IoT functions. The functions of fog computing architecture follow (17).

1. Eliminates the need to transfer large amounts of data to the cloud. Investigates the most time-critical data at the network's edge, where it is generated by devices.
2. Through fog computing, only selected data is sent to the cloud for analysis and long-term storage.
3. It uses rules to respond to the IoT data in milliseconds.

Various functions that are carried out are aggregated among fog computing architecture components (1).

7.5.2.1 IoT Devices

These are devices that connect to an IoT network via various wired and wireless technologies. Every day, these devices generate massive amounts of data (18). The IoT makes use of Zigbee, Zwave, RFID (radio-frequency identification), 6LoWPAN, HART (highway addressable remote transducer), NFC (near-field communication), Bluetooth, BLE (bluetooth low energy), NFC, ISA-100.11A, and other wireless technologies. In addition, IPv4, IPv6, MQTT (message queuing telemetry transport technical), CoAP (constrained application protocol), XMPP (extensible messaging and presence protocol), AMQP (advanced message queuing protocol), and other IoT protocols are used.

7.5.2.2 Fog Layer

Fog nodes are devices, such as routers, gateways, access points, base stations, and specific fog servers. They sit between end devices and cloud data centers. They can temporarily compute, transfer, and store data. They are used to dealing with routinely sensitive information.

7.5.2.3 Cloud Layer

The cloud layer is at the far end of the fog architecture. Unlike the fog layer, it provides permanent storage; typically, data that is not required in the users' proximity is present in the cloud layer. The cloud is linked to all the combined fog nodes (17, 18). Data that is not time-sensitive or has a lower priority is processed, analyzed, and stored in the cloud.

7.5.3 Layers of Fog Computing Architecture

According to previous research (19–22), the fog computing architecture consists of six layers: 1. physical and virtualization; 2. monitoring; 3. preprocessing; 4. temporary storage; 5. security; and 6. transport layer. Each layer has its own set of functions, and while they are all autonomous for operability, they are all pipelined for processing.

7.5.3.1 Physical and Virtualization Layer

This layer is made up of physical and virtual nodes. The nodes are dispersed throughout the network and perform the primary function of data collection. Sensor technologies are commonly used by nodes to record their surroundings. Several types of sensors are used at this node to collect data from the environment, which is then transferred to higher levels via gateways for further processing. The collected data is transmitted for processing using gateways. A node can be a standalone device, such as a smartphone, or a component of a larger device, such as a temperature sensor that is installed in a car (23).

7.5.3.2 Monitoring Layer

In this layer, nodes are monitored for a variety of reasons. This layer keeps track of the available sensors, fog nodes, and network components. The duration of node operation, their temperature and other physical characteristics, and the maximum battery life of the device can all be tracked. The performance and current state of applications are examined. The energy consumption of the fog nodes is monitored, i.e., how much battery power they consume when performing their functions (20, 21).

7.5.3.3 Preprocessing Layer

This layer handles a wide range of data activities, the majority of which are related to analysis. The data is cleansed and verified to ensure that it contains no potentially harmful information. When data impurities are removed, only meaningful data is collected. Data analysis at this level might entail extracting useful and relevant information from a large volume of data that is generated by end devices. Before using the data for a specific purpose, one of the most important characteristics to consider is data analysis (21, 22).

7.5.3.4 Temporary Storage

This layer is linked to data replication and nonpersistent dissemination. Storage virtualization, such as VSAN (virtual storage area network), is used in this layer. The preprocessed data is temporarily stored in the temporary storage layer. Data is removed from the temporary layer once it has been transported to the cloud (21, 22).

7.5.3.5 Security Layer

This layer is in charge of data privacy, integrity, encryption, and decryption. For fog computing data privacy, there are three options: 1. use-based privacy; 2. data-based privacy; and 3. location-based privacy. The security layer ensures that the data sent to the fog nodes is secure and private. Data integrity measures can also be used to protect it from tampering.

7.5.3.6 Transport Layer

The primary responsibility of this layer is to send partially processed and fine-grained encrypted data to the cloud layer for long-term storage. For efficiency, a portion of the data is gathered and uploaded. The data is routed through smart gateways before being uploaded to the cloud. Because the resources that are available for fog computing are limited, the communication protocols used were chosen to be lightweight and efficient.

A fog architecture is a model that consists of several layers. The model can be used to plan a fog network. The architecture depicts the numerous functions that are performed by the various tiers. Going through the fog architecture identifies the protocols that are used at various layers, as well as the individual devices used at various layers and their functionality and specifications.

7.5.4 Fog Data Flow

To construct an IoT system, the fog computing architectural design is composed of pieces of hardware and software. It is made up of IoT systems, fog nodes, and distant cloud storage databases, as shown in Figure 7.1.

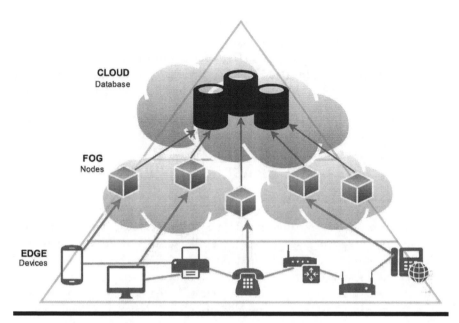

Figure 7.1   Fog data flow architecture.

7.6 Fog Computing with the IoT

According to research (24), for the IoT, the present hierarchical CC architecture faces significant hurdles. It cannot, for example, handle time-sensitive applications such as multimedia applications, games, or virtual reality (25). Furthermore, because it is a centralized paradigm, it lacks location-based services. Fog computing can help with these problems. Fog computing connects the IoT systems with large-scale cloud-based systems. Fog computing, according to Cisco (26), is a component of the cloud infrastructure that brings the cloud near to the network edge.

Almost all the data that is recorded by these sensor devices must be handled and evaluated in real-time to maximize the productivity of the IoT systems (27). Fog computing will provide cloud networking, computation, and memory capacity to the network's edge, which addresses the real-time issue of the devices while also ensuring secure and effective applications (28). Fog computing offers a range of services and operations that might be deployed across a large area. Through proxies and gateways that are positioned along lengthy roads and railways, fog can offer effective communication between diverse IoT applications, such as networked automobiles. Fog computing is seen to be the best option for systems that require low latency, such as those of video services, games, and wearable technology (29).

Combining fog computing with the IoT will help a variety of IoT applications. Fog helps to enable connections between IoT devices to minimize latency, which is especially helpful for time-critical IoT systems. Furthermore, fog computing can handle massive network architecture, which is a major issue with the ever-increasing number of devices, which will eventually number in billions. Fog computing has the potential to overcome many of the constraints of current computer systems that rely only on CC and terminal devices that connect to the IoT devices.

7.7 Fog–IoT Based Agricultural Applications

7.7.1 PA

PA refers to a set of agronomic management practices aimed at detecting and responding to changes in growing areas (e.g., soil, moisture, and organic matter), as well as crop optimization strategies. In terms of the environment, PA is a clever tool to achieve precise and targeted fertilizer application, which results in a significant reduction in pesticide usage. Researchers (4) created a fog-based IoT framework that uses two-tier fog and its resources to reduce data that is sent to the cloud, improve computational load balancing, and shorten wait times. It was designed by a three-tiered architect. The three-tier architecture was composed of the M2M (mobile to mobile) platform, gateway, and sensor nodes. The M2M platform is a cloud-based service that can be used for data storage, visualization, network management, and data reporting. Fog collector and fog aggregator nodes are the underlying layers. The communication between layers was defined using efficient protocols and IoT-appropriate technologies, both for resource conservation and the ability to reach remote locations.

The proposed fog computing technology is used in the burgeoning field of PA, which includes all agricultural land management methods. Furthermore, researchers simulated and demonstrated how the two-tier fog computing strategy could significantly reduce the amount of data that was transported to the cloud using this architecture. Based on the previous architecture, a prototype application to manage and monitor farms was proposed and explained, which could have a significant impact on commercial and environmental performances.

7.7.2 Smart Crop Disease Prediction

Pests and crop diseases have always posed a threat to agricultural output quality and quantity (30). As a result, their precise and timely forecasting could significantly reduce global economic losses while also reducing the negative environmental impact of fertilizers and pesticides. CC and the IoT could be used to create an interconnected network in this case. These frameworks aren't yet capable of dealing with computational problems. Fog computing attempts to bring processing capabilities closer to the target customers, reduce operational pressures, and avoid cloud resource misuse.

Agricultural disease outbreaks pose a significant risk to productivity (31), as many illnesses have significantly reduced crop output because of lockdown conditions, a lack of knowledge about crop development, and insufficient use of technology in farming areas. In the farming industry, IoT-based technology necessitates the collection of a large amount of data and the transmission of that data to a cloud server for illness categorization and detection, which is time-consuming and causes delays in diagnosis and treatment. In the literature (31), an IoT-based framework was presented for agricultural disease monitoring that used fog computing to perform timely disease monitoring in crops with the least delays. They proposed this framework for crop monitoring in a cloud–fog environment with minimal delays because it would improve the early warning and prediction system and provide on-time information to farmers, which allowed for well-timed measures to solve problems before they become destructive to productivity.

7.7.3 Fog Computing in Large Farms

Fog computing necessitates higher investment in computer and network design. Its infrastructure is still scarce, and as a result, it is mostly reserved for large farms. Furthermore, it is ideal for hard-to-reach areas. The advantage of fog in the open air is that you can see the fog and control its direction. The basic concept of fog is to reduce the cloud level to the farm level. Some of the key benefits of fog for large farms are that it takes video streams exclusively for farms, does not take them out of farms, does not require high bandwidth, and processes multiple videos simultaneously.

However, there are a few drawbacks. The maintenance of fog is a complicated process. The cost of hardware has increased. Furthermore, not all initiatives can be managed remotely, and maintaining infrastructure, such as fog, is more difficult.

7.8 Issues in Applications of Fog

Fog computing emerged from cloud technology as a cost-effective and monetized means of providing processing resources to consumers. The current developments in the growth of IoT gadgets (e.g., sensor systems and mobile phones), which have low-cost equipment, are becoming extremely important. The processing is done close to the edge, which decreases the cloud computation and data transferring charges while simultaneously providing security and privacy protection at the customer's end. However, technology on the edge faces numerous issues with networking, authentication, gadgets, and fog integration with the IoT, all of which are being researched. Fog computing operates in a decentralized architecture that takes a variety of factors into account. A brief review of the issues posed in producing fog alternatives in general, as well as in the agricultural business, is presented in the following section.

7.8.1 Challenges in the Device and Network

The following are some of the technology and network difficulties that are discussed: distributed architecture, connectivity tools, and gadget variation.

In a distributed architecture, fog computing's structure is distributed, which results in data redundancy. At the network edge, there is a recurrence of the identical code (32, 33). Therefore, the fog ecosystem should concentrate on eliminating distributed design inconsistency.

For the connectivity tools, the networking packets are spontaneously dispersed at the periphery of the fog system. This adds to the connectivity's intricacy. A good connection with components to retain a common pool of assets at the edge might be maintained to provide the services to the needed application.

In gadget variation, the fogs technology's edge devices are diverse. The essence of variability has resulted in more diversified structures (34). Fog-based software should take this element of variation into account at the system and networking levels.

7.8.2 Computing Difficulties

Computation at the fog stage is crucial because of computation at multiple levels and the distribution of computing capacity. Cloud services must always interface with fog technology. The fundamental goal of the fog technology should be to reply to customers during a certain timeframe at the bottom level when simultaneously carrying out its necessary calculations to the server, which would require more time. It is difficult to tell which computation should be performed in the cloud and which should be done in fog. It is possible that processing at the edge lacks the necessary tools. Additional nodes could be used to obtain similar materials. Therefore, because of this requirement it is now necessary to distribute resource calculations among numerous fog devices. Inside the fog computing environment pervasive computing is required (35). In the fog paradigm, mobility is a restriction. The fog infrastructure software must be created in such a way that there are fewer inconsistencies in the calculations (36, 37). These inconsistencies should be demonstrable. OpenFog is designated as an N-tier environment in relation to mobility. Nonetheless, the sudden growth in the population of fog level divisions might pose complications in the newly developed fog framework. In a fog computing atmosphere, commodity use is at its most brilliant and distinct. Using the resources available for fog computing is interesting, but it must be accompanied by the understanding of the resources' long-term behavior. This assumption is critical because, after the fog operation starts, and for a set amount of time, the location of the assets might change due to the needs of the desired applications, for which the fog device action is responsible.

Because fog gadgets are dispersed and their management is not consolidated, the likelihood of them breaking down is increased. As a result, fog nodes might fail for a variety of reasons, including end-user behavior, equipment failures, and system failure. The fog architecture manages hundreds of IoT systems that are receptive and uncooperative regularly. Obtaining services is a unique difficulty for the whole fog estate. Extensive research is required to determine the viability of fog-based technologies. Because there are so many detectors and connected devices made by so many firms in computing, choosing the best methodology has become challenging due to the various hardware layouts, programming models, and specific requests. Furthermore, in a few cases, maximal security needs to involve specified procedures and gadgets to function, which increases the system's maintenance time.

7.8.3 Privacy Issues

The fog infrastructure is made up of a variety of embedded systems. They might be subjected to a variety of methods, such as the person in the center approach in a fog computing environment (38). Information and networking are the most significant concerns in a fog computing environment.

7.8.4 Administrative Difficulties

A way of system computing through the network edge is the dissemination of resources above the fog nodes. Delivering tiny operations over fog devices; however, has its own set of problems. In the fog computing industry, the proper management of the infrastructure, and hence, the acquisition of resources is the most pressing challenge. In local service management, there are several challenges. Fog computing's structure enables it to modify and adapt to a variety of difficulties, which include resource scarcity and malfunctions. If any fog component fails, the system will be brought to a halt, with no capabilities accessible from the affected fog layer. In a fog computing environment, these services are simulated.

Many issues are associated with resource abstraction, which includes relocation, delay, and activation, and must be managed appropriately for services to be accessible during an outage. The fog architecture is made up of cloud and edge gadgets. The coordination of these diverse edge devices, as well as the cloud platforms that are used to execute computing and storage in a decentralized system (39), needs to be addressed. As a result, the final connection of fog devices and the cloud hosts must be loaded into the memory.

Clouds, fog, and edge-based systems have huge benefits in agricultural industries, but they also have a number of drawbacks. The obstacles and potential solutions are well described as follows.

1. Confidentiality (9–14, 40–43)

   Security and privacy issues, authentication and integrity, identification and encrypted communications, and adherence and laws are the major issues when it comes to smart agriculture that uses cloud technology (44). This is because smart farms create a massive quantity of data from numerous sources of data such as detectors, motors, and end devices. As a result, there is a risk of information leaks for information cloud storage. Farmers and agricultural enterprises may suffer significant financial losses because of this. To tackle this problem, apps must combine cloud (42) with greater computation power, such as edge computing, processing enormous data, machine intelligence capabilities, and high security.

2. Mobile assistance (40)

   Because smart farms constantly collect additional field data, they require transportation assistance and actual data analysis. These functions are not available if the farms are solely connected via the cloud. The properties of fog, on the other hand, allow for the real-time collection of information and interpretation in the field. Furthermore, there is a consistent high internet speed for real-time data analysis. Combinations of fog and edge have been proposed to overcome this problem since they have properties, such as low delay, bandwidth efficiency, and high flexibility (40).

3. Management and analysis (45, 40, 46, 47)

   In sustainable farming, data analysis and prediction are critical. In terms of actual data, smart fields that rely only on the cloud to evaluate and deliver outcomes will fall short. A hybrid of edge–cloud or fog–cloud might be an ideal option in this instance.

4. Power enhancements (45, 46, 48, 49)

   Cameras, motors, and portable devices are required for smart farming to function. To gather information and deliver it to other levels or for analysis on the network edge, all these sensors require electricity (50–52). Effective generation and energy management capabilities extend the life of cells. Sources of energy, such as solar electricity, can be employed as an option to extend the life of sensor networks (46, 49, 53).

5. High equipment expenses (45, 47, 54)

   In cloud-based smart agriculture, the act of posting and data analysis uses equipment and a number of cloud network services, such as cameras as well as other end devices to continually gather data and transfer it to the cloud. It also covers the implementation of the IoT in smart farms. To control operational cost difficulties in smart agriculture, effective price management is important.

6. Internet access (55, 56, 57)

 Among the most prevalent challenges in smart farming, particularly in remote regions, is an inadequate internet connection. To be a smart plantation, you must have internet access. Data leakage, computational inefficiencies, sluggish information upload speeds, and delayed response are all challenges that are caused by bad internet access in fields. Furthermore, if smart farming is simply connected to the cloud, the same issues will arise. Fog computing, on the other hand, could address these concerns because it operates local network and database servers. As a result, local data analysis is feasible since it includes offline operations.

The smart agricultural systems must dynamically establish the filtration period and frequency, and the software must understand the contextual conditions to complete the filtering. To put it another way, the smart agricultural system should modify the filters that depend on the evidence that is acquired from the crop field by the instruments.

7.9 Connectivity of Fog Elements to Cloud

Due to advances in the IoT and IT technologies, massive amounts of data will be generated that must be processed quickly and sustainably (58). To meet the growing demand for devices, by managing the process locally rather than in the cloud, fog computing performs on par with CC. Fog computing is a hybrid of the IoT and CC. The interconnectedness of fog and cloud has been revealed (59). Fog computing primarily provides real-time services to end users and brings CC capabilities closer to users. Fog is superior in a few areas. Low latency, no bandwidth issues, high security, power efficiency, and improved user experience are some of the fog's key advantages over CC. Because of these characteristics, opting for fog computing over CC is a wise decision.

The following are some distinctions between fog and CC.

1. The cloud's architecture is focused and contains massive amounts of data, whereas fog computing's architecture is distributed, with millions of small nodes that are placed as close to client devices as possible (58).
2. Fog connects data centers and hardware, bringing them closer to end users. If there is no fog layer, the cloud communicates with devices directly, which takes time.
3. CC's advantages over fog computing are its CC capabilities and storage capacity.
4. Fog performs short-term edge analysis due to its quick response, whereas the cloud focuses on long-term deep analysis due to its slower responsiveness (59).

There are several parallels. They are similar and complementary to one another. They collaborate so that the benefits of one offset the disadvantages of the other.

1. Both architectures are made up of multiple nodes that are linked to physical devices.
2. In cloud and fog computing, computer resources are placed between data sources and the cloud or any data centers (58).

7.10 Conclusions

In this chapter, a modern agricultural system was discussed, which was based on the framework of the IoT and fog computing, which extended the benefits of CC and reduced service delays. Through a more accurate and resource-efficient method, fog computing holds the promise of delivering more productive and sustainable agricultural production. Both are similar however edge is faster and has a higher latent value than fog and cloud. In a variety of ways, fog computing has benefited a wide range of industries, which has influenced profit growth. This work contributes by providing a comparative and comprehensive analysis of the issues and applications for fog computing in agriculture.

A comparison study aided in the most thorough investigation of the accuracy of all fog computing approaches, as well as a summary and conclusions on previous work. Fog computing and the IoT were concentrated on addressing agricultural production challenges, as well as previous research findings and diagrammatic overviews. As a result, the implementation of fog computing could provide additional benefits and new opportunities in the smart agricultural domain.

References

1. Kalyani Y, Collier R. A systematic survey on the role of cloud, fog, and edge computing combination in smart agriculture. Sensors. 2021; 21:5922. doi.10.3390/s21175922
2. Sucharitha V, Prakash P, Iyer G. Agrifog-a fog computing based IoT for smart agriculture. Int J Recent Technol Eng. 2019; 7:210–217.
3. Oliullah K, Tarafdar S, Whaiduzzaman MD. Fog computing and IoT based modern agricultural system. Topics in Intell Comput Ind Design. 2020; 2(1):88–92.
4. Guardo E, Di Stefano A, La Corte A, Sapienza M, Scata M. A fog computing-based iot framework for precision agriculture. J Internet Technol. 2018; 19(5): 1401–1411.
5. Malik AW, Ur Rahman A, Qayyum T, Ravana SD. Leveraging fog computing for sustainable smart farming using distributed simulation. IEEE Internet of Things J. 2020; 7(4):3300–3309.

6. Chew KT, Raman V, Hang Hui P. Fog-based WSAN for agriculture in developing countries. IEEE International Conference on Smart Internet of Things (SmartIoT); 2021; pp. 289–293. 13–15 August 2021, Jeju Island, South Korea.

7. Hsu T-C, Yang H, Chung Y-C, Hsu C-H. A creative IoT agriculture platform for cloud fog computing. Sustainable Computing: Informatics and Systems. 2020; 28.

8. da Costa Bezerra S, Filho ASM, Delicato FC, da Rocha AR. Processing complex events in fog-based internet of things systems for smart agriculture. Sensors. 2021; 21:7226. doi.10.3390/ s21217226

9. Nandhini S, Shivcharan Bhrathi D , Dheeraj G, Pranay K. Smart agriculture IOT with cloud computing, fog computing and edge computing. Int J Eng Adv Technol. 2019; 9(2):3578–3582.

10. Verma M, Bhardwaj N, Yadav AK. Real time efficient scheduling algorithm for load balancing in fog computing environment. Int J Inf Technol Comput Sci. 2016; 8(4):1–10.

11. Kim H-S. Fog computing and the Internet of Things: Extend the cloud to where the things are. Int J Cisco. 2016.

12. Anawar MR, Wang S, Azam Zia M, Khan Jadoon A, Akram U, Raza S. Fog computing: An overview of big IoT data analytics. Wirel Comm Mob Comput. 2018.

13. Chiang M, Zhang T. Fog and IoT: An overview of research opportunities. IEEE IoT J. 2016; 3(6):854–864.

14. Bonomi F, Milito R, Natarajan P, Zhu J. Fog computing: A platform for internet of things and analytics. Big Data and Internet of Things: A Roadmap For Smart Environments. Cham, Switzerland: Springer; 2014; pp. 169–186.

15. More P. Review of implementing fog computing. Int J Res Eng Technol. 2015; 4(6):335–338.

16. Zhu J, Chan DS, Suryanarayana Prabhu M, Natarajan P, Hu H, Bonomi F. Improving web sites performance using edge servers in fog computing architecture. IEEE Seventh International Symposium on Service-Oriented System Engineering; pp. 320–323. 25–28 March 2013, San Francisco, USA.

17. Qureshi R, Mehboob SH, Aamir M. Sustainable green fog computing for smart agriculture. Wirel Personal Comm. 202; 121(2):1379–1390.

18. Taneja M, Jalodia N, Malone P, Misha E. Methodical analysis of a Fog computing assisted animal-welfare software system in a real-world smart dairy farm IoT deployment. 2021 IEEE 7th World Forum on IoT (WF-IoT), 2021; pp. 857–864.14 June – 31 July 2021, New Orleans, USA.

19. Aazam M, Huh EN. Fog computing and smart gateway based communication for cloud of things. Proceedings of the 2014 International Conference on Future Internet of Things Cloud (FiCloud 2014); 2014; pp. 464–470. 07–09 August, Barcelona, Spain.

20. Mukherjee M, Shu L, Wang D. Survey of fog computing: Fundamental, network applications, and research challenges. IEEE Commun Surv Tutor. 2018; 20(3):1826–1857.

21. Aazam M, Huh EN. Fog computing micro datacenter based dynamic resource estimation and pricing model for IoT. Proceedings of Int Conf Adv Inf Netw Appl. 2015; 687–694.

22. Muntjir M, Rahul M, Alhumyani HA. An analysis of Internet of Things (IoT): Novel architectures, modern applications, security aspects and future scope with latest case studies. Int J Eng Res Technol. 2017; 6:422–447.

23. Liu Y, Fieldsend JE, Min G. A framework of fog computing: Architecture, challenges and optimization. IEEE Access. 2017; 4:1–10.

24. Atlam HF, Walters RJ , Wills GB. Fog computing and the Internet of Things: A review. Big Data Cognit Comput. 2018; 2(2):10.

25. Mouradian C, Naboulsi D , Yangui S , Glitho RH , Morrow MJ , Polakos PA. A comprehensive survey on fog computing: State-of-the-art and research challenges. IEEE Comm Surv Tutor. 2017; 20(1):416–464.

26. Networking, cloud, and cybersecurity solutions. Cisco. [Internet] [cited: 11 Jan 2022]. Available from: https:cisco.com/c/en/us/index.html

27. Atlam HF, Madini O, Alassafi A, Walters RJ, Wills GB. XACML for building access control policies in Internet of Things. Proceedings of IoTBDS. 2018; 253–260.

28. Ketel M. Fog-cloud services for IoT. Proceedings of the SouthEast Conference. 2017; pp. 262–264 April 2017, Kennesaw, USA.

29. Skarlat O, Schulte S, Borkowski M, Leitner P. Resource provisioning for IoT services in the fog. IEEE 9th International Conference on Service-Oriented Computing and Applications (SOCA). 2016; pp. 32–39. 04–06 November 2016, Macau, China.

30. Roy C, Das N, Swarup Rautaray S, Pandey M. A fog computing-based IoT framework for prediction of crop disease using big data analytics. AI, Edge and IoT-Based Smart Agriculture. Elsevier, USA: Academic Press. 2022; pp. 287–300.

31. Islam S, Jamwal S, Hussain Mir M. Leveraging fog computing for smart Internet of Things crop monitoring farming in Covid-19 era. Ann Romanian Soc Cell Biol. 2021; 25(6):10410–10420.

32. Tang B, Chen Z, Hefferman G, Wei T, He H, Yang Q. A hierarchical distributed fog computing architecture for big data analysis in smart cities. Proceedings of ASE BigData Social Informat. 2015:1–6.

33. Chiang M, Ha S, Risso F, Zhang T, Chih-Lin I. Clarifying fog computing and networking: 10 questions and answers. IEEE Commun. 2017; 55(4):18–20.

34. Bonomi F, Milito R, Natarajan P, Zhu J. Fog computing: A platform for internet of things and analytics. Big Data and Internet of Things: A Roadmap for Smart Environments. Cham, Switzerland: Springer; 2014; pp. 169–186.

35. Stojmenovic I. Fog computing: A cloud to the ground support for smart things and machine-to-machine networks. Australasian Telecommunication Networks and Applications Conference (ATNAC). pp. 117–122. 26–28 November 2014, Southbank, Australia.

36. Aazam M, Huh E-N. Dynamic resource provisioning through fog micro datacenter. IEEE International Conference on Pervasive Computing and Communication Workshops (PerCom workshops). pp. 105–110. 23–27 March 2015, St. Louis, USA.

37. Li S, Ali Maddah-Ali M, Salman Avestimehr A. Coding for distributed fog computing. IEEE Commun. 2017; 55(4):34–40.

38. Stojmenovic I, Wen S, Huang X, Luan H. An overview of fog computing and its security issues. Concurr Comput. 2016; 28(10):2991–3005.

39. Vilalta R, Mayoral A, Pubill D, Casellas R, Martinez R, Serra J, et al. End-to-end SDN orchestration of IoT services using an SDN/NFV-enabled edge node. Optical Fiber Communication Conference, W2A-42. Optical Society of America, 2016.

40. Symeonaki EG, Arvanitis KG , Piromalis DD. Cloud computing for IoT applications in climate-smart agriculture: A review on the trends and challenges toward sustainability. International Conference on Information and Communication Technologies in Agriculture, Food & Environment Cham, Switzerland: Springer. pp. 147–167. 21–24 September 2017, Chania, Greece.

41. Mehta A, Patel S. IoT based smart agriculture research opportunities and challenges. Int J Technol Res Eng. 2016; 4:541–543.

42. de Araujo Z, Rettore A, da Silva E, Carlos L , Albini P. Security challenges to smart agriculture: Current state, key issues, and future directions. Array. 2020; 8.

43. Khan MA, Salah K. IoT security: Review, blockchain solutions, and open challenges. Fut Gen Comput Syst. 2018; 82: 395–411.

44. Gupta M, Abdelsalam M, Khorsandroo S, Mittal S. Security and privacy in smart farming: Challenges and opportunities. IEEE Access. 2020; 8:34564–34584.

45. Zhang X, Cao Z, Dong W. Overview of edge computing in the agricultural Internet of Things: Key technologies, applications, challenges. IEEE Access. 2020; 8141748–8141761.

46. Rajasekaran T, Anandamurugan S. Challenges and applications of wireless sensor networks in smart farming: A survey. Advances in Big Data and Cloud Computing. Singapore: Springer; 2019. pp. 353–361.

47. Elijah O, Abdul Rahman T, Orikumhi I, Yen Leow C, Nour Hindia MHD. An overview of Internet of Things (IoT) and data analytics in agriculture: Benefits and challenges IEEE IoT J. 2018; 5(5):3758–3773.

48. Madushanki AAR, Surangi Wirasagoda WAH , Halgamuge MN, Syed, A. Adoption of the Internet of Things (IoT) in agriculture and smart farming towards urban greening: A review. Int J Adv Comput Sci Appl. 2019; 10(4).

49. Chung W-Y, Luo R-H, Chen C-L, Heythem S, Chang C-F, Po C-C, et al. Solar powered monitoring system development for smart farming and Internet of Thing applications. Meet Abstracts Electrochem Soc. 2019; 28:1371–1375.

50. Ruiz-Garcia L, Lunadei L, Barreiro P, Robla I. A review of wireless sensor technologies and applications in agriculture and food industry: state of the art and current trends. Sensors. 2009; 9(6):4728–4750.

51. Ojha T, Misra S, Raghuwanshi NS. Wireless sensor networks for agriculture: The state-of-the-art in practice and future challenges. Comput Electron Agric. 2015; 118:6–84.

52. Abbasi AZ, Islam N, Ahmed Shaikh Z. A review of wireless sensors and networks' applications in agriculture. Comput Standard Interf. 2014; 36(2):263–270.

53. Maddikunta PKR, Hakak S, Alazab M, Bhattacharya S, Gadekallu TP, Khan WZ, et al. Unmanned aerial vehicles in smart agriculture: Applications, requirements, and challenges. IEEE Sensors J. 2021.

54. Ratnaparkhi S, Khan S, Arya C, Khapre S, Singh P, Diwakar M, et al. Smart agriculture sensors in IOT: A review. Mater Today: Proc. 2020.

55. Pivoto D, Dabdab Waquil P, Talamini E, Pauletto Spanhol Finocchio C, Francisco Dalla Corte V, de Vargas Mores G. Scientific development of smart farming technologies and their application in Brazil. Inf Process Agric. 2018; 5(1):21–32.

56. Tzounis A, Katsoulas N, Bartzanas T, Kittas C. Internet of Things in agriculture, recent advances and future challenges. Biosyst Eng. 2017; 164:31–48.

57. Eitzinger A, Cock J, Atzmanstorfer K, Binder CR, Laderach P, Bonilla-Findji O, et al. GeoFarmer: A monitoring and feedback system for agricultural development projects. Comput Electron Agric. 2019; 158:109–121.

58. Masrat A, Gawde H, Ammar Makki M, Parekh U. Connecting fog and cloud computing. Int Res J Eng Technol. 2021; 8(9). Available from: www.irjet.net

59. Linthicum DS. Connecting fog and cloud computing. IEEE Cloud Computing. 2017; 4(2):18–20.

Chapter 8

Fog Computing and Vehicular Networks for Smart Traffic Control

Fog Computing-Based Cognitive Analytics Model for Smart Traffic Control

Deep Kumar

DIT University, Dehradun, Uttarakhand, India

Contents

DOI: 10.1201/9781003322931-8

8.1 Introduction

Traffic congestion on roads is a significant problem worldwide. Exhaust gas emissions, long travel delays, wastage of fuel consumption, and unsure travel timing are some of the issues that are created by unprecedented traffic congestion in urban areas. The intelligent management of vehicular traffic flow, real-time traffic monitoring, and real-time suggestions to commuters can reduce the acute impact of traffic congestion on the environment. This is the motivation behind the fog computing based cognitive analytics model for smart traffic control. The fog computing environment has multiple fog resources with the Internet of Things (IoT) sensors distributed over many geographic locations. This environment allows users to monitor real-time data and the summarized attributes for inference rules creation. Deployment of cloud applications for decision-making and to display the summarized results of IoT sensors on mobile devices is a common practice today (1). The IoT devices are proficient in generating and capturing signals for the creation of data in any system. Data gathered from IoT devices could be structured or unstructured (2). The manipulation of sensor data could be assisted by different technologies, such as cloud, edge, fog computing, and machine learning (ML).

1. Cloud computing

   In the last few decades, cloud computing platforms have provided a high computation environment with dynamic storage capability. Centralized cloud centers provide on-demand access to data storage, computing functions, and ML models (3). Data size is growing rapidly; however, data storage and analysis in cloud centers results in high latency, network congestion, and a delay in query response time.

2. Fog computing

   Fog computing provides auxiliary features to cloud computing by performing regional computation and abstraction from the central server to the edge network resources. The advances in fog computing have provided numerous choices for storage, networking, and data analysis in a fog environment (1). Some real-time applications, such as smart traffic systems require data processing and analysis instantly. So, fog computing constructs a low latency network interface between the IoT sensors to reduce the response time and make transmission and analysis faster (2).

3. Motivation

   The proper management of traffic flows, synchronization of traffic lights and distribution of information to commuters about the traffic status is a tough task to achieve in developing countries. A cognitive model for smart traffic control could help execute regional spatial queries locally and to achieve the goal of an intelligent traffic system. In most developed countries, traffic is lane-based, orderly traffic (Figure 8.1), which is easy to process for

Figure 8.1 Lane-based traffic.

Figure 8.2 Chaotic traffic.

insights. In developing countries, traffic is very much more chaotic as shown in Figure 8.2. In unordered traffic two and three-wheelers, cars, and heavy vehicles are intermingled on the same road chaotically. So, chaotic traffic requires significant research and a proper real-time insight model. Proper traffic optimization could be helpful in the avoidance of traffic congestion and reducing exhaust gas emissions. So, the deployment and optimization of fog resources within a cloud environment in a cognitive manner could reduce the use of cloud resources. The outcomes of these fog resources would be helpful in the creation of inference rules for decision-making. Therefore, with the help of middleware computing units in the fog environment, the local suggestions from regional inference rules that are created from those geographic regions can be optimized.

8.2 Related Work

8.2.1 Intelligent Transport System

An intelligent transport system (ITS) is an interdisciplinary combination of different research domains. Embedded research is required for the optimized construction and deployment of road sensors, such as acoustic, proximity, and magnetic loop sensors. A mobile computing background is necessary for the utilization of mobile sensors for sensing traffic density. Knowledge of signal processing and ML is required for analysis and pattern recognition in sensed data that is acquired from sensors. Synchronization and proper protocol communication between the IoT sensors with the traffic authority are required for optimized traffic control.

For traffic prediction and classification, different kinds of ML models could be used after preprocessing the sensor data. So, after deployment of the fog layer, a low latency network could be created for better real-time traffic prediction.

8.3 Proposed Cognitive Model for Smart Traffic Control

8.3.1 Phase 1: Deployment of Static Sensors at Highest Traffic Density Locations (IoT Layer)

1. Acoustic sensors
   Acoustic sensors are noise based and helpful for non-lane-based traffic recognition (4). The placement of these sensors will be at significant locations

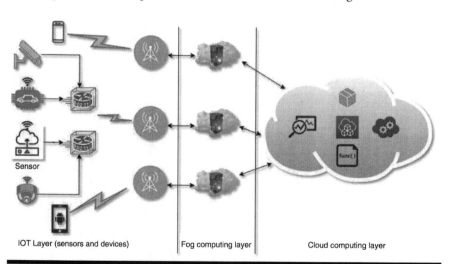

Figure 8.3   Fog computing architecture with layers.

to sense vehicle noises. The sensor's recorded data will be transferred to the nearest fog units for further processing. In the fog units, sensed attributes would be linked with location coordinates and geometric constructs for further analysis. The categorization of sensed noise attributes in various classes with spatial-temporal attributes would lead to the recognition of regional-based patterns.

2. Proximity sensors

   Proximity sensors are composed of transmitter–receiver pairs across the road to sense the obstacles between them. Here, a transmitter continuously sends the packets, and the facing receiver quantifies metrics like packet reception ratio and signal strength. Sensed attributes from these sensors will be shared with fog devices and correlated with location coordinates and geometric constructs allocated to their coordinates. Signal strength will be different according to the road width, which is why linking with spatial coordinates and geometric constructs is necessary for better predictions.

3. CCTV images and videos

   CCTV surveillance is common worldwide and depicts the traffic incidents and traffic density status in urban areas. There are various algorithms for object recognition, evaluating traffic density, and measuring vehicle speed from video footage (5, 6, 7, 8). In chaotic traffic, vehicle detection is a tough task to perform. The traffic coverage area on a road could easily be identified from static CCTV footage based on Haar features within a frame. The measured window of traffic density would be trained from these features for the approximation of traffic in each direction with locations and geographic constructs. This could be helpful in the prediction of the traffic coverage area for geometric constructs with spatiotemporal attributes. So, the task of vehicle recognition and continuous video analysis will be reduced to traffic window polygons that will be easily processed with geographic map polygons.

4. Mobile sensors

   GPS (global positioning system) on public transport and GPS and sensors on smartphones mapped to traffic polygons and geographic regions will be used for traffic polygons intensity and flow with time.

Accelerometer meter readings from smartphones could be used for brake identification within traffic polygons (9, 10, 11, 12). These values could be easily correlated to entry and exit times in traffic polygons and combined with other regional sensors for more precise patterns. All the sensed attributes within a specific bounding box could lead to the proper size and variation in traffic polygons with time. This would be helpful in route suggestions for users and overall traffic light synchronization for the traffic authorities, as shown in Figure 8.4.

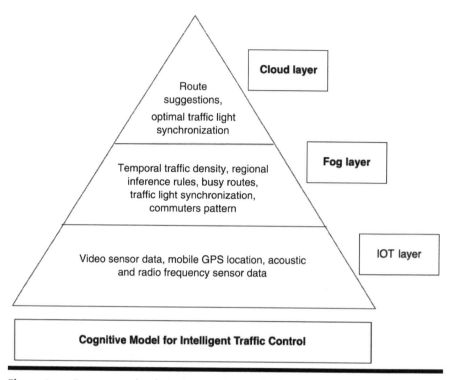

Figure 8.4   Fog computing based cognitive model for smart traffic control.

8.3.2 Phase 2: ETL Process for Sensed Attributes of Sensors in the Fog layer

This idea is implemented through the ETL (extract, transform, load) process of locally sensor data at the fog site and the creation of facts with inference rules locally. So, various parameters, such as busy routes, traffic density, and traffic light synchronization are correlated with spatial population, weather (e.g., rain and fog), and exhaust gas emission. The sensed attributes from all static sensors will be analyzed with their spatiotemporal attributes to create regional inference rules. These inference rules will be helpful in the creation of traffic density polygons with time in those specific regions. Therefore, users traveling in adjacent geographic polygons could be informed locally to reduce the efforts of the main cloud centers.

The implementation of a created knowledge base in a cognitive model could be helpful in the handling of spatial queries. Spatial queries at the fog sites could be handled efficiently using an indexing approach, such as an R tree with few bounding boxes for that region, which would have all the traffic polygons with the geographic polygons. The historical data from the traffic polygons for associated routes within a city could be used for daily traffic patterns, route suggestions, and traffic light synchronization. The inference rules created for that specific region would be optimized for better traffic prediction and suggestions in real-time. The spatial queries within the fog site could be executed in a distributed environment according to their spatial regions (i.e., bounding boxes). A knowledge base of the fog sites will be updated within the cloud environment for mapping of client suggestion layout with query execution.

8.3.3 Phase 3: Regional Traffic Geometric Constructs, Inference Rule and Knowledge Base Management in the Cloud Layer

The summarized attributes and regional patterns at the fog sites will reduce the computational time in the cloud servers. The users from spatial regions in the fog sites could be easily correlated with traffic polygons. The application dashboards of these users would receive summarized attributes of traffic polygons in real time when they reached the associated bounding boxes or spatial regions.

8.4 Conclusions

A fog-based cognitive analytics model could handle and suggest a regional knowledge base for smart traffic control. The inference rule created at the local fog spatial regions would be helpful for the creation of generalized spatial inference rules in the cloud environment. The complexity of the model would depend on the traffic and geographic polygons rather than the object recognition and analysis, which was why the implementation could be real-time computable at the fog sites or on smart CCTVs. This model is optimal for chaotic traffic sensing, real-time route suggestions, and low latency networks. The creation of a further knowledge base that uses multiple IoT sensors could be helpful in smart city models.

References

1. Hosseinioun P, Kheirabadi M, Tabbakh SRK, Ghaemi R. A new energy-aware tasks scheduling approach in fog computing using hybrid meta-heuristic algorithm. Journal of Parallel and Distributed Computing. 2020; 143:88–96.
2. Sood SK, Kaur A, Sood V. Energy efficient IoT-fog based architectural paradigm for prevention of Dengue fever infection. Journal of Parallel and Distributed Computing. 2021; 150:46–59.
3. Yadav AK, Tomar R, Kumar D, Gupta H. Security and privacy concerns in cloud computing. Comput Sci Softw Eng. 2012; 2(5).
4. Agarwal S, Swami BL. Road traffic noise annoyance in Jaipur city. Int J Eng Stud. 2009; 1(1)3946.

5. Palubinskas G, Kurz F, Reinartz P. Detection of traffic congestion in optical remote sensing imagery. IEEE International Geoscience and Remote Sensing Symposium. 07–11 July 2008, Boston, USA.
6. Li L, Chen L, Huang X, Huang J. A traffic congestion estimation approach from video using time-spatial imagery. First International Conference on Intelligent Networks and Intelligent Systems. 01–03 November 2008, Wuhan, China.
7. Kastrinaki V, Zervakis M, Kalaitzakis K. A survey of video processing techniques for traffic applications. Image and Vision Computing. Science Direct. 2003.
8. Chauhan AK, Kumar D. Study of moving object detection and tracking for video surveillance. International Journal of Advanced Research in Computer Science and Software Engineering. 2013; 3(4).
9. Mohan P, Padmanabhan VN, Ramjee R. Nericell: Rich monitoring of road and traffic conditions using mobile smartphones. SenSys. 2008; 1.
10. Thiagarajan A, Biagioni J, Gerlich T, Eriksson J. Cooperative transit tracking using smart- phones. Sensys. 2010; 11.
11. Koukoumidis E, Peh L, Martonosi M. Signalguru: Leveraging mobile phones for collaborative traffic signal schedule advisory. MobiSys. 2011; 1:127–140.
12. Thiagarajan A, Ravindranath L, Balakrishnan H, Madden S, Girod L. Accurate, low-energy trajectory mapping for mobile devices. NSDI. 2011.

Chapter 9

Virtualization Concepts and Industry Standards in Cloud Computing

Devesh Kumar Srivastava, Vijay Kumar Sharma,
Akhilesh Kumar Sharma, and
Prakash Chandra Sharma
School of Computing Information Technology, Manipal University, Jaipur, Rajasthan, India

Contents

DOI: 10.1201/9781003322931-9

9.1 Introduction

Industry 4.0 is the fourth mechanical revolution where mechanical worldview, PCs, and computerization will combine in another creative manner. Industry 4.0 is a lot of mechanical changes that are intended to allow a clear construction to be introduced into the assembling cycle. It is the utilization of digital actual frameworks, the Internet of Things (IoT), appropriated processing, and intellectual figuring into the collecting and administration platform. Virtualization (1) is referred to as the backbone of cloud computing, a procedure that is used to optimize the full use of the capabilities of computers. It is a technique used to make many OS (operating system) applications work on our workplace desktops.

In Industry 4.0, virtualization will contain a few innovation patterns that include distributed computing, versatility, and the IoT. Strong, high-accessibility networks that give representatives, machines, PCs, and applications access to information from any gadgets, which assemble a proficient IoT framework are much more effective. Virtualization is one of the plan standards alongside interoperability, decentralization, seclusion, administration advances, and ongoing ability that are shaping Industry 4.0 applications. A virtualized cloud framework will take on various issues that are faced effortlessly. Virtualization has some advantages: it decreases the number of actual assets required and gives an approach to fragmenting organizations, applications, or cycles. Virtualization can work at an association, laborer, or singular stage level. It licenses you to run various meetings for different people or simultaneously or to disconnect a singular work region into two virtual machines (VMs).

With virtualization (2, 3) and the increasing presence of the web, people have on-demand permission to numerous PCs as they need, and the way that these PCs exist remotely in some data centers does not affect an individual's ability to manage and use a machine. Nowadays, about a million servers are virtualized into VMs. These structures have better stability and availability. Virtualization-based consolidation no longer affects servers, but it improves the performance of the whole server and its components, such as storage, network, and centers. As cooling and space become vital issues for the server farms, the power saving limits of virtualization through computer programs are logically critical. Organizations are currently watching their virtualization stack as an approach to work on information technology (IT) assets to make their cycles more proficient, as shown in Figure 9.1.

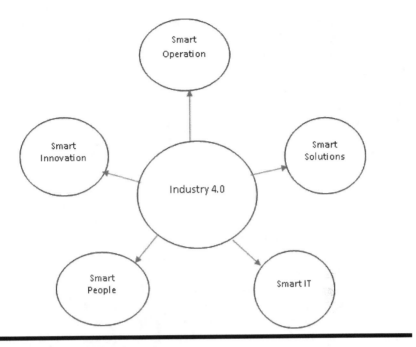

Figure 9.1   Smart services by Industry 4.0.

9.2 How Does Virtualization Work?

Virtualization is the route toward running a virtual PC framework in a layer that is disconnected from a PC system in a layer within the actual equipment. It allows the running of simultaneous working frameworks on a solitary foundation/environment. With this development, significant IT organizations are using resources that, for the most part, are bound to equipment. It licenses the use of an actual machine's full cutoff by distributing its capacities among various customers or conditions. Hypervisor (4), also known as a virtual machine monitor (VMM), is software, hardware, or firmware that enables various virtual operating systems to run on a single computer system simultaneously. A host machine is a computer on which a hypervisor runs, and guest machines are individual virtual operating systems. Hypervisors consume your valid resources and then divide them up so that virtual environments might make use of them. With virtualization, partitioning, isolation of physical servers, and hardware independency is achieved, and all the data is securely encapsulated.

All the virtual operating systems are independent of the host hardware but share all the related resources of the host machine such as memory, processors, and storage. This helps in reducing energy, maintenance, and space requirements.

The main role of the hypervisor is to fulfill the needs of virtual operating systems and manage them effectively. Each machine is independent; therefore, they do not interfere with each other and when one virtual operating system crashes or faces an issue, the other virtual operating systems continue to work normally. Therefore, the hypervisor translates requests between the virtual and physical resources.

A VM (5, 6) is a software application that runs on software rather than a physical device. On a physical hardware device, a VM is a virtual world that acts as a virtual operating system with its memory, processor, network interface, and storage. In addition, although they all run on the same host, each virtual machine runs its operating system independently of the others. A hypervisor divides the computer's resources from the hardware and configures them so that they can be accessed by the VM. This ensures that a virtual Mac OS virtual machine, for instance, will run on a real PC.

Virtualization allows you to work a few frameworks without any delay (e.g., Windows, Linux, and Mac OS) on that actual machine. This service essentially replaces your IT department, which allows you to cut costs when increasing revenue. With virtual work area facilitation, you can access your documents at any time and from any location. This frees you from actual hardware and programming issues, reduces your business expenses, and gives you more opportunities to grow your business, because you no longer have to worry about IT issues. For most people and organizations, virtualization is an energy-effective framework. Virtualization offers better uptime, and it allows for the faster deployment of resources. Virtualization permits you to simplify and amplify your assets, which lowers the amount of actual hardware you need and offers more benefits and uses for the servers you do utilize.

9.3 Virtualization Helps Applications: Hardware Independence

Through virtualization, hardware independence is easily achieved. It is the correct method to achieve it, and isolating the administration you depend on from the equipment and hardware is a significant advantage that virtualization offers. A virtual environment (7, 8) means less actual hardware use; therefore, your IT group will invest less energy and time in maintenance. Virtualization exists at the compute, storage, network, desktop, and application levels.

9.3.1 Compute Virtualization

Compute virtualization refers to the method of concealing the physical hardware from the system and allowing many operating systems to run simultaneously on one single or clustered physical machine. This process combines an OS and an application into a transportable VM.

A VM appears to be and works the same as a physical machine. Each OS runs on its own VM. For virtualizing the compute area, a virtualization layer is put between the hardware and the VM. The virtualization layer is additionally referred to as the hypervisor.

9.3.2 Storage Virtualization

Storage virtualization is a technique for providing a logical view of the physical storage resources to the host when covering the more complex parts of those storage resources. The logical view appears as the physical storage that is directly connected to the host. Tape storage virtualization, disc addressing, hot based management of volume, and LUN (logical unit number) (9) development are a few examples of storage virtualization. The virtualization layer handles the logical-to-physical storage mapping. It conceals the identities of the physical storage devices and establishes a storage pool by combining storage resources from multiple heterogeneous storage arrays.

Increased storage usage, adding or removing storage without impacting an application's availability, storage management simplification, and nondisruptive data migration are all major advantages of storage virtualization, as shown in Figure 9.2.

9.3.3 Network Virtualization

This refers to the software abstraction of a previously delivered hardware-based network infrastructure. Numerous physical networks can be merged into a software-based network, and a single physical network can be divided into discrete and distinct virtual networks. This program also enables administrators to transfer VMs between realms without reconfiguring the network. The software creates a network overlay that enables numerous virtual network layers to run on top of a single physical network fabric.

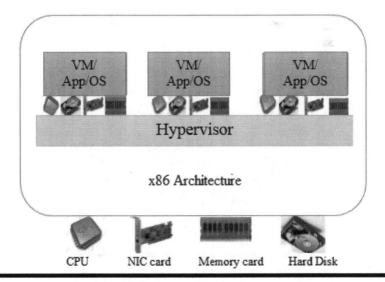

Figure 9.2   Compute virtualization.

9.3.4 Desktop Virtualization

Desktop virtualization technology aims to centralize the operating system of personal computers in the data center. End users can access desktops that are hosted at the data center using several endpoint computers, which act as VMs within the virtual data center, as shown in Figure 9.3. Application execution and data management are handled locally at the data center, rather than at the endpoint computers, as shown in Figure 9.4.

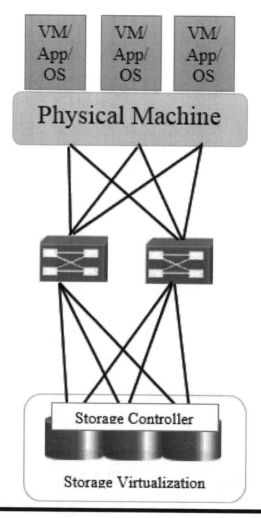

Figure 9.3 Storage virtualization.

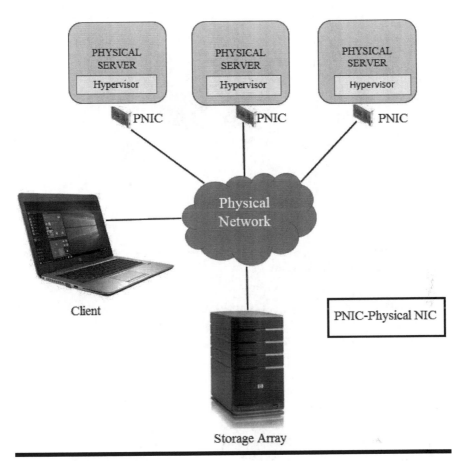

Figure 9.4   Network virtualization.

It is a software technology that enables users to easily deliver, protect, and manage desktops and applications while controlling costs and ensuring that end users can work from any device at any time. In addition, virtual desktops give the IT team greater consistency over system settings and policies. It decouples the desktop environment and its associated application software from the physical client device that accesses it, as shown in Figure 9.5.

9.3.5 Application Virtualization

This reduces system joining and association costs by keeping a regular programming standard across differently arranged PCs in an association. Fewer combinations secure the working framework and different inefficient applications.

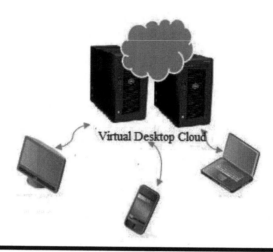

Figure 9.5   Desktop virtualization.

Application virtualization moreover deals with application performance and scalability.

A VM compensates for a biological system that intelligently isolates itself from the basic hardware. Virtualization has advantages, such as server consolidation and better use of hardware resources.

Therefore, virtualization helps when reevaluating the hardware utilized, removes additional energy costs, and limits the utilization of specific assets. It assists companies with sharing assets; therefore, they buy less actual equipment. One server hosts many servers, therefore reducing spending. Reduced hardware requirements mean less power is consumed to run them with lower cooling costs. Therefore, less cash and energy are invested in maintenance and actual administration, prompting additional cost savings.

9.4 VMware

VMware (10) is a hypervisor for VMs that communicates with the host's physical machine. It allots resources to a variety of guest operating systems. The guest operating system utilizes the VMs resources. The hypervisor isolates each visitor's operating system, which allows each to operate independently. If one visitor's operating system crashes, becomes unstable or is infected with malware, this does not affect the performance or activity of the visitors that run on the host. This ensures virtualization, which allows for more efficient use of physical compute resources. Each VM includes a setup file that stores the VMs settings, a virtual circle file that acts as a software-based hard drive, and a log file that records the VMs activities, such as system crashes, hardware changes, VM relocations from one host to the next, and the VM's status.

9.5 vSphere

VMware vSphere (11) is the company's enterprise virtualization platform, which is composed of ESXi hypervisor software and the vCenter Server management platform that manages multiple hypervisors. Standard, Enterprise Class, and Platinum editions of vSphere are available. Each enables strategy-driven VM stockpiling, real-time responsibility movement, and built-in network security. The higher-quality options include encryption at the VM level, container management, load balancing, and unified network management. Platinum provides security solutions and integration with third-party security solutions.

9.6 vMotion

Migration of VMs that starts with one actual host and then moves to the next with no downtime can be achieved with vMotion. This technology permits the VM cycles to continue to run during the migration. Of note is that VMware upholds the cold relocation mode, which implies that movement can be performed when the VM is killed or suspended. As the live relocation is carried out, the VM holds its current memory content, network characteristics, and associations, and all the extra data that characterizes it. On a gigabit ethernet organization, the cycle of relocation takes <2 s according to VMware documentation.

9.7 vCenter

One of vSphere's significant segments is vCenter Server (12). This is the administration part of vSphere. It permits VM organizations to be supervised by a huge assortment of host workers. It dispenses VMs to hosts, dispenses assets for them, screens executions, and mechanizes work processes.

9.8 Hardware and Software Separation Using Virtualization

Virtualization is the route toward running a virtual PC framework in a layer that is disconnected from a PC structure in a layer removed from the actual physical hardware. It refers to running concurrent operating systems on a single infrastructure or

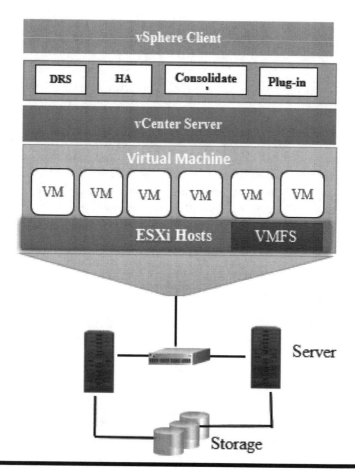

Figure 9.6 VMware vSphere framework.

environment It isolates the hardware structure, which makes it very adaptable for organizations and companies, as shown in Figure 9.6.

Virtualization is the innovation that permits clients to carry out specific activities in a virtualized climate. By virtualizing workers, accumulating, association, or applications, the move toward comparative functionalities without being near the hardware can be achieved. It could be the best technique to help associations cut down IT costs, support efficiency, and move toward a planned strategy. One of the primary concerns behind virtualization is taking actual machines and transforming them into virtual ones. In summary, it reduces the hardware and equipment an association needs to purchase.

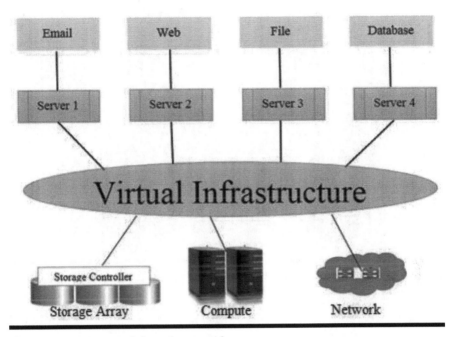

Figure 9.7 VMware vSphere framework.

Virtualization allows one PC to show two working frameworks. Each PC has enough computational capacity to compute multiple frameworks and fulfil multiple requests.

Because all the virtualization is carried out on a virtual arrangement, the upkeep of these assets turns out to be more cost-effective, and they require less electrical energy compared with an equivalent equipment arrangement. Similarly, there will be better help, and overhauls and fixes are simpler to utilize.

9.9 Comparison of Before and After Virtualization

Dual boot is the point at which a client divides the hard drive and introduces an alternate OS in each segment; therefore, when the PC is turned on, the client can choose which OS to startup. Hardware-based computing requires dedicated hardware for each network function, such as routers and firewalls. To make changes, broadband providers must manually update each hardware appliance. This arduous cycle can require weeks (or even months) when carrying out new administrations, especially if the network apparatus is remote. These slow and manual processes are

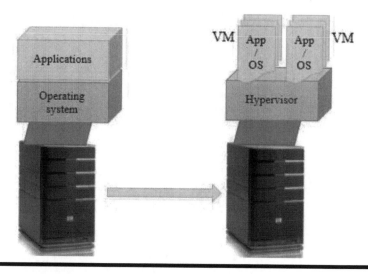

Figure 9.8   Concept of before and after virtualization.

also prone to errors. Therefore, legacy networks suffer from inflexible dedicated hardware and are prone to errors.

The expenses of buying, introducing, and designing machines are high. In addition, the huge upfront expense and restricted versatility of committed equipment mean that numerous broadband suppliers purchase more equipment than they need, in order to guarantee that they can meet high traffic demand later, as shown in Figure 9.8. Furthermore, for high demand, broadband providers need to buy more hardware.

A virtualized network is supported independently of the hardware, which saves time, resources, and money.

■ Since virtualization doesn't need real equipment segments to be utilized or introduced, IT departments discover it is a less expensive framework to maintain.

■ Most virtualization infrastructure providers and suppliers update the equipment and software that will be used.

■ Uptime has increased dramatically because of virtualization innovations. Several suppliers guarantee an uptime of 99.9999%. For example, cloud service providers (13) like GCP, AWS, and Azure give such uptime.

■ In virtualization, you can back up the entire virtual server and the virtual machine with frequent snapshots of the virtual machine to ensure data security and backup.

- A physical system tends to have a considerable loss when a disaster occurs; however, virtualization facilitates the easy recovery of up-to-date data even when a catastrophe occurs.
- Virtualization requires less physical hardware and time for the setup and maintenance of servers.

9.10 Virtualizing x86 Hardware

VMMs (14) work on implementing a specific rule. They alter the computer system according to some principle. VMMs do not allow strange software to run on a machine. They implement the layering of VMs and create hundreds of clones of the hardware and drive them on different OS. A VM is a stronger, better, faster version of a machine.

The distinct properties of VMMs are: 1. they give a medium for applications to function; 2. they make the programs run faster than the original one; and 3. VMMs keep a check on all the parts of the system.

1. Compatibility
   This allows it to run anything as it used to run in its natural habitat. There is no change in the environment and no limits.
2. Performance
   There will be a minor increase in running velocity and that could be classed as an upgrade. The new design systems should not be inferior to the previous ones. There should be some sort of improvement.
3. Isolating
   To run VMs independently without any effect from the other VM in the vicinity. This helps in performance and security, both of which are important. A code that is filled with a virus could ruin all the infrastructure; therefore, care should be taken.

There are four major challenges to the virtualization of x86 hardware.

1. The x86 hardware cannot be virtualized easily because some code in it was blocking the attempts. Trap-and-emulate and many other techniques failed to work. Experts thought that there was no way to alter the x86 hardware in the way they wanted to. This is a problem, which is a tough challenge.
2. The x86 architecture is very complicated and can't be comprehended by a novice. It takes a long time to build. With time, many new features have been included in it, to make it immaculate and enhance security, power, and overall quality.

3. They have a large number of attachments. Virtualizing these was time-consuming. It had a negative impact on many things, which engineers did not want.
4. The design of the graphic user interface or machine hardware had to be straightforward for clients that had no knowledge.

9.11 Techniques to Virtualize x86 Hardware

9.11.1 Full Virtualization

The hardware architecture is fully simulated in this hardware virtualization. Any program can run without any modifications. Administrators might use full virtualization to combine new and old systems to create something better and more effective. Virtualization necessitates simulating any component and function of the hardware in one of the VMs. Any program that can run on the hardware can run on the VM in this environment. The hypervisor, which operates at a higher privilege level than the operating system, is the gateway to completing the virtualization.

- ▪ This approach allows you to merge existing systems to create new systems with greater productivity and better hardware organization.
- ▪ This approach helps to reduce the maintenance costs associated with restoring and improving older systems.
- ▪ This technique can be used to improve less capable systems when reducing physical space and improving the company's overall efficiency, as shown in Figure 9.9.

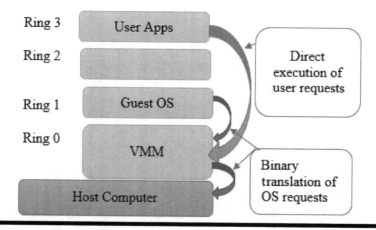

Figure 9.9 Full virtualization.

9.11.2 Paravirtualization

The hardware does not simulate this type of hardware virtualization, and the guest program runs its isolated device. Only the applications and programs that function for their websites are run precisely, without any hardware simulation. Since the paravirtualized OS is updated to be aware of the virtualization, the guest is aware of its surroundings when using paravirtualization. It is a technique that involves a guest that knows that it is a guest and works in that manner to its fullest extent. It does not have the authority to make demands for itself. It cannot perform high authority tasks because it is not allowed many resources. The meaning of the prefix 'para' is 'beside'. The hypervisor works on improving the machine and makes it more organized. Its task is to alter all the commands in the VM with calls. Kernel operations require calls from the hypervisor so that it can work on its basic features, such as managing errors, keeping track of time utilization, and reducing waste in the memory. If this technique is not used properly, it can cause huge problems; therefore, it must be implemented by experts.

- It improves performance by reducing the number of VMM calls and preventing the use of privileged instructions without permission.
- This technology is very beneficial because it improves server capacity without the expense of running the host software.
- With this type of virtualization, several OS can be run on one single server.

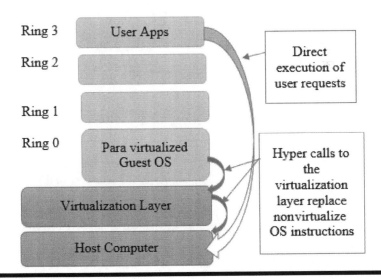

Figure 9.10   Paravirtualization.

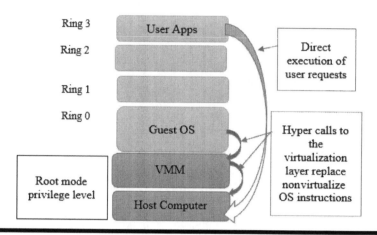

Figure 9.11 Hardware-assisted virtualization.

9.11.3 Hardware-Assisted Virtualization

Hardware-assisted virtualization is another version of full virtualization (15) in which the core can virtualize a system. This will change the system a lot, because it will give the guests some rights within the system processors, without harming the primary machine. This is the so-called hypervisor. Manufacturers of hardware devices are considering the future and trying to develop devices that are compatible with the newer and in-demand techniques. The customer base prefers newer technology-compatible systems. The newest systems are the only ones that include these facilities. In most cases, this technique is productive compared with other less advanced techniques. Software is now more flexible and can better incorporate changes, compared with older versions.

Conclusions

Throughout this chapter, the industry standard version 4.0-based virtualization was discussed, as well as the impact it has on business operations. How the concept of virtualization could be applied at the compute, storage, network, desktop, and application levels to improve the utilization of resources at the various levels of the organization was discussed. Virtualization technologies, such as VMware, vSphere, and vMotion were introduced at the hypervisor level. Under the heading of virtualization, the concepts of the hypervisor and x86 architecture were discussed in greater depth. In conclusion, virtualization plays a critical role in the industry, as it transitions to version 4.0.

Future scope for the technology:

1. Cloud service providers can enhance the security services.
2. Using cloud computing, market growth might increase rapidly.
3. Based on market needs, the storage capacity of data centers must be increased to capture the bandwidth.

References

1. Khayer A, Talukder MS, Bao Y, Hossain MN. Cloud computing adoption and its impact on SMEs' performance for cloud supported operations: a dual-stage analytical approach. Technol Soc. 2020; 60:101225.
2. Panda SK, Jana PK. An efficient request-based virtual machine placement algorithm for cloud computing. ICDCIT. LNCS. Cham, Switzerland: Springer. 2017. 10109:129–143. 26 November 2016, Bhubaneswar, India.
3. Qiu C, Shen H. Dynamic demand prediction and allocation in cloud service brokerage. IEEE Trans Cloud Comput. 2019. 9(4):1439–1452.
4. Panda SK, Jana PK. Efficient task scheduling algorithms for heterogeneous multi-cloud environment. J Supercomput. 2015; 71(4):1505–1533.
5. Introduction to Virtulization: www.vmware.com/solutions/virtualization.
6. Understanding Full Virtualization, Paravirtualization, and Hardware Assist. Whitepaper, VMware. 2007. [Internet] www.vmware.com/files/pdf/VMware paravirtualization.pdf
7. Blenk A, Basta A, Reisslein M, Kellerer W. Survey on network virtualization hypervisors for software-defined. IEEE Commun Surveys Tutor. 2016; 18(1):655–685.
8. de Jesus Gil Herrera J , Felipe Botero Vega J. Network functions virtualization: A survey. IEEE Lat Am Trans. 2016; 14(2):983–997.
9. History of Virtualization. VMware. 2009. [Internet] Available from: www.vmware. com/virtualization/ history.html. Accessed 10 Jan 2022.
10. Ge J-W, Deng Y-L, Fang Y-Q. Research on storage virtualization structure in cloud storage environment. Multimedia Technology (ICMT) International Conference. 29–31 October 2010, Ningbo, China.
11. Durairaj M, Kannan P. Study on virtualization techniques and challenges in cloud computing. Int J Sci Technol Res. 2014; 3(11).
12. Garg P, Sharma V. A survey on mobile cloud computing. IJCA Special Issue on Issues and Challenges in Networking, Intelligence and Computing Technologies ICNICT(6):1–5. November 2012.
13. Chun B-G, Ihm S, Maniatis P, Naik M. Clonecloud: Boosting mobile device applications through cloud clone execution. 2010. arXiv: 1009.3088V [Preprint]. Available from: https://arxiv.org/abs/1009.3088. doi: 10.48550/arXiv.1009.3088. Accessed: 14 March 2022.
14. Mainka C, Somorovsky J, Schwenk J. Penetration testing tool for Web services security. Proceedings of the 8th IEEE World Congress on Services. 15 September 2012, Honolulu, USA.
15. Almutairy NM, Al-Shqeerat KHA. A survey on security challenges of virtualization technology in cloud computing. IJCSIT. 2019; 11(3).

Chapter 10

Optimized Cloud Storage Data Analysis Using the Machine Learning Model

Devendra Prasad, Pradeep Singh Rawat, and Neeraj Rathore
Department of Computer Science and Engineering, School of Computing, DIT University, Dehradun, Uttarakhand, India

Contents

DOI: 10.1201/9781003322931-10

10.1 Introduction

Recent developments in the computing platform (cloud computing), network infrastructure [e.g., 5G and SDN (software defined network)], and self-learning algorithms [machine learning (ML)] have led to increased interest in the large quantity of medical data and have provided useful analysis for further decision-making in almost all sorts of businesses that include healthcare. Industry, particularly healthcare, has benefited from these systems especially ML and big data. Healthcare data referred to as EMRs (electronic medical records, e.g., 20% supervised and 80% unsupervised) is collected through a plethora of devices (e.g., smartwatches and fit bits) and processed by these intelligent systems for a long list of applications that includes smart records, medical imaging and diagnostics, drug discovery and development, reducing the cost of healthcare, and better establishing patient–doctor (or consumer–provider) relationships (1).

Traditionally, the old rule-based systems were very difficult to realize because of the structure (unstructured data) of the data and limited computing power. The cloud computing revolution made this possible today. Cloud computing technology components, especially, data centers, provide us with the required storage (e.g., S3) and deployment (i.e., of predictive analysis models) with long-term and lower cost and on-demand (easy access) basis (2). Kumar Sharma et. al. (2) carried out thorough research on the management techniques for a variety of healthcare data management systems over the cloud and highlighted the advantage of this technology during the COVID-19 pandemic along with a discussion of some future challenges. Security and privacy of medical data in the cloud are always a concern to researchers (3). For example, to restore privacy, one of the recent works with many encryptions is CBIR (content-based image retrieval) (3). This helped to develop applications for cloud computing in healthcare data, for example, the Internet of Medical Things (IoMT) and the successor of cloud computing, fog computing (4).

Optimization has a dominant place in cloud computing and ML. The huge amount of data processing over unlimited available resources in the cloud is badly affected if task-resource scheduling is not carried out properly. This task-resource scheduling can be of two types: 1. dependent and workflow; and 2. independent scheduling. Based on the two actors involved, for example, the consumer and provider, the optimization criteria are consumer-desired (e.g., makespan and time) and provider-desired (e.g., utilization and throughput). A comprehensive study (5–8) showed the prominent optimization techniques that were utilized for workflow scheduling; ant colony optimization, genetic algorithm (GA), particle swarm optimization (PSO), league championship algorithm (LCA), and bat algorithm. For the latest and modern approaches such as big-bang big-crunch, researchers (9–12) carried out a series of works. ML tasks along with optimization have been widely investigated and are still an interesting research area (13). In this work, optimization in the predictive analysis was focused on. This way, the optimization at different levels improved the overall performance of the system.

ML algorithms are deployed in the cloud environment for remote prediction (e.g., supervised or unsupervised classification and regression) on a huge amount of real-time data that is submitted. These algorithms require the data to be cleaned or transformed appropriately for further training and validation. Accuracy, confusion matrix, precision, recall, and ROC AUC (area under the receiver operating characteristic curve) are the well-known terminology for performance evaluation. ML in healthcare data analysis is popular today (14–16). A comprehensive survey by Dhillon et. al (15) summarizes the ML work to date for all types of healthcare data, clinical, omics, and sensors. Clinical data [HER (human epidermal growth factor receptor)] refers to patient records that are collected during ongoing treatment, and sensor data represents data collected from various wearable and wireless sensor devices. The omics data is composed of genome, transcriptome, and proteome data. The variability in healthcare data is suitably handled by clustering (e.g., unsupervised or semisupervised) compared with supervised learning (17).

To date, the literature discussed favored a healthcare data analysis setup in a local environment. The researcher trend has been inclined toward the real-time realization of this task and hence the integration of data, ML, and cloud platforms has become of interest among researchers (18, 19). The emergence (or advances) in the Internet of Things (IoT) fog, and big data have given a boost to a solution for this research challenge (20). Optimization has a must-to-implement concern now to obtain optimal and faster results (21–24). In this chapter, two important diseases, anxiety and depression (i.e., the psychological disorder and indicator of public mental health) and breast cancer, are focused on as examples for the theme of optimized cloud-deployed healthcare data analysis. In the recent literature on anxiety and depression, a study was conducted on college students (25), on all ages in the general population (26, 27), on the geriatric population (28), and on sailors (29–31). A survey on the population of Kenya stated that 50% of the population was depressed (32).

10.2 Motivation for This Work

The COVID-19 outbreak has negatively impacted the physical and mental health of the general population in every part of the world. Previously, other outbreaks had similar but more adverse effects, in 2003 (SARS), 2009 (H1N1), 2012 (MERS), and 2014 (Ebola) (33). The impact of stress, anxiety, and depression are prime among many psychological disorders that have been studied during pandemics (33, 34). Studies on the general populations of countries that include Turkey (34), the UK (35), Germany (36), Hong Kong (37), Denmark (38), and Ireland (39) have seriously advocated well-being and mental health status. New mutations of coronaviruses are emerging, and therefore, the prevention and cure of public mental health issues are of the utmost importance for everyone. In this chapter, a cloud-based framework is proposed to provide optimized real-time predictive analysis results, which covers all applications where some sort of predictive analysis is required for further decision-making. For testing and validation, the focus was on two diseases; anxiety and depression and breast cancer. The first appears to be the first initiative, to the best of our knowledge, in the previously mentioned context.

The rest of the chapter is organized as follows. Related work carried out to date for the development of these intelligent healthcare systems is summarized in Section 10.3. Section 10.4 presents the architecture of the proposed framework along with a detailed discussion of the components and their working. In this section, the empirical results are shown in two scenarios (e.g., with and without optimization) that utilize two different datasets (e.g., fabricated and benchmarked). Finally, the conclusions with the projected future scope are presented in Section 10.5.

10.3 Related Work

Researchers (40, 41) proposed a smart healthcare monitoring framework that was based on biomedical wireless sensor networks that employed state-of-the-art ML algorithms. However, their work did not show any evidence of optimization. In another work (42), the authors proposed a maintainable, scalable, portable, and discoverable deployment of healthcare services that was based on an emerging standard for interoperability [FIHR (fast healthcare interoperability resources)]. They referred to it as serverless on FIHR architecture. The researchers (43), in their distinguished work, attempted to optimize execution, data processing time, and system efficiency of a cloud-deployed healthcare service environment. They applied three optimization techniques, the Cuckoo search algorithm, PSO, and ABCO (artificial bee colony optimization), with the last one giving the best efficiency of 92.%. A similar work (18) also stated optimal VM (virtual machine) selection but used parallel PSO (PPSO) with their proposed model for chronic kidney disease diagnosis and prediction. Our focus on optimization was different than that of theirs because we focus on optimizing cloud-deployed ML algorithm performance. Before this, the authors (44) proposed optimization at various levels that included a deep searching algorithm, bitmap to select the best cloud clusters and optimized ML for prediction and diagnosis. The architecture in Chenyu et. al. (45) demonstrated the IoMT-based cardiovascular healthcare system with certain characteristics such as embedded system and cross-layer optimization. On average, 97% accuracy was achieved for any sort of disease prediction in their framework. Sometimes, selecting an appropriate cloud service (e.g., hardware and software) is itself a big challenge. Focusing on this, the authors (46) summarized the good work carried out to date and quoted that scalability and the ability to create multiple neural networks were the two prime factors when choosing the cloud service for the deployment of ML algorithms to predict as well as prescribe diseases. The clustering of different sets of patient–caretaker groups with a specialized technique called the k-centroid multi-viewpoint similarity algorithm was proposed (47). In a similar study, researchers (48) extended and optimized the work by employing whale optimization. A specifically focused study on breast cancer diagnosis and supervised ML algorithms was presented by the authors (49). They applied MLP (multilayer perceptron), decision tree, SVM (support vector machine), and kNN (k-nearest neighbors) classifiers successfully to Wisconsin data and found that MLP performed best among all with an accuracy of 97.7%. Therefore, after thoroughly studying this literature, it is clear that less optimization is being researched for predictive analysis tasks that are deployed in the cloud environment. However, the challenge of optimized VM selection and task-resource scheduling must be considered and requires further research. Healthcare service deployment requires these optimizations for better and timely responses for its stakeholders.

10.4 Proposed Framework

The proposed framework consists of three main components; cloud storage, ML model, and optimization module, as shown in Figure 10.1.

All three components are deployed in a cloud platform (data center). The description of the working of the overall framework and functions of these components follows.

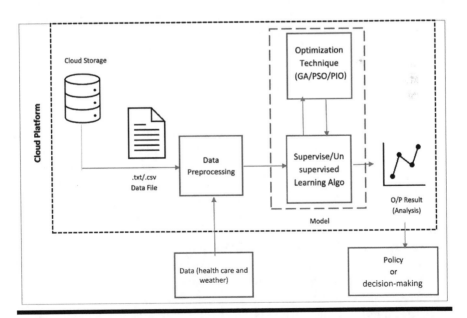

Figure 10.1   Proposed architecture for optimized cloud storage data analysis.

10.4.1 Cloud Storage and Data

The data received by the presentation interface is stored in the cloud storage (for this implementation S3 storage was used through AWS (Amazon web services)). The data could be structured (e.g., tabular data) or unstructured (e.g., image or signal) depending on the sensing devices and applications. Cloud storage offers unlimited, flexible, remote, and permanent arrangements for real-time data that is serviced through a relevant agreement (i.e., an SLA agreement). The best part of this storage is to reduce the limitations incurred by the local system without worrying about the privacy and security of the data. The disadvantage of some latency could arise if this cloud storage and the remaining framework are managed by different providers or are available in different data centers.

10.4.2 ML Model and Analysis

The ML model is composed of data preprocessing and a learning algorithm (e.g., any type from supervised, unsupervised, and semi-supervised). The data in cloud storage is fetched and transformed into the format that is required by the following ML algorithm. This module also splits the data into training and validation data sets. The trained ML algorithm is tested against real-time data, for instance, test data to produce an analysis (or result) that is further used by the decision-making module to deliver useful information to the outside. To enhance the throughput and reduce processing time, the training process is sometimes carried out and the real-time data received is tested immediately. This setup has advantages in scenarios with a huge amount of data and the analysis requires high-performance computing. Also, as in the storage cloud, the only drawback could be latency if deployed in different clouds or data centers.

10.4.3 Optimization and ML

The optimization module implements one or more optimization techniques to improve accuracy and any other performance parameter as required. Numerous nature-inspired optimization algorithms are available. PSO, GA, and PIO (predictive index optimization) are the most used optimizations. Optimization is mainly applied in the context of ML at the feature selection or reduction levels. The objective is to obtain the best near-optimal solution, for example, an accurate system within a certain time limit. In cloud deployment, optimization generally refers to task-resource scheduling. For a specific application, optimization at the cloud platform level could be ignored and the focus could be on optimization with ML tasks. There is also the option of one optimization technique from the many that are available. This flexibility is advantageous in this deployment, for instance, cloud deployment, otherwise has proved to be costly.

A few important things need to be highlighted. First, policy or decision-making modules can be inside the cloud platform (data center) or in the local client system.

For security concerns, these are implemented in the local system and for a timely response and good performance can be kept inside. Second, details of the sensors, communication technologies, and data center infrastructure are not visible and discussed clearly. These components are implicitly assumed whenever the proposed framework is discussed. The data centers consist of high-performance computers (HPCs), storage, accelerators [i.e., GPUs (graphics processing units)], and numerous security devices (50). Utilizing parallel or distributed computing concepts, along with high computing capability, the data centers offer intelligent real-time data analysis and support data mining to dig deep into the data. Generally, Hadoop is the architecture employed, with its two main components of a distributed file storage system (HDFS) and MapReduce (distributed data processing). The communication infrastructure contains SDN and 5G technology. Finally, the sensing equipment used includes biosensors, motion sensors, wearable devices with sensors, and some sensorless devices (50).

10.5 Performance Evaluation and Analysis

The performance of the system can be measured for the overall integrated system and specifically for predictive analysis. Overall, transmission time, latency, scheduling overheads, and throughput were considered along with the performance metrics for ML tasks. The performance measurements for the analysis task are focused on using the ML model and optimization.

10.5.1 Scenario 1: Without Nature-Inspired Optimization

A supervised ML algorithm was employed for the classification of a subject as healthy or not, based on whether anxiety, depression, or both were present in a fabricated dataset of 470 subjects of different age groups that had different working profiles in a few voluntary engineering institutions. A total of 11 nominal-type features and four numeric features were identified and collected in the dataset listed in Table 10.1.

As part of data preprocessing, nominal data was transformed to a standard scale using a One-Hot encoder and the numeric data used a standard normalization. The output class or target class was "Anxiety_Depression" which contained four labels {Anxiey and Depression, No Anxiety-No Depression, Only Anxiety, Only Depression}. To convert this task as a binary classification the labels anxiety and/or depression were considered as not healthy and the rest as healthy. The stratified data (90:10 ratio, e.g., 90% training data and 10% test data) was further used to obtain accuracy scores using random forest (RF) and ensemble (bagging) algorithms. Table 10.2 lists the transformed dataset.

The classification (e.g., binary or multiclass) algorithms' performance was measured in metrics: <accuracy, F1-Score, ROC AUC>. The F1-score contains two

Table 10.1   Feature Description of Fabricated Dataset

Feature Number	Feature	Feature Description	Feature Type	Feature Data Range
1	Employment status	Status of employment	Nominal	1 = regular; 2 = contractual
2	Job profile	Working role/ profile of the employee	Nominal	1 = teaching; 2 = nonteaching
3	Workplace	Workplace of the employee	Nominal	1 = university; 2 = college
4	Salary type	Type of salary structure	Nominal	1 = scale; 2 = consolidate
5	Age	Age of employee in years	Numeric	(24)
6	Marital status	Status of marriage	Nominal	1 = divorced; 2 = married; 3 = single
7	Family type	Type of family	Nominal	1 = joint; 2 = nuclear
8	Education	Highest qualification of employee	Nominal	1 = postgrad; 2 = grad; 3 = PhD
9	Monthly income	Average monthly income of the employee (INR)	Numeric	(6000,36666.67)
10	Duration service	Duration of service (years)	Numeric	(1,35)
11	htn	Hypertension	Nominal	1 = yes; 2 = no
12	DM	Diabetes mellitus	Nominal	1 = yes; 2 = no
13	IHD	Ischemic heart disease	Nominal	1 = yes; 2 = no
14	BMI	Body mass index	Numeric	(18.51, 28.06)
15	Anxiety_ Depression	Diagnosis of disease	Nominal	1 = anxiety and depression; 2 = no anxiety - no depression; 3 = only anxiety; 4 = only depression

Table 10.2 Overview of Transformed Dataset

Number of Instances	Output Feature				Number of Input Features	Number of Trained Samples	Number of Validation Samples
	No Anxiety – No Depression	Anxiety and Depression	Only Anxiety	Only Depression			
	Healthy	Not Healthy					
	241	67	137	18	18	(217, 60, 123, 23)	(24, 7, 13, 5)
470	241		229		18	(217, 206)	(24, 23)

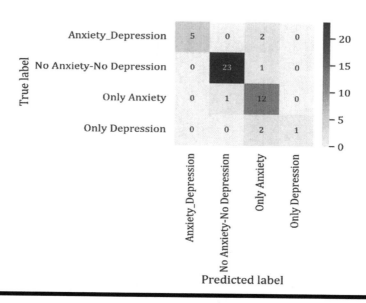

Figure 10.2 Confusion matrix for RF classifier.

components: precision and recall. It is a harmonic mean of these two. A high F1-score will result if precision and recall are high (51). ROC AUC measures the capability of the algorithm to separate true (predicted) versus true (actual) and false (predicted) versus false (actual) classifications accurately. ROC curve itself is a plot between true positive rate (TPR) and (1-TNR/specificity), where TNR stands for true negative rate. All these were computed using a confusion matrix. In this example, multiclass classification was carried out and the obtained confusion matrix is shown in Figures 10.2 and 10.3.

The module (composed of an ML algorithm and optimization as shown in Figure 10.1) implemented the experimentation. As part of this experimentation, an iterative procedure was carried out beginning with two random features that were selected. The best measurements of <accuracy, F1 score, ROC AUC> were obtained in 500 iterations but with capping at 50th, 100th, and 500th iteration. For optimization, when the first iteration after that measurement seems to be getting equal approximately to up to four precisions, the procedure gets stopped and these measurements are recorded. The task is repeated until all the features are selected and measured as per the procedure discussed above. Table 10.3 summarizes the results obtained. Figures 10.4 and 10.5 show the graphical analysis of the computed results.

The optimal performance in the best of the experimentations obtained for RF classifier was <accuracy = 87.23%, F1 Score = 0.867, ROC AUC = 0.899> and for ensemble (bagging) method was <accuracy = 85.10%, F1 Score = 0.843, ROC AUC = 0.867>. The analysis shows RF was better than the bagging approach on this fabricated dataset.

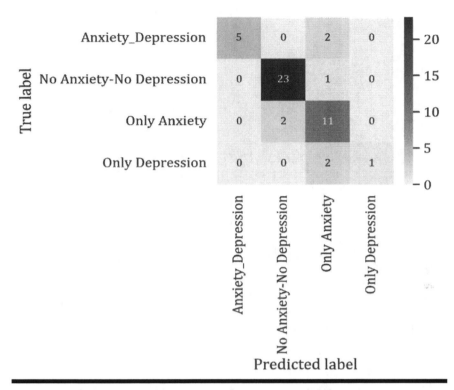

Figure 10.3 Confusion matrix for ensemble method (bagging).

10.5.2 Scenario 2: With Nature-Inspired Optimization

In the second example, the breast cancer problem was used (the Wisconsin Diagnostic Breast Cancer dataset). Researchers found this is a worldwide problem and rank it second after lung cancer (52). ML alone improved performance (classification) from traditional supervised learning to the modern neural network (49). Cloud computing platforms also boost the real-time interactions between the stakeholders (e.g., patients and doctors) in healthcare systems by providing breast cancer early detection (18). In this chapter, to measure the performance of the proposed framework with some sort of optimization, experiments were carried out on the Wisconsin Diagnostic Breast Cancer (benchmark dataset) and six well-known optimization techniques: PSO (particle swarm optimization), MVO (mean-variance optimization), GWO (grey wolf optimization), MFO (moth-flame optimization), CSO (cat swarm optimization), and the bat algorithm. Five iterations for each optimizer were performed with two cases of minimization and maximization. The best two scores obtained were selected. Further, the optimized accuracy levels achieved are summarized in Table 10.4 and the related analysis is shown in Figures 10.6 and 10.7.

Table 10.3 Empirical Results of Ensemble (Bagging) Method and RF Classifier for <Accuracy, F1 Score, ROC AUC>

Number of Features	Bagging Method				RF Classifier			
	Number of Estimators (Decision Trees)	F1 Score	ROC AUC	Accuracy	Number of Estimators (Decision Trees)	F1 Score	ROC AUC	Accuracy
2	45, 48, 53…	0.842	0.857	0.851	25	0.726	0.873	0.7446
3	150, 250	0.821	0.87	0.8297	350, 400	0.806	0.869	0.8085
4	26, 27, 200–500	0.796	0.872	0.8085	350	0.803	0.892	0.8085
5	24, 28	0.8	0.869	0.8085	82	0.868	0.885	0.8723
6	90	0.796	0.86	0.8085	24,	0.828	0.911	0.8297
7	34	0.779	0.86	0.7872	25	0.868	0.893	0.8723
8	5	0.676	0.832	0.7021	32	0.821	0.89	0.8297
9	6	0.703	0.842	0.7234	100	0.846	0.89	0.851
10	7	0.695	0.838	0.7021	200, 210	0.846	0.893	0.851
11	8	0.671	0.842	0.6808	150, 200, 250	0.821	0.897	0.8297
12	2	0.685	0.82	0.7021	200, 210	0.821	0.897	0.8297
13	4	0.704	0.826	0.7234	45, 48	0.823	0.898	0.8297
14	5	0.715	0.743	0.7234	58	0.846	0.894	0.851
15	2	0.693	0.759	0.7021	40	0.823	0.909	0.8297
16	2	0.695	0.838	0.7021	40	0.868	0.909	0.8723
17	8	0.695	0.838	0.7021	50, 60, 70,	0.821	0.914	0.8297
18	9	0.693	0.759	0.7021	12	0.865	0.925	0.8723

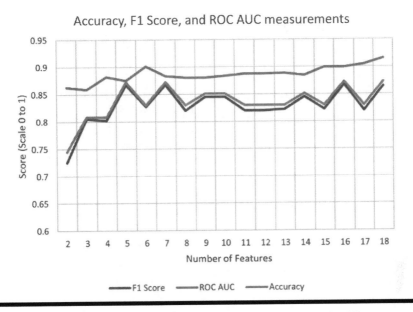

Figure 10.4   Linear (upward) growth of measurements for RF classifier.

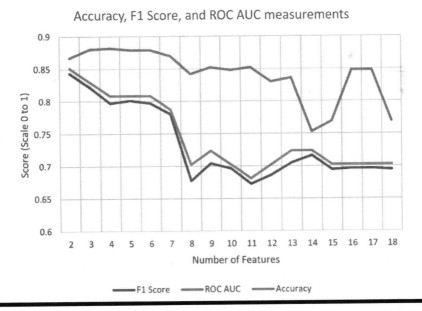

Figure 10.5   Linear (downward) growth of measurements for ensemble (bagging) method.

Table 10.4   Optimization Iteration Sand Results (Wisconsin Diagnostic Breast Cancer)

Optimization Technique	Test Accuracy
PSO	0.932773109
PSO	0.348739496
MVO	0.949579832
MVO	0.949579832
GWO	0.978991597
GWO	0.966386555
MFO	0.941176471
MFO	0.93697479
CSO	0.957983193
CSO	0.932773109
Bat	0.672268908
Bat	0.966386555

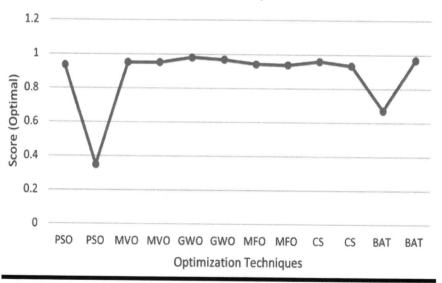

Figure 10.6   Analysis of min–max value; first appearance of optimizer indicates max entry and the second one is for min entry.

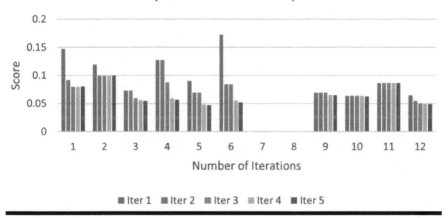

Figure 10.7   The score for each optimization technique in five iterations.

Figure 10.7 shows the score for each optimization technique. Six optimization techniques were used for two scenarios each and the experiments were repeated for five iterations. This figure shows a clear picture that the performance and quality of service were evaluated for the medical applications. Performance could be improved using multiple iterations with the Wisconsin Diagnostic Breast Cancer (benchmark dataset) and six well-known optimization techniques: PSO, MVO, GWO, MFO, CSO, and bat. Therefore, the performance and quality of service depended on the fitness or objective functions that were used in nature-inspired optimization techniques. As shown in Figure 10.7, the GWO second scenario gave the optimal value of the score parameter for Scenario 6.

10.6 Conclusion and Future Works

In this chapter, a framework was proposed to provide healthcare services through the integration of two modern technologies; a cloud computing platform and ML. Cloud computing involves S3 cloud storage for the huge amount of healthcare data and HPCs for real-time computing with the data to infer useful insights using a cloud-deployed ML model. Six optimization techniques were used to optimize the accuracy level of the supervised ML algorithms: PSO, MVO, GWO, MFO, CSO, and bat, and thorough studies were presented to support the improvement over nonoptimized systems. The systems were validated with two example scenarios. First, predicting whether a subject was healthy or not using a fabricated dataset that consisted of university and college employees and without employing any sort of optimization. Second, experiments were carried out for breast cancer prediction on a benchmarked Wisconsin Diagnostic Breast Cancer dataset with the six optimization techniques mentioned previously. Two limitations will be targeted in future work. First, for the overall system's performance, the latency involved in cloud computing was not considered in this work. The focus was on predictive analysis (ML) performance. Second, the optimization focus was on ML and not at the level of the cloud platform. Hence, performance and optimization were taken care of at the ML level that excluded the level of the cloud platform. In the future, the work will be expanded to overcome the previously mentioned limitation. The experiment that was carried out on a fabricated dataset will also be carried out with a few benchmark datasets with comparative analysis. Also, the framework performance comparison with real-time data on a single real dataset in both scenarios (e.g., with and without optimization) will be addressed in future research.

References

1. Bhardwaj R, Nambiar AR, Dutta D. A study of machine learning in healthcare. Proceedings of Int Compu. Softw Appl Conf. 2017; 2:236–241. Available from: doi:10.1109/COMPSAC.2017.164.
2. Kumar Sharma D, Sreenivasa Chakravarthi D, Ara Shaikh A, Al Ayub Ahmed A, Jaiswal S, Naved M. The aspect of vast data management problem in healthcare sector and implementation of cloud computing technique Materials Today: Proceedings. pp. 1–6. 31 July 2021. Available from: doi:10.1016/j.matpr.2021.07.388.
3. Majhi M, Pal AK, Pradhan J, Islam SH, Khan MK. Computational intelligence based secure three-party CBIR scheme for medical data for cloud-assisted healthcare applications. Multimed Tools Appl. 2021. Available from: doi:10.1007/s11042-020-10483-7.
4. Ullah A, Azeem M, Ashraf H, Alaboudi A, Humayun M, Jhanjhi NZ. Secure healthcare data aggregation and transmission in IoT: A Survey. IEEE Access. 2021; 9: 16849–16865. Available from: doi:10.1109/ACCESS.2021.3052850.
5. Kalra M, Singh S. A review of metaheuristic scheduling techniques in cloud computing. Egypt Informatics J. 2015; 16(3):275–295. Available from: doi:10.1016/j.eij.2015.07.001.
6. Pradhan A, Bisoy SK, Das A. A survey on PSO based meta-heuristic scheduling mechanism in cloud computing environment. J King Saud Univ Comput Inf Sci. 2022; 34(8):4888-4901. Available from: doi:10.1016/j.jksuci.2021.01.003.
7. Bothra SK, Singhal S. Nature-inspired metaheuristic scheduling algorithms in cloud: A systematic review. Sci Tech J Inf Technol Mech Opt. 2021; 21(4):463–472. Available from: doi:10.17586/2226-1494-2021-21-4-463-472.
8. Houssein EH, Gad AG, Wazery YM, Suganthan PN. Task scheduling in cloud computing based on meta-heuristics: Review, taxonomy, open challenges, and future trends. Swarm Evol Comput. 2021; 62(5):100841. Available from: doi:10.1016/j.swevo.2021.100841.

9. Rawat PS, Dimri P, Kanrar S, Saroha GP. Optimize task allocation in cloud environment based on big-bang big-crunch. Wireless Personal Communication. 2020; 115(2). Springer US.

10. Rawat PS, Dimri P, Saroha GP. Virtual machine allocation to the task using an optimization method in cloud computing environment. Int J Inf Technol. 2020; 12(2):485–493. Available from: doi:10.1007/s41870-018-0242-9.

11. Rawat PS, Dimri P, Gupta P, Saroha GP. Resource provisioning in scalable cloud using bio-inspired artificial neural network model. Appl Soft Comput. 2021; 99: 106876. Available from: doi:10.1016/j.asoc.2020.106876.

12. Kumar B, Ranjan RK, Husain A. A multi-objective enhanced fruit fly optimization (MO-EFOA) framework for despeckling SAR images using DTCWT based local adaptive thresholding. Int J Remote Sens. 2021; 42(14):5493–5514. Available from: doi:10.1080/01431161.2021.1921875.

13. Lohi S, Tiwari N. Assessment of suitability of metaheuristics and machine learning for task scheduling process: A review of aptness in heavy task environments. Smart Trends in Computing and Communications: Proceedings of SmartCom 2020. 419–425. 11–12 September, 2020.

14. Eedi H, Kolla M. Machine learning approaches for healthcare data analysis. J Crit Rev. 2020; 7(4):806–811. Available from: doi:10.31838/jcr.07.04.149.

15. Dhillon A, Singh A. Biology and today's world machine learning in healthcare data analysis: A survey. J Biol Today's World. 2018; 8(2)1–10. Available from: doi: 10.15412/J.JBTW.01070206.

16. Dhal P, Azad C. A comprehensive survey on feature selection in the various fields of machine learning. Applied Intelligence. 2022; 52:4543–4581.

17. Ambigavathi M, Sridharan D. Analysis of clustering algorithms in machine learning for healthcare data. International Conference on Advances in Computing and Data Sciences. Singapore: Springer. pp. 117–128. 11–12 September 2020, Bangkok, Thailand.

18. Abdelaziz A, Elhoseny M, Salama AS, Riad AM. A machine learning model for improving healthcare services on cloud computing environment. Measurement. 2018; 119:117–128. Available from: doi:10.1016/j.measurement.2018.01.022.

19. Abirami L, Karthikeyan J. A detailed study on implication of big data, machine learning and cloud computing in healthcare domain. International Conference on Innovative Computing and Cutting-edge Technologies. Cham, Switzerland: Springer. 2020. pp. 309–316.

20. Sarangi AK, Mohapatra AG, Mishra TC, Keswani B. Healthcare 4.0: A voyage of fog computing with iot, cloud computing, big data, and machine learning. Fog Computing for Healthcare 4.0 Environments. Cham, Switerland: Springer. 2021. pp. 177–210.

21. Firdaus H, Hassan SI, Kaur H. A comparative survey of machine learning and metaheuristic optimization algorithms for sustainable and smart healthcare. African J Comput. 2018; 11(4):1–17. Available from: https://afrjcict.net.

22. Surantha N, Lesmana TF, Isa SM. Sleep stage classification using extreme learning machine and particle swarm optimization for healthcare big data. J Big Data. 2021; 8(1). Available from: doi:10.1186/s40537-020-00406-6.

23. Zubar AH, Balamurugan R. Green computing process and its optimization using machine learning algorithm in healthcare sector. Mob Networks Appl. 2020; 25(4):1307–1318. Available from: doi:10.1007/s11036-020-01549-9.

24. Xiao C. Optimization and Machine Learning Methods for Medical and Healthcare Applications. University of Washington, USA. 2016. [Doctoral dissertation].

25. Meng X, Zhang J. Anxiety recognition of college students using a Takagi-Sugeno-Kang fuzzy system modeling method and deep features. IEEE Access. 2020; 8:159897–159905. Available from: doi:10.1109/ACCESS.2020.3021092.

26. Zulfiker MS, Kabir N, Biswas AA, Nazneen T, Uddin MS. An in-depth analysis of machine learning approaches to predict depression. Curr Res Behav Sci. 2021; 2(4):100044, Available from: doi:10.1016/j.crbeha.2021.100044.

27. Arif, M, Basri, A, Melibari, G, Sindi, T, Alghamdi, N, Altalhi, N. Classification of anxiety disorders using machine learning methods: A literature review. Insights Biomed Res. 2020; 4(1):95–110. Available from: doi:10.36959/584/455.

28. Sau A, Bhakta I. Predicting anxiety and depression in elderly patients using machine learning technology. Healthc Technol Lett. 2017; 4(6):238–243.

29. Sardar JC, Sau A, Sardar M, Karmakar, P. Mental health status of sailors of Haldia Dock Complex, West Bengal. Academia Edu. 2020; 7:7–12. Available from: https://academia.edu/download/64624955/IJRR0044.pdf.

30. Hurtado SL, Simon-Arndt CM, Hunter MA. Enhancing decision-making under stress among sailors. 2019; 19: Naval Health Research Center, San Diego, USA. Available from: https://researchgate.net/publication/338883246.

31. Sau C, Bhakta I. Erratum: Screening of anxiety and depression among seafarers using machine learning technology. Informatics Med Unlocked. 2019; 16(8):100228. Available from: doi:10.1016/j.imu.2019.100228.

32. Alharahsheh YE, Abdullah MA. Predicting individuals mental health status in Kenya using machine learning methods. 12th International Conference on Information and Communication Systems (ICICS). 2021. pp. 94–98. 24-26 May 2021, Valencia, Spain.

33. Salari N, Hosseinian-Far A, Jalali R, Vaisi-Raygani, A, Rasoulpoor, S, Mohammadi, M, et al. Prevalence of stress, anxiety, depression among the general population during the COVID-19 pandemic: a systematic review and meta-analysis. Global Health. 2020; 16(1):1–1.

34. Özdin S, Bayrak Özdin S. Levels and predictors of anxiety, depression and health anxiety during COVID-19 pandemic in Turkish society: The importance of gender. Int J Soc Psychiatry. 2020; 66(5):504–511, Available from: doi:10.1177/0020764020927051.

35. Shevlin M, McBride, O, Murphy, J, Miller, JG, Hartman, TK, Levita, L et al. Anxiety, depression, traumatic stress and COVID-19-related anxiety in the UK general population during the COVID-19 pandemic. BJPsych Open. 2020; 6(6)1–9. Available from: doi:10.1192/bjo.2020.109.

36. Bendau A, Petzold, MB, Pyrkosch, L, Maricic, LM, Betzler, F, Rogoll, J, Große, J et al. Associations between COVID-19 related media consumption and symptoms of anxiety, depression and COVID-19 related fear in the general population in Germany. Eur Arch Psychiatry Clin Neurosci. 2021; 271(2)283–291, Available from: doi:10.1007/s00406-020-01171-6.

37. Choi EPH, Hui BPH, Wan EYF. Depression and anxiety in Hong Kong during COVID-19. Int J Environ Res Public Health. 2020; 17(10). Available from: doi:10.3390/ijerph17103740.

38. Sønderskov KM, Dinesen PT, Santini ZI, and Østergaard SD. The depressive state of Denmark during the COVID-19 pandemic. Acta Neuropsychiatrica. 2020; 32(4):15–17, Available from: doi:10.1017/neu.2020.15.

39. Hyland P, Shevlin, M, McBride, O, Murphy, J, Karatzias, T, Bentall, RP et al. Anxiety and depression in the Republic of Ireland during the COVID-19 pandemic. Acta Psychiatr Scand. 2020; 142(3)249–256. Available from: doi:10.1111/acps.13219.

40. Bhandari KS, Seo C, Cho GH. Towards sensor-cloud based efficient smart healthcare monitoring framework using machine learning. Proceedings of 9th Intl Conf Smart Media Appl. 2020: 1:380–383, Available from: doi:10.1145/3426020.3426138.

41. Abdali-Mohammadi F, Meqdad MN, Kadry S. Development of an IoT-based and cloud-based disease prediction and diagnosis system for healthcare using machine learning algorithms. IAES Int J Artif Intell. 2020; 9(4):766–771. Available from: doi:10.11591/ijai.v9.i4. pp. 766–771.

42. Eapen BR, Sartipi K, Archer N. Serverless on FHIR: Deploying machine learning models for healthcare on the cloud, Preprint. 2020. Accessed: June 2022. Available from: http://arxiv.org/abs/2006.04748. Doi: https://doi.org/10.48550/arXiv.2006.04748.

43. Kumar P, Silambarasan K. Enhancing the performance of healthcare service in IoT and cloud using optimized techniques. IETE J Res. 2019; 68(2):1–10, Available from: doi:10.1080/03772063.2019.1654934.

44. Kumar TS, HS M, Mustapha SMFD, Gupta P, Tripathi RP. Intelligent fault-tolerant mechanism for data centers of cloud infrastructure. Mathematical Problems in Engineering. 2022.

45. Wang C, Qin Y, Han J, Kim I, Granados Vergara JD, Dong C, et al. A low power cardiovascular healthcare system with cross-layer Optimization from sensing patch to cloud platform. IEEE Trans Biomed Circuits Syst. 2019; 13(2):314–329. Available from: doi:10.1109/TBCAS.2019.2892334.

46. Kuzlo I, Strielkina A, Tetskyi A, Uzun D. Selecting cloud service for healthcare applications: From hardware to cloud across machine learning. CEUR Workshop Proc. 2018; 2122:26–34.

47. Sreedhar KC, Suresh Kumar N. An optimal cloud-based e -healthcare system using k -centroid MVS clustering scheme. J Intell Fuzzy Sys. 2018; 34(3):1595–607. Available from: doi:10.3233/JIFS-169454.

48. Ruthvik Reddy P, Sri Sai Nikhil G, Sreedhar KC, Shaik, M, Swathi M. A Cloud-Based Privacy Preserving e-Healthcare System using Whale Optimization. Cham, Switzerland: Springer, doi: https://doi.org/10.1007/978-3-030-46943-6_11.

49. Gupta M, Gupta B. A comparative study of breast cancer diagnosis using supervised machine learning techniques. Proceedings of 2nd International Conference on Computing Methodology and Communication (ICCMC). 997–1002. 15-16 February 2018, Erode, India. doi: 10.1109/ICCMC.2018.8487537.

50. Lin K, Xia F, Wang W, Tian D, Song J. System design for big data application in emotion-aware healthcare. IEEE Access. 2016; 4:6901–6909, Available from: doi:10.1109/ACCESS.2016.2616643.

51. Geron A. Hands-On Machine Learning with Scikit-Learn, Keras, and Tensorflow: Concepts, Tools, and Techniques to Build Intelligent Systems, 2nd Edition. 2019. O'Reilly Media, Inc., 2011.

52. Bhat JA, George V, Malik B. Cloud computing with machine learning could help us in the early diagnosis of breast cancer. Proceedings of 2nd IEEE International Conference on Advanced Computing Communication and Engineering. 2015; 4: 644–648. 01 May 2015, Dehradum, India, doi: 10.1109/ICACCE.2015.62.

Chapter 11

Resource Management in Fog Computing Environment Using Optimal Fog Network Topology

Pradeep Singh Rawat, Srabanti Maji, and
Devendra Prasad

*Department of Computer Science and Engineering, School of Computing,
DIT University, Dehradun, Uttarakhand, India*

Contents

DOI: 10.1201/9781003322931-11

11.1 Introduction

The internet-based computing paradigm supports services in a demand fashion across the globe. The types of computing node are mobile, sensor and cloud (1, 2). The nodes are interlinked for the sharing of the data, which is stored inside the cloud data center (1). When users need the data for various applications, data can be fetched from the cloud. It increases the network latency and data is not in the control of the end user who wants to use the data as a service. There might be unauthorized access to the data inside the cloud storage in the data center (3). The alternative solution is an extension of cloud computing, for instance, the fog computing environment. It supports low latency in an edge computing environment with better availability. The fog node provides the computing environment at the edge of the network where the data is generated by the fog node (e.g., sensor, camera, proxy servers, and actuators). The fog computing environment has wide, real-time applications that include surveillance applications that use detector and capturing nodes. Hence, in the decision-making process where real-time data is required, the fog node plays a prominent role that uses real-time processing at the edge. Health departments, smart parking and disaster management systems have wide applications in the fog computing environment, which is integrated with cloud computing storage as a service. The distributed data collection point is used, for instance, the fog nodes (4). The delay in computing places the demand on the fog computing environment. The processing and data analysis for decisions are performed at the edge of the network, for instance, the services delivered at the edge location of the distributed fog network (5). There is no requirement to access the storage in the cloud node inside the data center. The performance and quality of service can be improved using effective fog nodes that include sensors, actuators, gateways, and video cameras, and other fog devices according to the requirement of the users. This chapter focuses on the description of the physical topology that is required for resource management in the fog network and resource management policy implementation across the globe. The fog network combined the sensor node, actuators, and control devices to capture the live streaming data that was generated from user sites. The captured data could be used for analysis and evaluation purposes at the user end across the globe. The fog network connects with the data center node in the cloud to provide the services using SaaS (software as a service) and IaaS (infrastructure as a service) (6). The reliability of the information management system could be enhanced using technology transformation, for example, fog computing, the Internet of Things (IoT)-based computing, integration of fog and IoT computing with the cloud computing environment. The natural resources are limited; therefore, natural resources need to be conserved and data center availability provided 24 hours a day, without any disruption. The fog computing environment overcomes the limitations of cloud computing. Researchers have focused on developing an efficient model that uses intelligence away from the cloud to minimize the latency. The intelligence could be allocated at the access point (7). The nodes associated with the fog network process the information closer to the data sources, which is generated by the IoT devices. The local area network is used to connect the devices in a distributed environment. The intelligence might be transferred to a local area network and supports the processing of the data in the fog node or IoT-based gateway device (8). The primary focus of this chapter is the resource management methodologies in the fog computing environment that use fog network physical topologies. Resource management methodologies for comparative analysis have been focused on previously. Still, there is an opportunity to focus on the performance metrics of latency and energy consumed. This focus includes a case study on the fog network that includes fog devices (e.g., electroencephalography (EEG) sensor, area camera, ISP (Internet service provider) gateway, and cloud node).

11.2 Background and Related Work

This section covers the study of the service-oriented computing paradigm and its extension for optimal resource management. This section starts with the cloud and extends up to the edge computing environment, which includes fog and edge computing, and an IoT-based computing environment. It covers the role of optimization based resource management techniques for a better quality of service that uses a fog network topology architecture with optimal performance metrics. The edge of the network fog node provides a facility similar to the cloud node and things are connected to the fog node to provide the data for intelligent decisions (9). The processing capability of the node can be implemented at the edge of the network with minimum bandwidth cost and minimum delays. This process is known as offloading. The computing and processing happen at the edge node that has things. The things node lies at the edge that is connected with the high-speed internet (10). The accessible resources are assigned to the end users that use supporting optimal strategies in the cloud, fog, and edge computing environments (11). The researchers presented the administrative resource management in the fog computing environment. The administrative resource management focuses on controlled resource allocation in an integrated fog and cloud network (12). The researchers' primary focus was overcoming the major challenges in a cloud computing environment in a real-time scenario where delay could not be accepted. The computing, storage, and network resources were accessed at the edge using access points and software defined network nodes for the implementation of the resource management policy (13). The researchers presented a smart building system that used a fog computing environment (14). Hence, starting from communication systems, the computing paradigm shifted from traditional to automated and data center-aware remote computing. There are some pros and cons of the computing system, which are further enhanced using an on-demand on-site computing system that provides everything on-demand as per the requirement of the users (e.g., end users, developers, and business people). The optimal fog network topology includes the edge, root, and internal nodes that transfer the information. The resource management in the fog computing environment follows a three-layer architecture, which includes fog and cloud data centers, and a communication system that uses controlled internetworking hardware, for instance, a software-defined network system. The satisfaction of the client is the primary concern of service providers. The cloud and fog computing paradigms cooperate for service availability for the users across the globe (15). The resource management techniques in a service-oriented computing paradigm include five categories: 1. quality of service-aware; 2. load management; 3. power management of host and virtual machine level; 4. migration of virtual resources in online mode; and 5. offline mode respectively. The category includes the resources of the fog, cloud, and edge computing layers, respectively. The root node of the topology network follows the static approaches for resource management. It includes the round robin approach for the allocation of computing power to the adjacent node (16). The unlimited data can be served using an IoT network with the help of the fog computing environment. The advantages of the fog computing environment can be achieved using an effective resource management technique at the level of fog node and cloud (e.g., IaaS, PaaS (platform as a service), and SaaS) service layers. The data processing can be enhanced using an optimal fog network with an optimal hybrid technique. The novelty of the model depends on resource utilization costs, fog node utilization, and optimal power management. The incoming requests to the fog devices can be efficiently managed using appropriate mapping between tasks and the fog node.

11.2.1 Simulation Setup

The modeling and simulation of the computing paradigm play an important role in high-performance computing. The service-oriented cloud, fog, and edge computing environments can be simulated using simulation tools integrated with a Java-supported IDE (integrated development environment). In this chapter, all the simulation processes were implemented using an integrated environment with

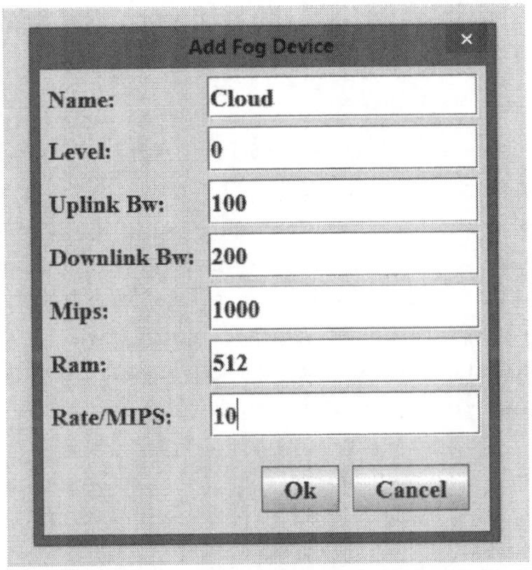

Figure 11.1 Fog device configuration parameters.

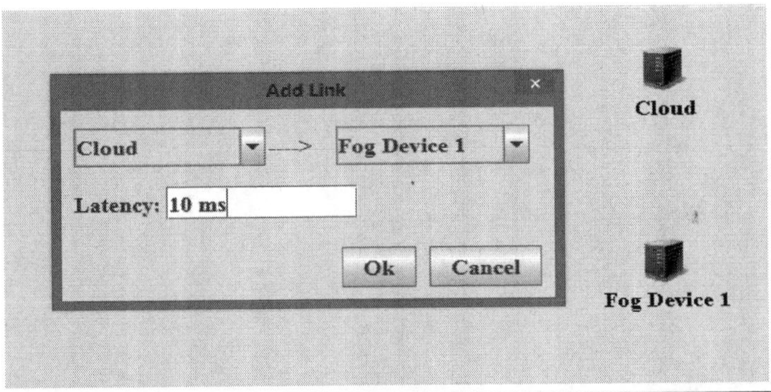

Figure 11.2 Link configuration information (cloud---->fog device 1).

Eclipse IDE for Java Developers (includes incubating components) Version 2020-12 (4.18.0)/NetBeans IDE 8.0.1, and an iFogSim simulation toolkit (17). The topology network was simulated using the fog Gui interface. The configuration parameters of the fog device was defined using the interface shown in Figure 11.1.

Figure 11.2 shows the communication link interface between any pair of nodes. In this case, a communication link is shown between the cloud node and Fog Device 1 with a latency period of 10 ms.

11.2.2 High-Level Architecture of Resource Management System Using Optimal Fog Network

Figure 11.3 shows the high-level architecture in the collaborative study of all computing paradigms, which provided services to the end users across the globe. Layer 1 is associated with capturing the on-site data that uses video objects. Layer 2 indicates the edge computing nodes that provide intelligence at the site of the resources. The fog computing node includes fog computing network nodes, which inculcate the computing and storage on cash mode. Layer 3 provides the optimization techniques used for resource management, data analysis, and visualization. The data analysis provides a clue about the data processed and outcomes of the captured information at the level data node. The lower layer included the data source area site and cloud computing nodes. Cloud computing provides unlimited computing, storage, and network as a service to the end users. Between the cloud node and user interface fog gateway, decisions are taken about the flow of the information. The quality of service degradation is supported by the cloud node in the fog network topology. So, on-site intelligence and computing power is taken care of. The power consumption and latency in a scalable environment cannot be ignored (18). Hence, the architecture

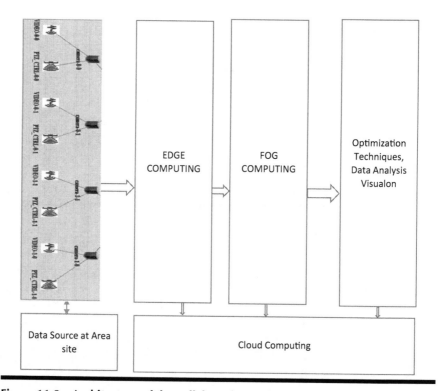

Figure 11.3 Architecture of the collaborative study of computing (e.g., cloud, edge, fog) environment.

shown in Figure 11.3 incorporates the low energy consumption and on-demand on-site resource availability. In between the cloud nodes and IoT devices, various intermediate nodes are offloaded for better resource utilization. The utilization of the network was also enhanced (19). The new computing paradigm ensured that a cloud computing environment was not sufficient to perform all the tasks; therefore, the data analysis required more than a cloud computing environment and included edge and fog computing, and an IoT-based computing environment. In a real-time scenario, the data analysis outcome required immediate decisions, for instance, all computing must be performed at the edge node without any communication delay. The architecture in Figure 11.3 shows that the optimization technique layer provides the resource management and optimal use of the fog network nodes. Hence, the optimal fog network topology was used for data processing and moving from the site to the cloud node as per the requirements. The optimal fog network might be helpful in real-time decisions for dam water level monitoring.

11.3 Resource Management in Fog Computing Environment

The responsibility of the resource management techniques was based on optimization, which concerned with the assignment of the resources to the concerned users across the globe. Resource assignment is a challenging concern for the consumers who want to use the services of cloud, fog, edge, and IoT-based computing environment to the end users (20).

The layered architecture of the fog node with the cloud node includes the following components as shown in Figure 11.4. Figure 11.4 shows that the cloud data center stores the data fetched from the edge of the network.

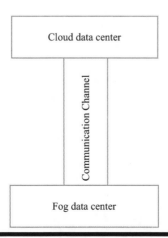

Figure 11.4 Layered architecture components of fog-cloud.

The cloud fog environment includes the communication channel for data transfer from the fog node to the cloud data center node. The direction of the flow of information takes place from bottom up as shown in this figure. The intelligence and computing power are available at the fog data center. The fog data center layer is known as Tier 1, a communication channel is known as Tier 2, and the cloud data center layer is known as Tier 3. Tiers 1, 2, and 3 contain multiple internet working hardware (e.g., router, switches, hub access point, and gateway devices). The orchestration of the cloud resources performs using resource management policy at the level of fog network and cloud data center. The expansion of cloud computing is the primary requirement of the users that have a high mobility of the data with a flight mode. The edge of the computing environment provides on-demand Tier 1, 2, and 3 resources with better scalability. The fog computing environment supports real-time optimization with better security and privacy. Hence, there are wide applications for three-tier architecture, including smart parking, surveillance, and water control at reservoir sites. In real-time applications, the three-tier computing environment supports computing, communication, and network cost minimization. The researchers focused on reliability improvement using the fog layer (21).

11.3.1 Fog Computing Topology Nodes and Configuration Parameters

Table 11.1 gives the fog computing node in a fog network using four different levels. The level zero contains the cloud node, which is connected to the adjacent fog nodes. The topology is shown in Figure 11.5 and uses the parameters for optimal resource management. The simulation setup uses the configuration parameters. The physical topology configuration efficiency was measured using the performance metrics of latency and energy consumed.

11.3.1.1 Level 0 Fog Node

Level 0 as shown in Figure 11.5 contains the cloud node. The configuration parameters of Level 0 are given in Table 11.1. The configuration parameters include computing power, storage, and bandwidth of the network link from the cloud node to fog node and fog node to cloud node, for example, the uplink and downlink bandwidth of the network. The cloud node provides infinite computing power that uses a large-scale distributed data center network. The backups and replicas of the data are contained inside the cloud node with multiple data centers DCN (data center number) 0, DCN_1,…DCN_n. The cloud node–Link–Fog Node 1 transfers the data for future backups.

Table 11.1   Fog Network Node Configuration Parameters

Serial Number	Level	Node	Configuration Parameters	Parameters Range	Link Status
1	0	Cloud node	Cloud	Cloud node with Unlimited Hosts	Cloud Node---Fog Node 1
			MIPS	47800	
			RAM	40000	
			UpBw	100	
			DownBw	10000	
			ratePerMips	0.01	
			busyPower	16*103	
			idlePower	16*83.25	
2	1	Fog Node 1 (proxy server)	MIPS	2800	Fog Node 1 --- Fog Node 2
			RAM	4000	
			UpBw	10000	
			DownBw	10000	
			ratePerMips	0.0	
			busyPower	107.339	
			idlePower	83.4333	
3	2	Fog Node 2 (access point)	MIPS	2800	Fog Node 2---Fog Node 3
			RAM	4000	
			UpBw	10000	
			DownBw	10000	
			ratePerMips	0.0	
			busyPower	107.339	
			idlePower	83.4333	
4	3	Fog Node 3 (camera)	MIPS	500	Fog Node 3--- Fog Node 4
			RAM	1000	
			UpBw	10000	
			DownBw	10000	
			ratePerMips	0	
			busyPower	87.53	
			idlePower	82.44	
5	4	Fog Node 4 (Actuator (LED) Display)	Latency	1 ms	Fog Node 4---Actuator

11.3.1.2 Level 1 Fog Node

Level 1, as shown in Figure 11.5, contains the fog node (i.e., proxy server). The configuration parameters of the proxy server at Level 1 include storage, computing, and network bandwidth of the fog node with the adjacent cloud node and fog node 2. The fog node 2 has some limited computing power to perform some basic operations of intelligence. The fog node contains the link with the cloud node–link–fog node 1, fog node 1–link–fog node 2.

11.3.1.3 Level 2 Fog Node

Level 2, as shown in Figure 11.5, contains the router or access point that takes some routing decisions when the data flows from the leaf node toward the cloud node in the topology network. The access point at Level 2 acts like a fog device that has intelligence regarding computing power and network bandwidth. The fog node has a link status fog node 2–fog node 3–fog node 4. The configuration parameter details are given in Table 11.1.

11.3.1.4 Level 3 Fog Node

The Level 3 fog node shown in Figure 11.5 contains the camera node. The camera node at Level 3 acts as a fog device that has intelligence regarding computing power and network bandwidth. The fog node at Level 3 has a link status fog node 3–fog node 4. The configuration parameters are given in Table 11.1. The camera node works on-site at the study area and has intelligence with storage. The camera node forwards the information to the adjacent node to take the routing decisions for information forwarding.

11.3.1.5 Level 4 Fog Node

The Level 4 fog node shown in Figure 11.5 contains actuator (LED display) sensors. The actuators in the fog area display the information with an efficient routing decision. Level 4 is the leaf level that acts as a source of information. The source of information in the study fog area provides the information that flows from the bottom to the top level up to the cloud node at Level 0.

The number of cameras depends on the number of fog areas. The number of nodes in the leaf level is shown by the equation number of fog node = number of areas x the number of cameras per study area.

11.4 Simulation of Fog Computing Environment

The simulation of the fog computing environment allows the following procedure. The simulation procedure includes the following steps.

Step 1: Initialize the parameters and number of fog users
Step 2: Define the configuration parameters of individual fog nodes
Step 3: Define the levels of the fog network topology using tog topology creator
Step 4: Start the simulation process
Step 5: Print the results of the execution time, delay, and energy consumed

11.5 Results

This section shows the information on the performance metrics that were used to evaluate the configuration of the fog topology network. The energy consumption and time estimates for the different scenarios that used four levels as shown in Figure 11.5 and Table 11.1. The parameters are associated with the node (e.g., start and target nodes), and the connecting link between the target node and start node with high bandwidth and low latency.

The performance metrics given in Table 11.2 provide information on the optimal fog configuration network. The performance metrics given in Table 11.2 exhibit the execution delay inside the cloud node at Level 0 in the topology network. The power consumption includes at the level of fog nodes that are connected with the cloud node using uplink and downlink bandwidth parameters. The primary focus was to set up an optimal topology network that would provide efficiency improvement, which was measured using performance metrics 1–6 given in Table 11.2.

The energy consumption parameter was measured at all the levels of the fog–cloud–integrated environment. Table 11.3 shows various levels of computing and energy consumption.

11.5.1 Fog Network Physical Topology of the Simulation

Figure 11.5 shows the tree topology network with the root node for the cloud node, which was connected with the ISP gateway. The data center network of the fog environment used the area gateways, which were directly connected with the on-site camera node for capturing the information.

Table 11.2   Performance Evaluation Parameters

Serial Number	Parameter
1	Execution time (ms)
2	Energy consumed (KW·h)
3	Cost of execution in cloud (USD)
4	Network use (Mb/s)
5	CPU execution delay (ms)
6	App loop delay (ms)

Table 11.3 FOG Computing Experimental Setup

Serial No	Node	Parameters
1	Level 0 (cloud node)	Energy consumption
2	Level 1 (proxy Server)	Energy consumption
3	Level 1 (Fog Node 2)	Energy consumption
4	Level 2 (Fog Node 3)	Energy consumption
5	Level 3 (Fog Node 4)	Energy consumption
6	Level 4 (leaf node)	Energy consumption
7	Level (root node) (cost)	Energy consumption
8	Level 4 (leaf node)	Energy consumption

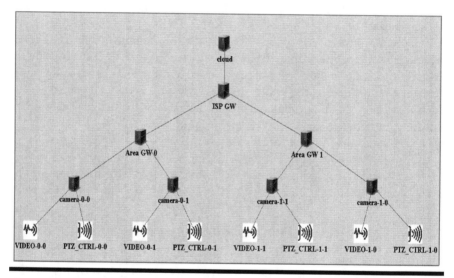

Figure 11.5 Tree base physical topology fog network.

Source: (21)

11.6 Performance Evaluation and Analysis

Table 11.4 lists the values of the performance metrics at different link states that used the path for Levels 0, 1, 2, and 3, respectively. The level of the cloud and fog nodes had some energy consumption, with the cost of execution being inside the cloud node, for instance, dependent on the latency of the network from the root to leaf node with high-level resource optimization.

Figure 11.6 shows the levels of the parameters versus simulation experimental values. The independent variable shows that parameter Level 0 indicated the execution

Table 11.4   Performance Metrics

Execution Time: 3646
Cloud: Energy Consumed = 1.3334336162582325E7
proxy-server: Energy Consumed = 834332.9999999987
d-0: Energy Consumed = 1048622.3287600018
Link (m-0-0): Energy Consumed = 846283.437000042
Link (m-0-1): Energy Consumed = 846283.437000042
Link (m-0-2): Energy Consumed = 846283.437000042
Link (m-0-3): Energy Consumed = 846283.437000042
Cost of execution in cloud = 21685.714285692997
Total network usage = 11611.12

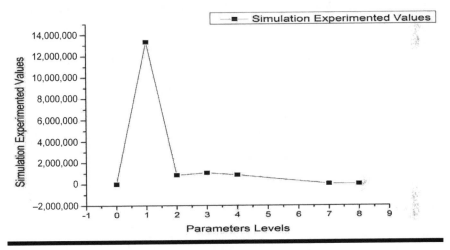

Figure 11.6   Parameters levels versus simulation experimented values.

time: 3646, Parameter level 1 indicates the cloud: Energy Consumed = 1.33 kw, and parameter level 2 indicates the proxy server: Energy Consumed = 834332.9999999987, parameter 2 indicates the d-0: Energy Consumed = 1048622.32 and Link (m-0-0): Energy Consumed = 846283.43 indicates the parameter level 3 and Cost of execution in cloud = 21685.714 parameter 4 and Total network usage = 11611.12 presents the parameter level 5. The results are shown in Figure 11.6, which indicates the variations in the performance metrics. The results were obtained using a fixed scenario at the cloud and fog nodes. The parameters showed cost, time, and energy for the performance evaluation and analysis.

11.7 Conclusions

The extension of cloud computing plays an important role in real-time data analysis scenarios. The computing and communication required are on-demand across the globe. Resource management and intelligence are required at the edge of the network. The fog computing environment fulfils the requirements with high scalability and reliability. In this chapter, the primary focus was resource management using optimal network topology. The resource management and optimal configuration of the fog and cloud nodes were evaluated using performance metrics time (ms), cost (USD), and energy consumption (kWh).

11.7.1 Future Directions

Future work will be implemented in real-time traffic management and surveillance systems for banking fraud detection that includes credit card fraud management with an optimal cloud and fog integrated environment. It will be also implemented for crop soil health management that uses real-time data analysis. This will increase the productivity of crops at the farmer's end. The integrated environment will be tested in real cloud scenarios using Amazon EC2 cloud and Microsoft Azure services. It will provide support to the healthcare departments for real-time patient monitoring and dam water management. In the future, the on-demand and edge computing environments will be helpful to control natural disasters, for example, earthquakes and landslides. The leaf node will include the sensor node to capture the data from the area site using point to control. The sensor node will be connected directly with the fog node with decision-making intelligence.

References

1. Sangeetha KS, Prakash P. Big data and cloud: A survey. Adv Intell Syst Comput. 2015; 325:773–778.
2. Shiva Jegan RD, Vasudevan SK, Abarna K, Prakash P, Srivathsan S, Gangothri V. Cloud computing: A technical gawk. Int J Appl Eng Res. 2014; 9(14):2539–2554.
3. Mandlekar VG, Mahale VK, Sancheti SS, Rais MS. Survey on fog computing mitigating data theft attacks in cloud. Int J Innov Res Comput Sci Technol. 2014; 2(6):13–16.
4. Elahi R. Fog computing and its ecosystem. SNIA Global Edu. 2015.
5. Luan TH, Gao L, Li Z, Xiang Y, We G, Sun L. Fog computing: Focusing on mobile users at the edge. Networking and Internet Architecture. 2016. pp. 1–6
6. Gai K, Li S. Towards cloud computing: A literature review on cloud computing and its development trends. Proceedings of the 2012 4th International Conference on Multimedia Information Networking and Security; 2012. 03–05 November, Nanjing, China.

7. Karagiannis V, Schulte S. Comparison of alternative architectures in fog computing. Proceedings of the 2020 IEEE 4th International Conference on Fog and Edge Computing (ICFEC); 2012. 11–14 May, Melbourne, Australia.

8. Naha RK, Garg S, Georgakopoulos D, Jayaraman PP, Gao L, Xiang Y, et al. Fog computing: Survey of trends, architectures, requirements, and research directions. IEEE Access. 2018; 6: 47980–8009.

9. Tordera EM, Xavi MB, Alminana J, Jukan A, Ren GJ, Zhu J, et al. What is a fog node a tutorial on current concepts toward a common definition. arXiv: 1611.09193 [Preprint]. 2016. doi: 10.48550/arXiv.1611.09193. Accessed: 22 March 2022.

10. Li H, Ota K, Dong M. Learning IoT in edge: Deep learning for the internet of things with edge computing. IEEE Netw. 2018; 32: 96–101.

11. Premsankar G, Francesco M, Taleb T. Edge computing for the Internet of Things: A case study. IEEE Internet of Things J. 2018; 5:1275–1284.

12. Agarwal S, Yadav S, Yadav AK. An efficient architecture and algorithm for resource provisioning in fog computing. Int J Inf Eng Electronic Bus (IJIEEB). 2016; 8:48–61.

13. Qi Q, Tao F. A smart manufacturing service system based on edge computing, fog computing, and cloud computing. IEEE Access. 2019: 7:86769–86777.

14. Javaid S, Javaid N, Saba T, Wadud Z, Rehman A, Haseeb A. Intelligent resource allocation in residential buildings using consumer to fog to cloud based framework. Energies. 2019; 12:815.

15. da Silva RAC, da Fonseca NLS. Resource allocation mechanism for a fog-cloud infrastructure. Proceedings of the 2018 IEEE International Conference on Communications. 2018. 20–24 May, Kansas City (MO).

16. Javaid S, Javaid N, Saba T, Wadud Z, Rehman A, Haseeb A. Intelligent resource allocation in residential buildings using consumer to fog to cloud based framework. Energies. 2019; 12:815.

17. Gupta H, Vahid Dastjerdi A, Ghosh SK, Buyya R. IFogSim: A toolkit for modeling and simulation of resource management techniques in the Internet of Things, edge and fog computing environments. Software: Practice and Experience. 2017; 47(9):1275–1296.

18. Tedeschi P, Sciancalepore S. Edge and fog computing in critical infrastructures: Analysis, security threats, and research challenges. Proceedings of the 2019 IEEE European Symposium on Security and PrivacyWorkshops (EuroS & PW); 2019. 17–19 June 2019, Stockholm, Sweden.

19. Masip-Bruin X, Marin-Tordera E, Jukan A, Ren G. Managing resources continuity from the edge to the cloud: Architecture and performance. Fut Gener Comput Syst. 2018; 79:777–785.

20. Agarwal S, Yadav S, Yadav AK. An efficient architecture and algorithm for resource provisioning in fog computing. Int J Inf Eng Electronic Bus (IJIEEB). 2016; 8:48–61.

21. Javaid S, Javaid N, Saba T, Wadud Z, Rehman A, Haseeb A. Intelligent resource allocation in residential buildings using consumer to fog to cloud based framework. Energies. 2019;12:815.

Chapter 12

Applications of Fog in Healthcare Services

Ujjwal Bhushan, Srabanti Maji, and
Pradeep Singh Rawat

School of Computing, DIT University, Dehradun, Uttarakhand, India

Contents

DOI: 10.1201/9781003322931-12

12.1 Introduction to Fog Computing

Because the size of devices is shrinking and the volume of data is growing at an exponential rate, finding alternative useful ways to deal with the data has become a requirement. Many in the healthcare industry are now finding it difficult to collect, analyze, visualize, and use data. These figures are derived from the use of the Internet of Things (IoT) devices. The IoT enables us to develop gadgets that are more powerful, intelligent, and efficient. The technology of the IoT helps us to connect devices. In healthcare systems, this can be achieved using devices, such as tracking cameras, medical sensors, and monitoring equipment, such as an electrocardiogram (ECGs), heart rate, and blood pressure. The main purpose of IoT devices is that a device can be accessed remotely and can be monitored from anywhere. Currently, IoT devices are helping to improve quality of life and accessibility.

The IoT is being used in various areas of life, such as smart cities, smart home appliances, and voice-controlled devices. Due to the incorporation of the IoT with fog computing, medical services and healthcare have shown a significant improvement in patient care and aid services.

12.2 Characteristics of Fog Computing

Fog computing has the following characteristics.

1. Edge location
   Fog computing architecture consists of endpoints that have services at the end of the network. These services have short latency and requirements (1).
2. Heterogeneity
   Fog computing is a platform that connects distant devices to cloud computing by storing computation and network services. Fog systems are highly virtualized systems that are used to store and analyze sensor data. The cloud and fog computing systems are built on these resources.
3. Sensor networks
   Fog computing works on the principle of distributed systems. The systems require storage resources and distributed computing. Thus, to monitor these environments, fog computing has a large-scale sensor network that monitors the grid of the fog systems (2).
4. Real-time interactions
   Real-time interactions are preferred in fog computing applications rather than batch processing.
5. Mobility
   Fog computing applications require communication directly with mobile devices. Thus, it requires mobility support techniques. This protocol

dissociates the sender identity from the receiver identity. This process requires a distributed system.

6. Geographical distribution

   Cloud computing uses a centralized architecture and fog computing leans toward widely distributed services. It provides high-quality services to edge-located components. Thus, fog computing applications generally rely on a widely distributed architecture.

7. Interoperability

   To support certain services, such as live streaming, fog computing requires collaboration between providers. The fog components must have interoperability and the services must be distributed across the domains.

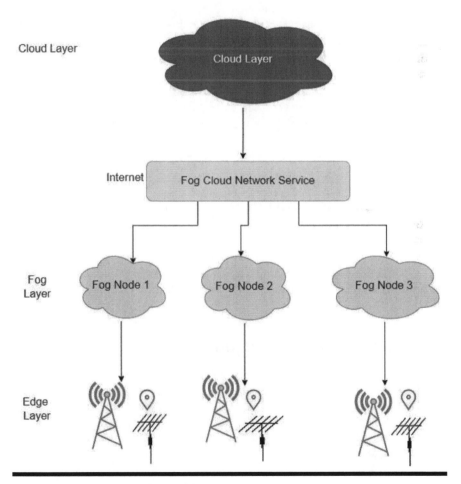

Figure 12.1   Fog computing architecture.

12.3 Fog Computing Architecture

Fog computing is designed to overcome the problems that have arisen in cloud computing. Fog computing is also known as edge computing (3).

The fog computing architecture has been designed to accommodate physical and logical elements. These consist of hardware and software components. These components are used to implement the IoT network.

Figure 12.1 shows the fog computing architecture with different layers from bottom to top.

1. Terminal layer

   This is the most basic layer of fog architecture. The terminal layer has devices like mobile devices, sensors, and readers. These devices are used for the monitoring and collection of data. These devices are spread across geographical locations and can be accessed using adjacent nodes. These devices show optimum performance in mixed environments and each node might contain several means of communication.

2. Fog layer

   The fog layer consists of devices, such as gateways, routers, base stations, and servers. These are known as fog nodes. The storage, transfer, and computation take place through these fog nodes. These fog nodes ensure services to end devices. Cloud data centers and fog nodes are enabled using IP networks. Cloud computing enhances interaction and collaboration using enhanced storage capacities and processing.

3. Cloud layer

   This consists of servers that provide large storage and high-performance machines. These servers are used to store data permanently and to analyze the data. The data is also stored in the backup and the user has access to it. A cloud layer is formed using large data centers with high computation capabilities. Hence, in fog architecture, the cloud layer is situated at the end. It is a backup and permanent storage for the processed data in the fog systems.

12.4 Working of Fog Computing

Fog computing works on various kinds of data. Thus, it is used to collect, monitor, process, and analyze the data it receives from devices. The fog nodes nearest to the devices receive the data from the sensors (4).

The most time-sensitive data are analyzed and then the action is transmitted to the device. The summary of this action is then stored in the cloud for future reference by the user. Figure 12.2 shows the working of the fog computing environment in an integrated environment using the fog network. Data that is less sensitive is sent to the nodes for analysis. After this analysis is performed, the node sends the result to the device using its neighboring node. This process takes a few minutes for

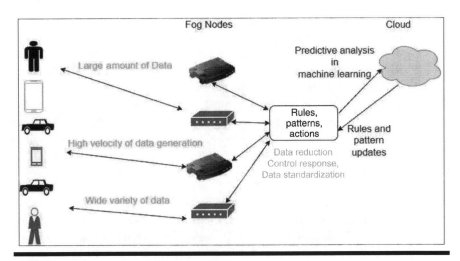

Figure 12.2   Working of fog computing.

processing (5). The time-insensitive data takes a large amount of time to process and analyse. This is later stored in the cloud for long-term storage and analysis.

12.5 Literature Review

12.5.1 Literature Review on Fog Computing in Healthcare Systems

Fog computing is one of the most evolved technologies in the last decade. In this chapter, research works are included that are based on fog computing with the IoT and cloud computing. Most of these works were motivated by the idea of making healthcare services more efficient and smarter. The main objective of this research work was to make it possible for the patients to have a consultation with healthcare professionals and receive effective aid for their disease.

The principle for the use of IoT technologies is to implement collaboration between fog and cloud computing to produce efficient healthcare services for the patients. The proposed systems include the implementation of fog technology for health monitoring, data security and confidentiality, and data protection.

1. Mutlag et al. (6) published a review paper that analyzed the use of fog technologies that were implemented and their impact on healthcare services. They reviewed various research works that are based on the architecture of the fog systems proposed, their performance, and their evaluation.
2. Kumari et al. (7) proposed a model for patients in healthcare architecture. This is a three-layer model that works in real-time to collect data, process it, and transmit the results to the cloud.

3. Al-Khafajiy et al. (8) focused on healthcare systems. The work proposed a three-layered architecture that contained sensors, fog nodes, and a cloud data center. The paper proposed the framework that combined this architecture. The proposed model offered cooperation between fog nodes when managing the resources of the system and job allocation. This process helped in achieving low latency in the healthcare system.

4. Atlam et al. (9) presented research work based on the integration of fog computing with the IoT. This process highlighted the profits and implementation challenges to the model. The purpose of using such a fog model was to show how fog computing architecture and developing IoT applications could be enhanced.

5. Kraemer et al. (10) presented a review on healthcare informatics that used fog computing. The paper explored, classified, and discussed applications of fog computing in healthcare services. The tasks of fog computing were categorized by applications into case classes. The tasks that were executed by the system were recorded in the application that could be handled by fog computing (11).

6. Gia et al. (12) proposed a fog-based monitoring system that was low cost and provided remote monitoring. The system was made of gateways and well-organized IoT sensors. Besides, the sensors collected ECG signals, respiration rate, and body temperature. This data was sent remotely to gateways for analysis to produce alerts following the results.

7. Sood et al. (13) proposed a model to predict a diagnosis in patients infected with Chikungunya virus (CHV) that used a healthcare system that was based on fog and cloud computing. The three-layered system was made of fog and cloud layers that were integrated with wearable IoT sensors. The system was designed for the prediction, identification, and control of the CHV virus. Fuzzy-C means (FCM) was used for the diagnosis of the infected patients and alerts were generated accordingly.

8. For heart attacks and brain strokes, a healthcare application was proposed by Zohora et al. (14) which was time sensitive. In this proposed model, fog computing was used to predict the symptoms and send alerts immediately. In these applications, fog computing enhanced the execution time and the cost of energy consumed by the system.

9. Rahmani et al. (15) describe how fog computing was different from other solutions regarding the IoT systems in healthcare. This system architecture could withstand the issues in healthcare systems, such as mobility, energy awareness of the system, and reliability.

10. Ahmad et al. (16) proposed a fog-based healthcare model that considered important features of healthcare applications, such as data privacy and security. This model implemented a fog layer as an intermediate layer between the cloud and end devices. To enhance the edge of the network, privacy and security were controlled using a cloud access security broker (CASB).

11. Chakraborty et al. (17) proposed a model platform that was designed to deal with latency in healthcare services using fog computing. A programming

model was used to control the distributed systems in fog computing in a wide geographical area. Using fog computing, the accuracy and consistency of data were improved by monitoring the service delivery time of the system.

12. Moosavi et al. (18) proposed that fog computing can tackle a variety of devices and sensors in healthcare systems. These devices are also equipped with managing and processing local data and storage. This research work was conducted on the principle that fog computing is the optimum technique to handle healthcare systems using specific features.

13. Dubey et al. (19) proposed a system architecture based on fog computing to authenticate and analyze the health data of the patients. The patterns were identified in the data through instances and then these results are stored in the cloud for future use. The system works on the principle of processing large amounts of data while using fewer fog resources.

14. Gia et al. (20) proposed to enhance the health monitoring system by utilizing the principle of fog computing at smart gateways. This model provides advanced techniques and services such as distributed storage, advanced data mining, and alert service at the edge of the network. During the process of feature extraction, an ECG was chosen as the most promising feature, because it is used to diagnose many types of cardiac diseases.

15. Craciunescu et al. (21) addressed the technical challenges faced due to the architecture of cloud computing and the requirements of smart connected object applications within the sensing environment. They investigated the possibility that executing cloud tasks, such as storage and data signal processing that take place at the edge of the network would decrease the latency associated when performing tasks within the cloud.

16. Fratu et al. (22) presented a distributed fog computing strategy for chronic obstructive pulmonary disease (COPD). This algorithm could be used to predict mild dementia patients. The data utilized in this study was collected in accordance with Romanian healthcare legislation to fulfil the process's needs. The planned surveillance system was a wall. Fog computing was used to connect huge numbers of geographically dispersed devices. Real-time connectivity, mobility assistance, interoperability, heterogeneity, and data preparation in the cloud were all considered by the system. Table 12.1 summarizes all the findings from the survey on fog computing research in health care.

12.5.2 Literature Review Related to Frameworks and Models in Healthcare Systems Using Fog Computing

This section describes the techniques that are used to design the frameworks and models in healthcare applications that use fog computing. The main parameters that were considered for the literature review were how the frameworks and models were designed for the healthcare systems using fog, IoT, and cloud computing. Fog

Table 12.1 Various Techniques Based on Fog Computing in Healthcare

Number	Author	Publication and Year	Methodology or Technique
1	Mutlag et al.	Science Direct 2019	A review paper that analyzes the use of fog technologies that have been implemented and their impact on healthcare services. They reviewed various research works based on the architecture of the fog systems proposed, their performance, and evaluation.
2	Kumari et al.	Elsevier 2018	Proposed a model for patients in healthcare architecture. This is a three-layer model that works in real time to collect data, process it, and transmit the results to the cloud.
3	Al-Khafajiy et al.	ACM Press 2018	The research work proposed a three-layered architecture containing sensors, fog nodes, and a cloud data center. The paper proposed the framework that combined this architecture. The proposed model offers cooperation between fog nodes when managing the resources of the system and job allocation. This process helps in achieving low latency in the healthcare system.
4	Atlam et al.	Big Data and Cognitive Computing	The research work is based on the integration of fog computing with the IoT. This process highlights the profits and implementation challenges of the model. The purpose of using such a fog model was to show how fog computing architecture and developing IoT applications could be enhanced.

Table 12.1 (Continued)

Number	Author	Publication and Year	Methodology or Technique
5	Kraemer et al.	IEEE Access 2017	A review on healthcare informatics that used fog computing. The research paper explored, classified, and discussed applications of fog computing in healthcare services. The tasks in fog computing were categorized by applications into case classes. The tasks executed by the system were recorded in the application that can be handled by fog computing.
6	Gia et al.	IEEE 2017	A fog-based monitoring system that is low cost and provides remote monitoring. The system is made of gateways and well-organized IoT sensors. Besides, the sensors collected ECG signals, respiration rate, and body temperature. This data was sent remotely to gateways for analysis to produce alerts following the results.
7	Sood et al.	Science Direct 2017	The model predicts the diagnosis of patients infected with CHV that used a healthcare system based on fog and cloud computing. The three-layered system is made of fog and cloud layers integrated with wearable IoT sensors. The system is designed for the prediction, identification, and control of CHV. FCM is used for the diagnosis of the infected patients and alerts are generated accordingly.

(continued)

Table 12.1 (Continued)

Number	Author	Publication and Year	Methodology or Technique
8	Zohora et al.	IEEE 2017	For heart attacks and brain strokes, a healthcare application was proposed which was time sensitive. In this proposed model, fog computing was used to predict the symptoms and send alerts immediately. In these applications, fog computing enhances the execution time and cost of energy consumed by the system.
9	Rahmani et al.	Elsevier 2017	Describes how fog computing is different from other solutions regarding IoT systems in healthcare. This system architecture can withstand the issues in healthcare systems such as mobility, energy awareness of the system, and reliability.
10	Ahmad et al.	Springer Link 2016	Proposed a fog-based healthcare model that considered important features of healthcare applications such as data privacy and security. This model implemented a fog layer as an intermediate layer between the cloud and end devices. To enhance the edge of the network, privacy and security were controlled using a CASB.
11	Chakraborty et al.	IEEE 2016	Proposed a model platform that was designed to deal with latency in healthcare services using fog computing. A programming model was used to control the distributed systems in fog computing in a wide geographical area. Using fog computing, the accuracy and consistency of data were improved by monitoring the service delivery time of the system.

Table 12.1 (Continued)

Number	Author	Publication and Year	Methodology or Technique
12	Moosavi et al.	Science Direct 2016	Proposed that fog computing could tackle a variety of devices and sensors in healthcare systems. These devices are also equipped to manage and process local data and storage. This research work was conducted on the principle that fog computing is the optimum technique to handle healthcare systems using specific features.
13	Dubey et. al.	Arxiv 2016	To validate and assess detected raw health data, a fog computing system architecture was presented. Embedded computer instances were confined by resources during this operation. Instances were used to identify relevant patterns, which were subsequently forwarded to the cloud. The main goal of this system was to handle large amounts of data while employing low-power fog resources.
14	Gia et al.	IEEE 2015	Proposed a system architecture based on fog computing to authenticate and analyze the health data of the patients. The patterns were identified in the data through instances and then these results were stored in the cloud for future use. The system works on the principle of processing large amounts of data while using fewer fog resources.

(*continued*)

Table 12.1 (Continued)

Number	Author	Publication and Year	Methodology or Technique
15	Craciunescu et al.	IEEE 2015	Within the sensing environment, addressed the technical issues posed by cloud computing architecture and the requirements of smart connected item applications. The concept of executing cloud functions, such as storage and data signal processing, at the network's edge was examined to reduce the latency associated with doing tasks within the cloud.
16	Fratu et al.	IEEE 2015	A distributed fog computing approach was proposed for COPD. This model also predicted people suffering from mild dementia. The data used in the research was collected according to Romanian healthcare regulations. To meet the requirements of the process eWall was used as the proposed monitoring system.

computing has shown the use of smart gateways at the edge of networks and the use of adjacent fog nodes for the transmission of data from the device to the cloud. The research also considered the enhancement in healthcare systems by analyzing the performance of the system, execution time, and selection of features for the analysis of the data.

1. Rajagopalan et al. proposed a smart e-health gateways network. This network aided in data preparation. The simplicity of data available from the cloud and sensors aided this process in reducing further processing (23).
2. Jararweh et al. established a framework that blended software-defined systems (SDS) and mobile edge computing (MEC) systems. This aids in the creation of a ubiquitous MEC that serves as a global controller for connecting a large number of local controllers (24).
3. Rahman et al. (25) proposed an MEC framework. This framework showed how services for people in diverse locations could be supported in real-time and could be personalized. The use of a hybrid cloud at the end of the server

along with terminal fog computing (FCTs) on the edge of the network, can be used.

4. According to research work by Distefano et al. (26), the IoT–Cloud framework could manage edge nodes using the proposed framework Stack4Things. This framework can compute how latency can be reduced by allocating resources closer to offloading processing.

5. Chaudhry et. al. proposed how security can be monitored for patient data by applying the security provisioning model (AZSPM) in fog environments (27).

6. According to Lu et al. (28), to serve as an on-request environment for execution, the cloud at the edge of the fog network could serve as a virtual platform. This helps to micromanage services near the data sources, such as sensor devices. This is different from micromanaging the devices themselves. The gateways in the fog network are placed so that the connection between the gateway distribution and the aggregation is affected.

7. Hamid et al. (29) proposed a protocol of triparty, one-round key authenticated agreement that used fog computing techniques. The cryptography was considered that uses bilinear pairing. This produced a session key between the entities to ensure that the communication was secure.

8. Wu et al. proposed a new computational framework (30), which used fog computing. This framework facilitated the use of remote real-time monitoring and sensing of data for analysis. The model has high performance for the prediction and diagnosis of diseases in healthcare systems.

9. Elmisery et al. (31) proposed that for IoT devices and healthcare cloud systems, personal gateways could act as a bridge between the intermediate fog nodes that are geographically deployed in the fog system.

10. For the dynamic allocation of resources in healthcare systems, fog computing was used for the smart gateway (micro data center) in the edge network. This model was proposed by Aazam et al. (32).

11. Oueis et al. (33) suggested an approach that clustered tiny cells to promote resource sharing between them.

12. Kliem et al. advocated the use of cloud computing to mitigate the IoT resource management by sharing the device resources of users (34).

Table 12.2 lists the frameworks and models proposed in fog computing in healthcare systems.

12.6 Edge and Fog Computing Comparisons

Edge computing technology was created to improve cloud computing at the network's edge. To meet the critical needs, it provides edge services near the data source. In mobile network base stations, this technique distributes intermediary

Table 12.2   Frameworks and Models Proposed in Fog Computing in Healthcare Systems

Number	Author	Publication and Year	Methodology or Technique
1	Rajagopalan et al.	IEEE 2017	Proposed a network of smart e-health gateways. This network helped in preprocessing the data. This process helps in alleviating further processing by the ease of data access from the cloud and sensors.
2	Jararweh et al.	Oxford University Press 2017	SDS and MEC systems were combined in this framework. This aided in the creation of a ubiquitous MEC that served as a global controller for connecting a large number of local controllers.
3	Rahman et al.	IEEE 2017	Offered an MEC paradigm. This design depicted how people in various regions could receive real-time and customized services. At the server end, you can utilize a hybrid cloud, and at the network's edge, you can FCTs.
4	Distefano et al.	Springer 2017	The IoT–cloud framework could manage edge nodes using the proposed framework Stack4Things. This framework can compute how latency can be reduced by allocating resources closer to offloading processing.
5	Chaudhry et al.	IEEE 2017	Proposed how security can be monitored for patient data by AZSPM in fog environments.
6	Lu et al.	IEEE 2017	According to this research, to serve as an on-request environment for execution, the cloud at the edge of the fog network can serve as a virtual platform. This helps to micromanage services near the data sources, such as sensor devices. This is different from

Table 12.2 (Continued)

Number	Author	Publication and Year	Methodology or Technique
			the process of micromanaging the devices themselves. The gateways of the fog network are placed in such a way that the connection between the gateway distribution and the aggregation is affected.
7	Hamid et al.	IEEE 2017	The paper proposed a protocol of triparty, one-round key authenticated agreement that used fog computing techniques. The cryptography was considered using the bilinear pairing. This in turn produced a session key between the entities to ensure that the communication was secure.
8	Wu et al.	Elsevier 2017	Proposed a new computational framework that used fog computing. This framework facilitated the use of remote real-time monitoring and sensing of data for analysis. The model has high performance for the prediction and diagnosis of diseases in healthcare systems.
9	Elmisery et al.	IEEE 2016	Proposed that for IoT devices and healthcare cloud systems, personal gateways could act as a bridge between the intermediate fog nodes that were geographically deployed in the fog system.
10	Aazam et al.	IEEE 2015	For the dynamic allocation of resources in the healthcare system, fog computing was used for a smart gateway (micro data center) in the edge network.

(*continued*)

Table 12.2 (Continued)

Number	Author	Publication and Year	Methodology or Technique
11	Oueis et al.	IEEE 2015	A method was presented to cluster tiny cells to simplify resource sharing among them.
12	Kliem et al.	IEEE 2015	The research stated that by sharing user device resources, the mitigation of IoT resource management could be achieved using cloud computing.

nodes. These intermediate nodes can compute and store data. Edge computing uses cloud computing to reduce latency and improve context awareness within the radio area network (RAN) (35). It lowers network activity by doing calculations at the network edge. In fog and edge computing, the cloud's storage and network power are transported to the edge network. Edge and fog computing improve efficiency and allow for the development of new services. For design, the function and location of nodes, and the number of nodes, fog computing was compared with edge computing.

Edge computing refers to computing at the network's perimeter or any network site that is closer to the user than the cloud. The devices use a cellular network to connect with the node at the base station. Non-IP-based technologies like BLE (Bluetooth low energy) and wi-fi are supported by fog computing. The edge's proximity decreases the latency to milliseconds and ensures that users have a stable connection. The difference between edge and fog is that isolated edge nodes use edge computing; however, fog computing is used for node-to-node interconnections.

12.7 Limitations and Challenges in Fog Computing

Although the use of fog computing provides efficient and effective results, every technology has its limitation and challenges to overcome. A few of the challenges that could occur due to the use of fog technology are listed in the following sections.

12.7.1 Control of Access

In fog computing, one of the major questions that might arise is how the architecture of fog computing will be designed. This is carried out so that it might not cause

Table 12.3   Characteristic Comparison of Fog and Edge Computing in Healthcare Systems

Number	Features	Edge Computing	Fog Computing
1	Devices	Server runs at the base station	Gateways, access points, switches, routers
2	Location	Radio network controller	Ranging from cloud to IoT nodes
3	Proximity	Only single hop	One to multiple hops
4	Access mechanism	Cellular networks	Bluetooth, cellular networks, wi-fi
5	General use cases	Video caching, traffic management, and local video monitoring	Smart delivery, IoT, connected automobiles, connected city, surveillance cameras assistance with health
6	Operators	Network infrastructure providers or local businesses	Users and service providers in the cloud
7	Various types of facility	Local	Global
8	Distance from users	Close	Relatively closer
9	Application type	Low bandwidth computation	High computation with low bandwidth
10	Architecture	Localized or distributed	Decentralized or hierarchical
11	Security	On edge devices	On participant nodes
12	Service Access	At the edge of the Internet	Through intelligent devices from the edge to the heart

any conflict when the access needs to traverse from client to fog to cloud where the data is stored. To ensure the security of the system it is necessary to have access control. The data owner can expand its access control in the cloud. Some research work has shown that several encryption techniques could be built together to provide an efficient way to access data in the cloud (36).

Dsouza et al. (36) proposed a system that was based on controlling access resources in fog computing. In the future, it might be possible to develop more techniques that deal with access control, which aim to support secure access and interoperability between mixed resources in fog computing.

12.7.2 Authentication

Devices that operate on fog computing might face issues, such as authentication and data trust. The reliability of authentication in cloud central servers is not a good selection, because authentication needs to collaborate with personnel devices to run locally when there is no remote authentication. A few research works have described the problem of authentication in fog computing; however, the issue remains unsolved (37).

Figure 12.3 shows the authentication issues in the fog computing environment from a security perspective.

12.7.3 Security and Privacy Issues

Fog computing devices might have security vulnerabilities because they are used in contexts when protection and monitoring are not available. As a result, devices are more vulnerable to attacks that could compromise the system and allow harmful operations, such as eavesdropping and data theft.

Several solutions could solve security-related issues in cloud computing; however, they do not necessarily work on fog computing devices because they are based

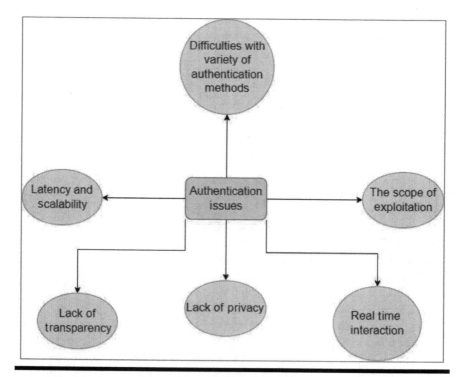

Figure 12.3 Authentication issues in fog computing.

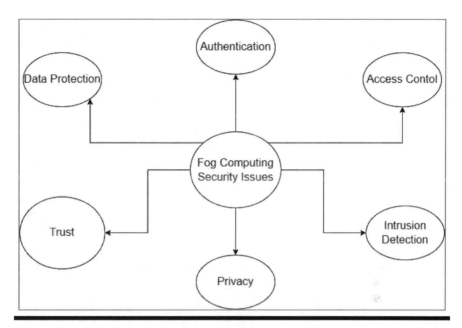

Figure 12.4   Security issues in fog computing.

on edge networks. The working of fog devices might have threats that are not necessarily found in cloud computing.

Figure 12.4 shows the major components that are associated with security issues in fog computing.

12.7.4 Fault Tolerance

In case of failure in networks, platforms, and specific sensors fog computing can provide services and function smoothly (38). Multiple fog nodes are distributed throughout the system. Using these nodes, the users could access the neighboring nodes when the services in the system are irregular.

12.8 Conclusion and Future Works

The integration of fog computing with the IoT makes it possible for us to have more intelligent and efficient devices in healthcare systems. The IoT is now being used in various sectors, such as robotics, smart devices for homes, traffic control, and agriculture. Using computing with the IoT technologies in healthcare and hospital systems will help when tackling emergencies. This will help health professionals to provide immediate aid in real-time and prevent adverse events. Cloud computing could serve as an aid when tracking the health of patients, their information in a database, and other relevant information. This chapter aimed to provide information on the research that has been conducted on fog computing and to present recent cloud–IoT–fog-based architecture. The latest development, difficulties, and obstacles observed were also discussed. Future work on fog computing could involve the expansion of cloud-based applications when integrating with fog computing. In addition, fog computing could be used when iterating various configurations that could be used in the infrastructure of smart cities.

References

1. Bonomi F, Milito M, Natarajan P, Zhu J. Fog Computing: a platform for the Internet of things and analytics. Big Data and Internet of Things: A Roadmap for Smart Environments. Springer International Publishing; 2014. pp. 168–185.
2. Kumari S, Singh S, Radha. Fog computing: Characteristics and challenges. Proceedings of Int J Emerg Trend Technol Comput Sci (IJETTCS). 2017; 6(2):113.
3. Dastjerdi AV, Gupta H, Calheiros RN, Ghosh SK, Buyya R. Fog Computing: Principles, architectures, and applications. Sci Direct. 2016; 1:61–75.
4. Hua P, Dhelima S, Ninga H, Qiuc T. Survey on fog computing: Architecture, key technologies, applications and open issues. J Network Comput Appl. 2017; 98:27–42.
5. Pareek K, Tiwari1 PK, Bhatnagar V. Fog computing in healthcare: A review. IOP Conference Series: Materials Science and Engineering. 2021; 1099(1):12–25.
6. Mutlag AA, Ghani MKA, Arunkumar N, Mohammed MA, Mohd O. Enabling technologies for fog computing in healthcare IoT systems. Sci Direct. 2019; 90:62–78.
7. Kumari A, Tanwar S, Tyagi S, Kumar N. Fog computing for Healthcare 4.0 environment: Opportunities and challenges. Computers and Electrical Engineering. 2018; 72:1–13.
8. Al-khafajiy M, Webster L, Baker T, Waraich A. Toward Fog driven IoT healthcare: Challenges and framework of fog computing in healthcare ICFNDS. Proceedings of the 2nd International Conference on Future Networks and Distributed Systems; 26–27 June 2018, Amman, Jordan.
9. Atlam H, Walters R, Wills G. Fog computing and the Internet of Things: A review. Big Data Cogn Comput. 2018; 2(2):10.
10. Kraemer FA, Eivind Braten A, Tamkittikhun N, Palma D. Fog computing in healthcare: A review and discussion. IEEE Access. 2017; 5.
11. Nguyen Gia T, Jiang M, Sarker VK, Rahmani AM, Westerlund T, Pasi Liljeberg P, et al. Low-cost fog-assisted healthcare IoT system with energy-efficient sensor nodes. 13th International Wireless Communications & Mobile Computing Conference. 1765–1770. 26–30 June 2017, Valencia, Spain.
12. Sood SK, Mahajan I. Wearable IoT sensor-based healthcare system for identifying and controlling chikungunya virus. Comput Ind. 2017; 91:33–44.

13. Zohora FT, Khan MRR, Bhuiyan MFR, Das AK. Enhancing the capabilities of IoT-based fog and cloud infrastructures for time-sensitive events. Proceedings of Int Conf Elect Eng Comput Sci. 2017; 224–30. 22–23 August 2017, Palembang, Indonesia.

14. Rahmani AM, Nguyen Gia T, Negash B, Anzanpour A, Azimi I, Jiang M, et al. Exploiting smart e-Health gateways at the edge of healthcare Internet-of-Things: A fog computing approach. Futur Gener Comput Syst. 2017; 78(2):641–658.

15. Ahmad M, Amin MB, Hussain S, Kang BH, Cheong T, Lee S. Health fog: A novel framework for health and wellness applications. J Supercomput. 2016; 72(10):3677–3695.

16. Chakraborty S, Bhowmick S, Talaga P, Agrawal DP. Fog networks in healthcare application. Proceedings of 13th Int Conf Mob Ad Hoc Sens Syst (MASS). pp. 386–387. 10–13 October 2016, Brasilia, Brazil.

17. Moosavi SR, Nguyen Gia T, Nigussie E, Rahmani AM, Virtanen S, Tenhunen H, et al. End-to-end security scheme for mobility enabled healthcare Internet of Things. Futur Gener Comput Syst. 2016; 64:108–124.

18. Dubey H, Yang J, Constant N, Amiri AM, Yang Q, Makodiya K. Fog data: Enhancing telehealth big data through fog computing. Proceedings of ASE BigData Soc. 2015; 14:1–6.

19. Gia1 TN, Jiang M, Rahmani A-M, Westerlund T, Liljeberg P, Tenhunen H. Fog computing in healthcare Internet of Things: A case study on ECG feature extraction. IEEE International Conference on Computer and Information Technology 26–28 October 2015, Liverpool, UK.

20. Craciunescu R, Mihovska A, Mihaylov M, Kyriazakos S, Prasad Simona Halunga R. Implementation of Fog Computing for Reliable EHealth Applications IEEE. 2015

21. Fratu O, Pena C, Craciunescu R, Halunga S. Fog computing system for monitoring Mild Dementia and COPD patients: Romanian case study. 12th Int Conf Telecommun Mod Satell Cable Broadcast Serv (TELSIKS). 2015. pp. 123–128. 14–17 October 2015, Nis, Serbia.

22. Rajagopalan A, Jagga M, Kumari A, Ali ST. A DDoS prevention scheme for session resumption SEA architecture in healthcare IoT. 3rd IEEE International Conference. pp. 1–5. 09–10 February 2017, Ghaziabad, India.

23. Jararweh Y, Alsmirat M, Al-Ayyoub M, Benkhelifa E, Darabseh A, Gupta B, et al. Software-defined system support for enabling ubiquitous mobile edge computing. The Computer Journal. 60(10):1443–1457.

24. Rahman A, Hassanain E. Toward a secure mobile edge computing framework for Hajj. IEEE Internet of Things J. 2017; 5:1–20.

25. Distefano S, Bruneo D, Longo F, Merlino G, Puliafito A. Personalized health tracking with edge computing technologies. BioNanoScience. 7(2):439–441.

26. Chaudhry J, Saleem K, Islam R, Selamat A, Ahmad M, Valli C. AZSPM: Autonomic zero knowledge security provisioning model for medical control systems in fog computing environments. IEEE 42nd Conf Local Comput Networks Work. pp. 121–127. 09 October 2017, Singapore.

27. Lu D, Huang D, Walenstein A, Medhi D. A secure microservice framework for IoT. Proceedings of 11th IEEE Int Symp Serv Sys Eng (SOSE). pp. 9–18. 06–09 April 2017, San Francisco, CA, USA.

28. Al Hamid HA, Rahman SMM, Hossain MS, Almogren A, Alamri A. A security model for preserving the privacy of medical big data in a healthcare cloud using a fog computing facility with pairing-based cryptography. IEEE Access. 2017; 5:22313–22328.

29. Wu D, Liu S, Zhang L, Terpenny J, Gao RX, Kurfess T, et al. A fog computing-based framework for process monitoring and prognosis in cyber manufacturing. Journal of Manufacturing Systems. 2017; 43:25–34.

30. Elmisery AM, Rho S, Botvich D. A fog-based middleware for automated compliance with OECD privacy principles in the internet of healthcare things. IEEE Access. 2016; 4:8418–8441.

31. Aazam M, Huh EN. Fog computing micro datacenter-based dynamic resource estimation and pricing model for IoT. Proceedings of Int Conf Adv Inf Netw Appl (AINA). pp. 687–694. 24–27 March 2015, Gwangju, South Korea.

32. Oueis J, Strinati EC, Sardellitti S, Barbarossa S. Small cell clustering for efficient distributed fog computing: A multi-user case. IEEE 82nd Vehicular Technology Conference (VTC2015- Fall). pp. 1–5. 06–09 September, Boston, MA, USA.

33. Kliem A, Kao O. The Internet of Things resource management challenge. IEEE Int Conf Data Sci Data Intensive Syst. pp. 483–490. 11–13 December 2015, Sydney, Australia.

34. Yu S, Wang C, Ren K, Lou W. Achieving secure, scalable, and fine-grained data access control in cloud computing. Proceedings of IEEE International Conference on Computer Communications. 2010; pp. 1–9.

35. Dolui K, Datta SK. Comparison of edge computing implementations: Fog computing, cloudlet and mobile edge computing. Global Internet of Things Summit (GIoTS). 06–09 June 2017, Geneva, Switzerland.

36. Dsouza C, Ahn GJ, Taguinod M. Policy-driven security management for fog computing: Preliminary framework and a case study. Proceedings of the IEEE International Conference on Information Reuse and Integration. 2015; 1175 16–23. 13–15 August 2014, Redwood City, CA, USA.

37. Yi S, Qin Z, Li Q. Security and privacy issues of fog computing: A survey. International Conference on Wireless Algorithms, Systems, and Applications. pp. 685–695. 10-12 August 2015, Qufu, China.

38. Dastjerdi AV, Buyya R. Fog computing: Helping the Internet of Things realize its potential. Computer. 2016; 49(8):112–116.

Chapter 13

Roles and Future of the Internet of Things-Based Smart Health Care Models

Dheeraj Rane, Sathish Penchala, and Rakesh Jain
Indore Institute of Science and Technology Indore, Madhya Pradesh, India

Vaishali Chourey
Nirma University, Ahmedabad, India

Contents

DOI: 10.1201/9781003322931-13

223

13.1 Introduction

The goal of smart health care is to make patients' life simpler by providing them with information about medical problems and how to solve them. In the event of a medical emergency, smart health care allows patients to take appropriate actions quickly (1). It allows for remote diagnosis and check-ups, thereby lowering treatment costs and helping health care providers expand their services beyond the limits that are imposed by geographical boundaries. Smart health care further allows enhanced diagnostic mechanisms and smart solutions to improve patient care by monitoring data in real time. Through technological advances, gadgets, such as smartwatches, are being extensively used to diagnose and track a plethora of ailments. It would not be wrong to say that these technological advancements have transformed a hospital-centric health care model into a patient-centered system (2, 3). For example, several clinical tests can now be conducted at home without the assistance of a health care expert. These include monitoring blood pressure (BP), glucose levels, oxygen statistics, and several others. The information about these statistics can be transmitted from remote locations to health care centers. These health care centers need to run a server on the cloud and the entire process can be automated quite easily. Naturally, and looking at the overall mechanism and the growth of these technologies, we could say that the era of smart health care looks promising.

One of the ways to achieve a smart and digital health care environment is via the Internet of Things (IoT). The IoT has expanded a human's ability to engage with the outside world while increasing their freedom. The IoT links a wide array of devices to the internet, including wireless sensors, household appliances, and electrical gadgets (4). Moreover, the IoT can link automobiles (5, 6), household appliances (7, 8), and even medical infrastructures (1, 8) to the internet, thereby transforming a dumb sensor into a smart device. The IoT is a network made up of a range of physical items that have inbuilt communication and sensing technology. It also creates a worldwide ecosystem in which devices might share their measured data and collaborate to build new applications without requiring any human interaction. The IoT further describes how IoT devices might help people lead better lives. Such devices could be connected via Bluetooth, wi-wi, or IEEE 802.11 (Wi-Fi). In the context of health care, we can say that the devices possess the natural capacity to address a wide array of problems. Issues such as automating medical image classification, analyzing health records, and making predictive inferences are now just a touch away. Additionally, sensors could be used to capture physiological data from a patient. This includes attributes such as temperature, BP, heart rate, electrocardiography (ECG), or electroencephalography (EEG) (9, 10). Naturally, this raw data could aid in predicting essential information about the patient's health. However, this notion is not without problems. Due to the volume of data generated, and therefore collected, finding relevant patterns is challenging. This is further exacerbated because the data comes from a variety of sources. There are challenges like data storage, accessibility, and interoperability in the IoT ecosystem. Moreover, there is a privacy issue. It is understood that the dissemination of a patient's data happens over the internet. For a successful and secure transmission, users, patients, and the communication module must work together. The majority of the IoT devices have a user interface that allows health care workers to manage, visualize, and interpret data. In the literature, there is a lot of information on the advances in the IoT system in health care monitoring, control, security, and privacy (11). However, preserving the quality-of-service parameters, such as privacy when information sharing, security, cost, dependability, and availability is the primary consideration when designing an IoT device. In this regard, techniques, such as artificial intelligence (AI), machine learning (ML), and blockchain could come in handy. These paradigms have a natural tendency to tackle the challenges that are imposed by the IoT in the health care domain. Moreover, due to the amount of raw data available on any cloud server, it would be natural to try and apply big data analytics to find useful insights. This idea is mesmerizing. However, successfully executing such an undertaking is a problem.

Considering the challenges highlighted in this section, a discussion of how the IoT could improve health care models in the future is presented in this chapter. Understanding the IoT from multiple points of view is focused on. This includes ML, AI, and cloud computing. The goal of this chapter is to give a comprehensive analysis of IoT-based health care systems' supporting technologies, services, applications, and problems, and to outline recent advances in the field. The importance of statistical techniques and automated methodologies that could help answer a few questions in health care will be highlighted. Moreover, a discussion on the combined use of these technologies to make patient care more effective is included. It should be noted that the overall objective of this chapter is to present a methodology and a set of recommendations that could help future work when designing effective mechanisms in health care. Moreover, a few guidelines to integrate state-of-the-art technologies to produce a more secure and problem-free system for patient care are presented.

13.2 Digital Health Care: Use of ML and Cloud Computing Technologies

In this section, the ideas behind ML and the deployment of ML-driven health care on the cloud infrastructure are discussed. The discussion starts with ML.

13.2.1 ML

ML includes inferences, data processing, and analysis to make informed decisions. Recently, ML has been a key enabler for IoT devices. From cloud-based big data processing to embedded intelligence, ML is a realistic and promising option in a variety of IoT application domains, including health care. ML can create models based on experiences, which might subsequently be used to anticipate future data or find trends. There are four basic categories for this. These are shown in Figure 13.1. In addition to this, ML techniques can be divided into several classes, which deal with data and build models accordingly.

1. Supervised learning
   In supervised learning, the training dataset is labeled with the appropriate output. The learning process is completed with an instruction dataset in supervised learning. Even if a training dataset is used, the task may be regarded as a mentor who monitors the learning process. The algorithm can assist in creating predictions based on data collected throughout the training phase and obtaining changes made by the teacher. A conclusion may indicate if the algorithm has achieved an acceptable level of performance or not.

2. Unsupervised learning
   Unsupervised learning deals with the collection of unlabeled training data to find an underlying pattern. It differs from supervised learning in the sense that there are no correct replies, and the numbers are not communicated to the teacher. Unsupervised learning employs a technique that introduces data

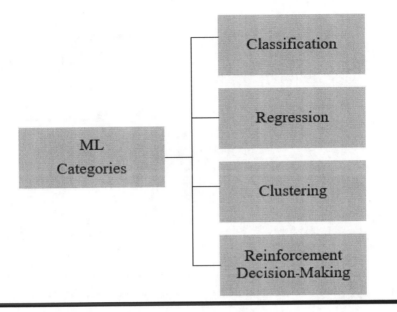

Figure 13.1   Four main categories of ML.

with few, if any, matching variables. The basic goal of this learning is to aid learners when grasping the knowledge by helping them model the underlying framework.

3. Reinforcement learning

   In reinforcement learning, accurate results are not supplied a priori; however, the predicted result might be evaluated by rewards, such as positive and negative, which reflect how good or bad the projected output was. Unlike other ML algorithms, reinforcement learning can learn the environment with only a few parameters to learn. It addresses the optimization problem by interacting with the environment and automatically adjusting the settings.

13.2.2 Cloud in Health Care

In the new era of innovation, cloud computing plays a crucial role in terms of minimizing health care integration costs and maximizing the utilization of resources. Cloud computing allows users to have ubiquitous and transparent access to shared resources and infrastructure, thereby allowing them to deliver on-demand services through the network and undertake activities that adapt to changing demands. In the context of health care, sensors capture biosignals from users (e.g., heart rate and ECG) and data from their surrounding environment. The data could then be

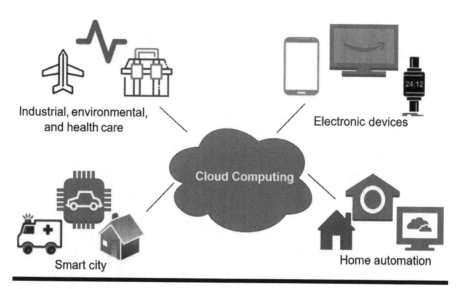

Figure 13.2   Importance and integration of IoT devices over the cloud.

transmitted over the web to a mobile device or straight to the cloud infrastructure, which depends on the wireless technology employed (12). Current trends call for information to be accessible at any time from any location, which might be accomplished by shifting health care data to the cloud. The capacity to interchange data between two different servers will be one of the most important benefits. This is a skill that health care information technology sorely requires. For example, cloud computing might let health care systems communicate the information, such as a doctor's reference, medication, test outcome, and insurance information that is stored on many systems. This idea is implemented in situations where institutions want to save money on storage. Figure 13.2 shows the importance and integration of IoT devices.

13.2.3 Usage of ML and Cloud Computing Technologies in Smart Health Care

The IoT is a network made up of a range of physical items that have inbuilt communication and sensing technology. Most IoT devices, such as smart televisions or smartphones might help people live more securely and freely. Soon, IoT devices will generate a massive amount of big data streams. Big data is in high demand across all sectors, such as manufacturing, automobiles, and health care. Those that attempt to understand their clients' businesses and challenges will be able to find big data solutions that are suited for their needs in advance, thereby giving them a competitive advantage over their rivals. The ability to find insights that are concealed in the large and increasing amount of data is essential for the fulfillment of the IoT. Due to the pace, diversity, and volume of data that is generated by the IoT, new systems with unique mining techniques are required.

The IoT environment is demanding, necessitating quick algorithms that consume a short amount of time and memory. They must be adaptable to changes, and never stop learning. These types of algorithms should be distributed and operated on big data platforms. The key difficulty for the IoT analytics systems soon will be to accomplish this accurately in real-time. Data arrives rapidly in health care. Algorithms that process such data streams must work within very difficult space and time-specific limitations. As a result, the design of data mining algorithms will be complicated. Therefore, ML-based algorithms must function within resource constraints (e.g., time and memory). Further, they must deal with data that is changing in terms of its type or distribution. The IoT further creates a worldwide ecosystem in which devices might exchange their measured data and collaborate to build new applications without requiring human engagement. Most of the communication devices that are used in the IoT networks have inbuilt communication technologies like Bluetooth Zigbee, LiFi, wi-fi, 5G, and other protocols. The data that is created and communicated might be examined and utilized for

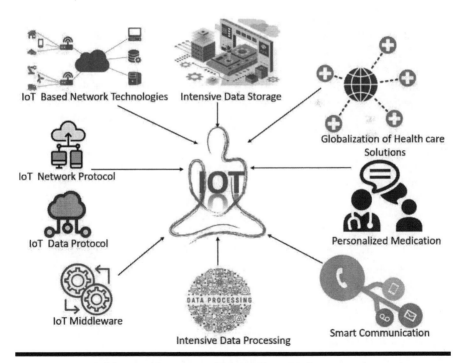

Figure 13.3   Various components used in IoT-based infrastructure.

classification, decision-making, and planning purposes. Such ideas coupled with ML techniques could open a new dimension of work that could make health care smarter. Furthermore, IoT devices could monitor physiological and remote data. The IoT enables adaptability and convenience when transmitting diverse settings for monitoring and communication purposes, thanks to the interaction of many types of smart devices (13). ECG signals, BP, oxygen saturation levels, and other parameters might be measured with embedded sensors and IoT devices. The main purpose of IoT devices in smart health care systems is to lower expenses, follow-up on daily patients' medical issues, decreased clinic-driven treatment, increase patient care, and deal with privacy and security issues (14). Naturally, this plethora of functionalities requires the use of some components. These components are shown in Figure 13.3. Using cloud computing-based technologies, these parts can now be easily integrated on a remote server, thereby enabling a seamless mechanism for efficient patient care.

From the discussion presented in this section, the existing health care infrastructure could be complemented via the use of ML and cloud computing technologies.

13.3 Health Care and IoT Technologies

In smart health care systems, an IoT framework makes it easier to combine the advantages of sensing technologies and cloud computing. In a health care environment, we are dealing with a lot of protocols; therefore, it is imperative to maintain a balance between them. These protocols are needed to transfer patient data from sensors to the cloud environment. The Healthcare IoT (HIoT) combines several components into a grid-like infrastructure. Each part of the network and cloud serves a unique role. These roles must be predefined very well to ensure that every part runs smoothly.

In the real world, patient monitoring via HIoT has provided many structural alteration theories that have been implemented in the past. It is critical to make a list of all relevant actions related to the intended health application. The overall outcome of the IoT system is determined by how well it meets the needs of health care practitioners. Because each condition necessitates a complicated set of health care actions, the topology must conform to medical guidelines and their diagnosis. In this respect, the technologies required to create an HIoT system are also critical. This is because the use of certain technologies could improve an IoT system's capability (15). As a result, a variety of cutting-edge technologies have been used to link diverse health care applications with an IoT system. In this section, emphasis is placed on the use of various technologies in HIoT.

13.3.1 Identification of IoT Devices

A very important element required in the design of an HIoT system is accessibility. Accessing data of patients from permitted nodes (sensors) must be made easy so that the overall process of information sharing is easy. However, this is only possible if the nodes in the network correctly can be identified. Identification is the process of allocating a unique identifier (UID) to every node in the network, thereby enabling it to be easily identified. In this respect, one of the solutions is to identify the potential stakeholder nodes within the health care infrastructure and assign them one UID (16). Of note is that sensors can be easily recognized and handled independently. This enables the smooth and coherent integration of resources. However, the unique identification of a component might change during the life cycle of an IoT system due to the continual progress in IoT-based technologies. The device must provide a mechanism to update this information to keep the health care equipment and system in working order. This is because a configuration change has an impact on the process of tracking the network component(s) and could potentially result in an inaccurate diagnosis.

13.3.2 Communication Technology

Different elements in an HIoT network can connect due to communication technology. There are two types of communication technologies; short and medium range (17). In the following sections, each of the components that use short and medium-range equipment is described in detail.

13.3.2.1 Radio Frequency Identification

Radiofrequency (RF) identification (RFID) uses a tag and reader to uniquely mark an object. The tag contains an antenna with an onboard chip that could be used to identify any object. The reader receives the information from the antenna and identifies the object. In the IoT, the data stored in the tag is stored as an electronic product code. Medical equipment could be found and tracked more quickly thanks to RFID technology. In addition, many technologies in the health care industry come with such an identifier. However, they only operate over a short radius.

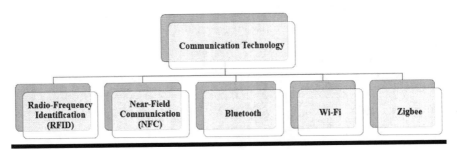

Figure 13.4 Information on communication technologies.

13.3.2.2 Near-Field Communication

The electromagnetic induction between two loop antennas that are positioned close to each other is the fundamental notion of near-field communication (NFC). This technology is related to RFID, which similarly transmits data by electromagnetic induction. Active and passive modes are available for NFC devices. Only one device generates RF in the passive mode when the other serves as a receiver. In the active mode, both devices can create RFs at the same time and communicate data without the need for pairing (18). NFC's key benefits are its ease of use and a reliable wireless communication network. It is, however, only suitable for a very limited communication range.

13.3.2.3 Bluetooth

Bluetooth uses radio waves at ultra-high frequencies and operates at short ranges. Medical devices may now connect wirelessly thanks to this technology. The frequency band used by Bluetooth is 2.4 GHz. The communication range of the Bluetooth protocol is ≤100 m. Authentication and encryption are provided by Bluetooth to ensure data security. The low cost and energy efficiency of Bluetooth are its advantages. During data transmission, it also assures less interference between linked devices. However, when it comes to long-range communication in health care, this technology falls short.

13.3.2.4 Wi-Fi

Wi-fi is an IEEE 802.11-compliant wireless local area network. Compared with Bluetooth, it has a longer range and widespread acceptability. Wi-fi allows for the creation of a fast and reliable network quite efficiently. These networks are often in places with high concentrations of people. For instance, hospitals and cinema halls. Wi-fi networks are also used in combination with cellphones and IoT devices.

13.3.2.5 Zigbee

Zigbee is a standard protocol for interconnecting and transmitting data between medical equipment. It has a comparable frequency range to Bluetooth (2.4 GHz). However, compared with Bluetooth devices, it has a longer communication range. A mesh network topology is used by this technique. End nodes, routers, and a processing center are all part of the network. The data analysis and aggregation are handled by the processing center. Even if one or two devices fail, the mesh network guarantees that other devices stay connected. Low power consumption and a large network capacity are all advantages of Zigbee.

13.4 Services and Applications of HIoT

Medical gadgets can now carry out real-time analysis, which was previously impossible for clinicians. This aids in the medical system, facilitating many individuals at once with minimum cost. Various technologies in the literature, such as big data and cloud computing, provide improved and simplified communication between patients and physicians. As a result, this reduces the financial burden, and more patients are involved in the treatment process. Recently, the IoT aided the HIoT applications, which provide various advantages, such as affordability for end-to-end users, simultaneous monitoring and reporting, easy diagnostics, fitness management, and remote medical assistance. The former consists of rules that are employed when developing an HIoT device, and the latter refers to health care apps that are used to diagnose or monitor health indicators. In the following subsection, the services and applications are discussed to easily understand health care fundamentals.

13.4.1 Services

By answering numerous health care concerns, services and concepts have altered the health care business. With rising health care demands and technological advances, more services are being introduced daily. These are increasingly becoming an important element of the HIoT system design process. In the HIoT context, each service delivers a collection of health care solutions. These concepts or services are not defined uniquely. The applications are what make HIoT systems stand out. As a result, defining any idea in a broad sense is difficult. Figure 13.5 shows the most extensively utilized IoT health care services.

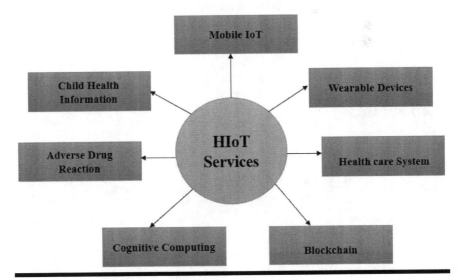

Figure 13.5 Information on HIoT services.

13.4.1.1 Mobile IoT

Tracking patient health data and other physiological states using mobile computers, sensors, communication technologies, and cloud computing is referred to as the mobile Internet of Things (m-IoT). Researchers (19) proposed a framework to provide effective internet medical services via communication links between mobile devices and personal area networks. Most of the research was carried out on mobile computing (20–22). These technologies are accessed by health care practitioners and help in different services, such as therapy and patient data. Research (23) has dealt with the challenges and focused on different learning, including network security, technical policies, technical, and physical protection. Figure 13.6 shows the generalized environment of the m-IoT.

13.4.1.2 Wearable Devices

Wearable gadgets serve a variety of health conditions at a lower cost to health care providers and individuals. Many of the devices used in our daily lives include wristbands, hats, shirts, handbags, and other items (24). The connected sensor is utilized to collect information about the surroundings and the patient's health. Then, the data is posted to the server and databases. Through health apps, several wearable devices are linked to smartphones. Many researchers have focused on mobile devices and wearable services to develop real-time monitoring systems (25–28). The device's computing capacity is increased by connecting it to a mobile application. The program could be used for simple data processing and visualization.

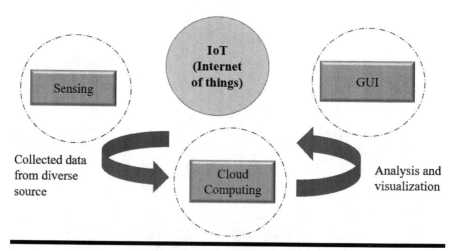

Figure 13.6 Generalized m-IoT environment.

13.4.1.3 Community-Based Health Care Services

The concept of community-based health care monitoring focuses on creating smart networks for a local community. This could include private clinics, local residential areas, and hotels. In this regard, research (29) presented an IoT-based cooperative medical network to enable remote health care monitoring. Various authentication and authorization procedures were used to secure the networks. In addition, a community medical network that functions as a virtual hospital was also proposed (30). This aided in the provision of medical services to those in need.

13.4.1.4 Blockchain

Communication between several medical devices and health care providers is a critical task in an HIoT network. Data fragmentation is one of the significant concerns in the safe exchange of data. It can also create information gaps between specialists that the same patient examines. Sometimes, treatments are delayed by a lack of or wrong information. Therefore, (31) proposed the idea of blockchain technology being utilized to reduce the problems that occurred in data fragmentation and assist medical organizations in connecting data repositories throughout the network. This helps the patients and their specialists. At the same time, it protects sensitive medical information. Blockchain can be regarded as a qualitative study, a collaboration between organizations and professionals. Figure 13.7 describes the overall health monitoring system. Blockchain technology provides three varieties to serve the safe transfer of data. First, is a fixed ledger that helps anybody easily control, access, and ensure that the records of data cannot be changed once it has been uploaded to the ledger. The second is the distributed system, which is used for different devices and computers. Finally, blockchain is followed with smart contracts and used for data exchange policies. Some researchers (32–34) launched a blockchain health care business that handled EMR (emergency medical records) data, drug discovery devices, and other clinical pathways. Health care data gateway is a famous platform for blockchain where users can share their information and data. Other research (35) focused on a patients' privacy framework for managing and sharing their information without violating the underlying policy.

13.4.1.5 Adverse Drug Reaction

Adverse drug reaction (ADR) describes the side effects of taking the wrong prescription. Sometimes, it comes from long-term use, or it might be possible when patients take two different drugs simultaneously, which causes an unpleasant response. The ADR is unrelated to the type of drug or ailment being treated, and it differs from person to person. One work identified the unique barcode with the help of IoT-based ADR systems (36). Drug combinations in patients' bodies are examined by

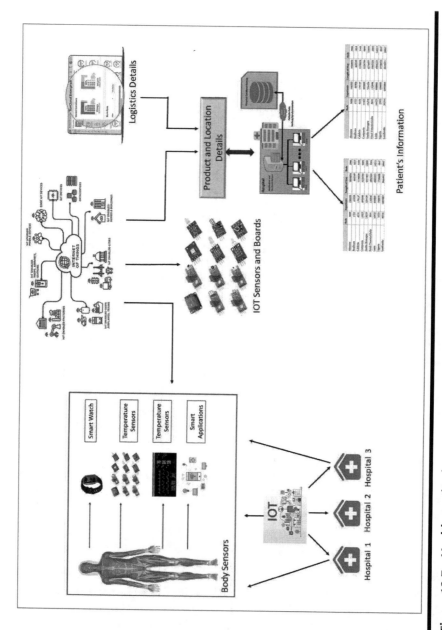

Figure 13.7 Health monitoring systems.

pharmaceutical intelligence information. Using e-health records, the information system tracks each patient's allergy profile. A judgment is made as to whether the drug is suitable for the patient or not after examining the allergy profile and other crucial health facts. Other research (37) proposed new variants of drug reactions for IoT systems, for example, prescription adverse drug event (prescADE), which might enhance patient safety by minimizing ADRs.

13.4.1.6 Child Health Information

This follows the idea of increasing a child's health awareness. The main objective of child health information is to develop awareness for children and their parents about health care systems, which includes emotional, physiological, and nutritional values. Researchers contributed to the work with the help of the IoT to build a platform that helps to monitor physical and mental health (38) remotely. In an emergency, physicians and parents could assist in taking the required precautions. Researchers (39) built mobile applications that are easily connected to medical equipment. Height, temperature, and heart rate were the three bodily characteristics that the device collected. The app makes this information available to doctors and other health care providers. Teachers and parents might monitor children's eating habits using an m-health service (40). The app was used to help youngsters achieve healthy nutritional levels.

13.4.1.7 Cognitive Computing

Cognitive computing refers to the process of evaluating a problem in the same way that the human brain does. Recently, sensor technology and artificial cognitive computing that were integrated with IoT devices found hidden patterns in large amounts of data (41). Sensors that can simulate the human brain in problem-solving are increasingly integrated with IoT devices. To provide effective health services, all sensors in a cognitive IoT network collaborate with other smart devices. In the literature (42), a smart health care monitoring system that was based on EEG was proposed. The main objective of this work was to enable health care providers to properly monitor patients' data. The patient's pathological condition was determined via cognitive computing. To establish a patient's state, the EEG data was coupled with additional sensor data, such as posture, gesture, bodily movement, voice, and facial expressions. One of the major concerns in cognitive computing is that it must be adaptive enough to learn as the knowledge and goals change. To do this, AI and sensor devices, such as pattern recognition, natural language processing, and data mining are helpful. Furthermore, it encourages prompt aid in the event of life-threatening situations. Another study (43) offered the idea of conveying cognitive data that worked with detecting, recording, and determining patient health daily. In the event of an emergency, the data of a patient in a critical condition is delivered as soon as possible.

13.4.2 Applications of HIoT

As mentioned in 13.4.1, two different sections, such as services and applications were focused on. In this section, the applications of IoT in health care are focused on. In this regard, a range of IoT-based applications has been built that use the HIoT services and concepts. Researchers in these fields have proposed several solutions and applications. Therefore, the ideas are oriented toward developers, and applications are geared toward users. Due to the improvements in IoT technologies, medical equipment has become cheap. Due to this advantage, the application area of HIoT has seen tremendous growth. Figure 13.8 shows the potential HIoT-based applications. In the following sections, each of these applications will be expanded on in detail.

13.4.2.1 ECG Monitoring

The electrical activity of the heart can be monitored via an ECG. This is very popular for diagnosing cardiac disease and captures the effect of heart muscles. Naturally, there could be several abnormalities associated with the human heart. For example, arrhythmia and myocardial ischemia. ECG monitoring has been improved by IoT technology to diagnose cardiac problems. The IoT has been used in most research areas in ECG monitoring (44, 45). In this field, there is a large amount of data available, and storage issues are handled by big data. Of note, researchers (46) attempted to address the difficulty of wearable power consumption. In the literature (47), the authors focused on EEG monitoring systems and IoT-based fall detection systems

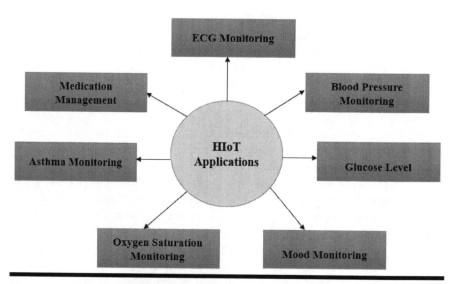

Figure 13.8   Various applications of HIoT.

with the help of cloud-based services and mobile applications. This system was created to offer continuous ECG and accelerometer data to elderly patients to enable real-time monitoring. Based on the literature, the IoT can monitor heart conditions in real-time and send the information to the doctor seamlessly.

13.4.2.2 BP Monitoring

BP measurement is one of the mandatory processes in every diagnostic procedure. The most common technique in BP pressure measurement necessitates the participation of at least two people. BP monitoring systems, with and without a cuff, have been constantly developed and improved. Continuous BP monitoring without the need for a cuff deals with home health care at a low cost and reduces the workload in a hospital setting. It might be measured by a variety of noninvasive procedures. The integration of the IoT and other sensor technology; however, changed how BP was measured. Researchers (48) presented a method to measure BP that utilized an ECG signal and a photoplethysmogram that was collected from the fingertip. Most of the continuous and noncontinuous techniques can be found in the literature to measure BP, such as arterial tonometry, plethysmography, and pulse transit time. Furthermore, these readings could be sent to a health care provider in real-time, and any issue arising from any complication could be fixed quickly using IoT-based technologies.

13.4.2.3 Glucose Level Monitoring

Glucose levels are high in chronic diabetic conditions. It is one of the most common human illnesses. To diagnose the illness, multiple tests are used. Fingerpicking, followed by blood glucose level monitoring, is the most widely used approach for diabetes diagnosis. Recently the IoT has worked on different wearable gadgets for monitoring glucose levels that are safe and noninvasive. Research (49–51) proposed the idea of a noninvasive m-IoT-based glucometer to monitor the actual data on blood glucose levels. Health care professionals used IPV6 (Internet Protocol version 6) connections for wearable sensors. Another research study (52), proposed the IoT architecture for glucose level monitoring that used double moving average techniques. Optical sensors, such as infrared LEDs have been used recently. Other researchers (53) proposed the concept of glucose level monitoring that used light signals reflected from the patient's body. This huge and growing body of work highlights that the IoT could help when diagnosing and managing glucose levels in an efficient and noninvasive manner.

13.4.2.4 Mood Monitoring

Mood monitoring helps to track emotional health and manage a healthy mental level. Mood monitoring is a technique for keeping track of a person's emotional state and ensuring mental well-being. It also helps health care providers manage mental diseases, which include anxiety and bipolar disorders. Self-awareness of one's emotional condition helps one better understand one's mental state. The CNN (convolutional neural network) also places a person's mood into different categories where human emotions, such as happy, thrilled, sad, calm, angry, and stress are reduced (54). Similar research (55), used an interactive technology, Meezaj, to evaluate mood in real-time. This software deals with real-time mood monitoring and identifying the importance of happiness. Stress might now be diagnosed ahead of time using the heart rate thanks to the inclusion of an advanced ML system. Additionally, the device might communicate with the patient about their stress level (56). This all is possible because of IoT-based technologies and their integration into a framework that enables efficient health care.

13.4.2.5 Oxygen Saturation Monitoring

The IoT has also found its way into oxygen saturation monitoring. In this respect, pulse oximetry detects oxygen saturation that might be useful in medical research. The noninvasive technique eliminates the disadvantages of the previous method and enables real-time monitoring. Pulse oximetry has improved because of IoT-based technologies. Researchers (57) proposed the concept of a noninvasive tissue oximeter that monitors the heart rate oxygen levels and observes pulse diagnostics. Furthermore, it was suggested that the transmission of data takes place over a variety of methods such as Zigbee or wi-fi. A medical intervention choice was taken based on the reported data. Other researchers (58) discovered the idea of an alarm system that could inform patients whether oxygen saturation levels were critical or not. Different types of sensors are used in the literature to connect pulse oximeters. Furthermore, (59) discovered the concept of multispectral sensor devices to reduce the adverse effects of a single LED. Low power and minimum cost monitoring systems have been proposed (60). Real-time monitoring is possible with this gadget. Therefore, the IoT has vast applications in oxygen saturation monitoring.

13.4.2.6 Asthma Monitoring

Asthma is a sustained lung disease that affects breathing and covers many health issues, such as breathlessness, an increase of mucus, and chest pain. Asthma patients suffer from this problem all the time, and the use of an inhaler or nebulizer is the only treatment solution. Recently, researchers have proposed real-time monitoring situations based on IoT systems (61, 62). Sometimes, monitoring devices do not convey the best solutions, and patients could refer for the proper medication and contact their physicians (63). Furthermore, the device could evaluate the surrounding environment and tell a patient to leave an area that was harmful to health. Tracking asthma problems, ML, big data, and cloud computing have been collaborating with

IoT devices (64, 65). Researchers (66), presented a list of services that might be included in an IoT-based asthma monitoring system as it considers future expansion.

13.4.2.7 Medication Management

In health care, following a strict medication schedule is a prevalent issue. Patients' dangerous health issues might be exacerbated if they do not take their medications on time. Nonadherence is very frequent among the elderly as they grow older and develop clinical disorders, such as cognitive decline and dementia. Therefore, it is difficult for them to carefully follow their doctor's orders. Several studies have focused on using IoT to track a patient's medication compliance (67). A smart medical box that can remind individuals to take their medicine was proposed (68). Each tray in the box has medication for three distinct periods (e.g., morning, afternoon, and evening). Once the important information is captured, it is sent to the cloud server. Communication was then initiated between doctors and patients based on this information. Furthermore, research (69) described an adaptive IoT-based smart pharmaceutical system that used fuzzy logic to interpret data that was obtained from a temperature sensor. The device effectively treated illness by continually monitoring body temperature and automatically modifying the time and amount of medicine given during medication. Overall, the paradigm of the IoT could therefore help achieve the goal of smart medicine.

13.5 Challenges

Recently, health care has received a lot of attention in the literature. This has truly helped health care services; therefore, making it easy for a patient to work with their ailments with ease. In this regard, the IoT has helped and effectively altered the paradigm of health care by combining sensors, ML, and cloud computing. The IoT, like any other technology; however, is not without issues. These issues need new oversight, and additional efforts must be made to address the challenges. Some challenges are discussed in the following list.

1. Data privacy and security
   Cloud computing has changed the way real-time patient care is achieved. However, with cloud computing comes the risk of cyber attacks. Specifically, attacks on a hospital's networks. Several preventive steps must be therefore implemented during the design of an HIoT system to protect it from this malicious assault. Network protocols like Wi-Fi and Zigbee, for instance, must be secured using state-of-the-art procedures (70).
2. Identification
   Health care workers often deal with patients and their relatives. In much the same way, if a patient has a disease, they are treated by many doctors. To

minimize the overall hassle in the process and enable a seamless operation, it is therefore important to interchange the identities of patients, nurses, and doctors. Sometimes, this must be accomplished within a single session. This is one of the significant factors that the IoT must address effectively without compromising on patient care. Moreover, the process should be confusion free (71).

3. Scalability

The capacity of health care technology to escalate itself according to the evolving dynamics of the operating conditions is frequently referred to as scalability (70). A system that is highly efficient in terms of scalability typically runs smoothly; therefore, maximizing the use of available resources. As a result, creating a network that can address scalability is critical. One way to overcome this issue is using decentralized IoT networks (i.e., fog computing). Moreover, to ensure privacy, ideas like blockchain could help in this case (72).

4. Interoperability

Because IoT devices are diverse, interoperability is a huge problem. The setup and installation processes for the IoT devices from different vendors are, without a doubt, expected to vary. There are semantic and syntactic problems between devices from various suppliers, because their operational characteristics differ by a large amount. Without addressing semantic ambiguity, it is tough to add a new device to an existing network. When these devices function together in an interoperable environment, it is possible to give high-quality treatment to patients. It will automate hospitals in the health care business, which will allow doctors to remotely monitor patients (73). Physicians will be able to swiftly obtain information on their patients and offer recommendations. It will allow patients' records to be quickly accessed from various IT storage systems.

5. Big data

Using the example of a hospital or health care provider, improperly handled patient data raises the potential of misdiagnosis, wrong treatment, or lost or corrupted test findings. There is the possibility that two touchpoints on a patient's treatment path (e.g., a GP and a specialist) might have separate databases for the same person. The IoT should be able to handle time, resources, and processing capabilities, because connected devices continually and concurrently create massive volumes and different forms of data (74). As a result, placing health care datasets on a big data server would provide practitioners with a single, unchanging resource for utilization when treating patients.

13.6 Conclusion

The primary goal of digital health care is for consumers to employ smart solutions in their daily life. This is accomplished by incorporating the IoT into health care.

The growth of IoT technology; however, is not without issues. There are difficulties such as interoperability, heterogeneity, security, and resource management. To tackle these issues, research is increasingly bringing innovative approaches and strategies. Despite these challenges, the IoT brings in machine learning that helps when monitoring and diagnosing a variety of health concerns. At the same time, it provides a mechanism to diagnose health issues remotely. This has resulted in a shift in the health care industry. More specifically, the paradigm is now focused on a patient-centric model. This contrasts with earlier approaches that followed a hospital-driven method. In this chapter, several applications of the IoT in health care were discussed. Emphasis was placed on the importance of ML techniques and how cloud computing could help to bridge the gap between decentralized monitoring and centralized control. Additionally, it discussed the use of ML and AI techniques that have transformed the health care industry. However, the use of these technologies brings additional challenges in IoT-driven health care. Finally, the problems of designing and producing ML-compliant IoT devices were highlighted in detail. The objective was that in the future, these challenges could serve as a benchmark for future research.

References

1. Sundaravadivel P, Kougianos E, Mohanty SP, Ganapathiraju MK. Everything you wanted to know about smart health care: Evaluating the different technologies and components of the Internet of Things for better health. IEEE Consum Electron Mag. 2017; 7:18–28.
2. Yang G, Xie L, Mantysalo M, Zhou X, Pang Z, Xu LD, et. al. A health-IoT platform based on the integration of intelligent packaging, unobtrusive biosensor, and intelligent medicine box. IEEE Trans Industr Informatics. 2014; 10(4):2180–2191
3. Yan Y. A home-based health information acquisition system. Health Inf Sci Syst. 2013; 1:12.
4. Khan M, Han K, Karthik S. Designing smart control systems based on internet of things and big data analytics. Wirel Pers Commun. 2018; 99(4):1683–1697.
5. Menon VG. An IoT-enabled intelligent automobile system for smart cities. Internet of Things J. 2022; 18:100213.
6. Qin V. Cloud computing and the internet of things: technology innovation in automobile service. Proceedings of the International Conference on Human Interface and the Management of Information; 2013. 21–26 July 2013, Las Vegas, NV, USA.
7. Froiz-Míguez I, Fernández-Caramés T, Fraga-Lamas P, Castedo L. Design, implementation and practical evaluation of an IoT home automation system for fog computing applications based on MQTT and ZigBee-WiFi sensor nodes. Sensors. 2018; 18(8):2660.
8. Mathew PS. Applications of IoT in healthcare. Cognitive Computing for Big Data Systems over IoT. Berlin, Germany: Springer. 2018; pp. 263–288.
9. Jagadeeswari V. A study on medical Internet of things and Big Data in personalized healthcare system. Health Inf Sci Syst. 2018; 6:14.

10. Peng H, Tian Y, Kurths J, Li L, Yang Y, Wang D. Secure and energy-efficient data transmission system based on chaotic compressive sensing in body-to-body networks. IEEE Trans Biomed Circuits Syst. 2017; 11(3):558–573.

11. Gatouillat A, Badr Y, Massot B, Sejdic E. Internet of medical things: A review of recent contributions dealing with cyber-physical systems in medicine. Internet of Things J. 2018; 5(5):3810–22.

12. Shimrat O. Cloud computing and healthcare. San Diego Physician. 2009; pp. 26–29.

13. Nguyen Gia T, Jiang M, Sarker VK, Rahmani AM, Westerlund T, Liljeberg P, et al. Low-cost fog-assisted health-care IoT system with energy-efficient sensor nodes, 13th IEEE Int Wirel Commun Mob Comput Conf (IWCMC). 2017; pp. 1765–1770.

14. Ahmad M, Amin MB, Hussain S, Kang BH, Cheong T, Lee S. Health Fog: A novel framework for health and wellness applications. J Supercomput. 2016; 72(10):3677–3695.

15. Yuehong Y. The internet of things in healthcare: An overview. J Ind Inf Integr. 2016; 1:3–13.

16. Shanmugasundaram G, Sankarikaarguzhali G. An investigation on IoT healthcare analytics. Int J Inform Eng Electron Bus. 2017; 9(2):11.

17. Lee J-Y, Scholtz RA. Ranging in a dense multipath environment using a UWB radio link. J Sel Areas Commun. 2002; 20:1677–1683.

18. Cerruela Garcia G, Luque Ruiz I, Gomez-Nieto M. State of the art, trends and future of Bluetooth low energy, near field communication and visible light communication in the development of smart cities. Sensors. 2016; 16(11):1968.

19. Tabish R. A 3G/WiFi-enabled 6LoWPAN-based U-healthcare system for ubiquitous real-time monitoring and data logging. Proceedings of the 2nd Middle East Conference on Biomedical Engineering. pp. 277–280. 17–20 February 2014, Doha, Qatar.

20. Mora H, Gil D, Terol RM, Azorin J, Szymanski J. An IoT-based computational framework for healthcare monitoring in mobile environments. Sensors. 2017; 17(10):2302.

21. Tyagi S. A conceptual framework for IoT-based healthcare system using cloud computing. Proceedings of the 2016 6th International Conference-Cloud System and Big Data Engineering (Confluence). pp. 503–507. 14–15 January 2016, Noida, India.

22. Nazir S. Internet of Things for Healthcare using effects of mobile computing: a systematic literature review. Wirel Commun Mob Com. 2019; 2019:5931315.

23. Al Motoring SH. Mobile health (m-health) system in the context of IoT. Proceedings of the 2016 IEEE 4th International Conference on Future Internet of Things and Cloud Workshops (FiCloudW). 22–24 August 2016, Vienna, Austria.

24. Singh K. Role and impact of wearables in IoT healthcare. Proceedings of the 3rd International Conference on Computational Intelligence and Informatics. pp. 735–742. 18 March 2020, Berlin, German.

25. Mendonca M. An IoT-based healthcare ecosystem for home intelligent assistant services in smart homes. Proceedings of the EAI International Conference on IoT Technologies for Health Care. 04-06 December 2019, Braga, Portugal.

26. Mauldin T, Canby M, Metsis V, Ngu A, Rivera C. SmartFall: A smartwatch-based fall detection system using deep learning. Sensors. 2018; 18(10):3363.

27. Kraft D, Srinivasan K, Bieber G. Deep learning based fall detection algorithms for embedded systems, smart-watches, and IoT devices using accelerometers. Technologies. 2020; 8(4):72.

28. Erdem NS. Gait analysis using smartwatches. Proceedings of the 2019 IEEE 30th International Symposium on Personal, Indoor and Mobile Radio Communications (PIMRC Workshops). 08 September 2019, Istanbul, Turkey.

29. Wang W. The Internet of Things for resident health information service platform research. Proceedings of the IET International Conference on Communication Technology and Application (ICCTA 2011). 14–16 October 2011, Beijing, China.

30. Kelati A. Biosignal monitoring platform using Wearable IoT. Proceedings of the 22nd Conference of Open Innovations Association FRUCT; 08 May 2018, Petrozavodsk, Russia.

31. Satamraju KP, Malarkodi B. Proof of concept of scalable integration of internet of things and blockchain in healthcare. Sensors. 2020; 20(5)1389.

32. Zhang X, Poslad S. Blockchain support for flexible queries with granular access control to electronic medical records (EMR). Proceedings of the 2018 IEEE International Conference on Communications (ICC). 20–24 May 2018, Kansas City, MO, USA.

33. Zhang X. Block-based access control for blockchain-based electronic medical records (EMRs) query in eHealth. Proceedings of the 2018 IEEE Global Communications Conference (GLOBECOM). 09–13 December 2018, Abu Dhabi, UAE.

34. Norfeldt L. Crypto pharmaceuticals: increasing the safety of medication by a blockchain of pharmaceutical products. J Pharm Sci. 2019; 108:2838–2841.

35. Yue X, Wang H, Jin D, Li M, Jiang W. Healthcare data gateways: found healthcare intelligence on blockchain with novel privacy risk control. J Med Syst. 2016; 40:218.

36. Jara AJ. A pharmaceutical intelligent information system to detect allergies and adverse drugs reactions based on internet of things. Proceedings of the 2010 8th IEEE International Conference on Pervasive Computing and Communications Workshops (PERCOM Workshops). 13–15 April 2010, Mannheim, Germany.

37. Nakhla Z, Nouira K, Ferchichi A. Prescription adverse drug events system (PrescADE) based on ontology and internet of things. Comput J. 2019; 62(6):801–805.

38. Nigar N, Chowdhury L. An intelligent children's healthcare system by using ensemble technique. Proceedings of International Joint Conference on Computational Intelligence. 14–15 December 2018, Dhaka, Bangladesh.

39. Sutjiredjeki E, Basjaruddin NC, Fajrin DN, Noor F. Development of NFC and IoT-enabled measurement devices for improving health care delivery of Indonesian children. J Phys Conf Ser. 2020; 1450.

40. Vazquez-Briseno M. A proposal for using the internet of things concept to increase children's health awareness. Proceedings of CONIELECOMP, 22nd International Conference on Electrical Communications and Computers. 27–29 February 2012, Cholula, Mexico.

41. Behera RK, Bala PK, Dhir A. The emerging role of cognitive computing in healthcare: A systematic literature review. Int J Med Inform. 2019; 129:154–156.

42. Amin SU, Hossain MS, Muhammad G, Alhussein M, Rahman MA. Cognitive smart healthcare for pathology detection and monitoring. IEEE Access. 2019; 7: 10745–10753.

43. Kumar MA, Vimala R, Britto KRA. A cognitive technology-based healthcare monitoring system and medical data transmission. Measurement. 2019; 146: 322–332.

44. Agu E. The smartphone as a medical device: assessing enablers, benefits and challenges. Proceedings of the 2013 IEEE International Workshop of Internet-of-things Net-working and Control (IoT-NC). June 2013, New Orleans, USA.

45. Liu M-L. Internet of things-based electrocardiogram monitoring system. Chinese Patent. 2012; 102:118.

46. Djelouat H, Al Disi M, Boukhenoufa I. Real-time ECG monitoring using compressive sensing on a heterogeneous multicore edge-device. Microprocess Microsyst. 2012; 72:102839.

47. Al-Kababji A, Shidqi L, Boukhennoufa I, Amira A, Bensaali F, Gastli MS. IoT-based fall and ECG monitoring system: wireless communication system based firebase realtime database. Proceedings of the 2019 IEEE SmartWorld, Ubiquitous Intelligence & Computing, Advanced & Trusted Computing, Scalable Computing & Communications, Cloud & Big Data Computing, Internet of People and Smart City Innovation; 19–23 August 2019, Leicester, UK.

48. Dinh A. Blood pressure measurement using finger ECG and photoplethysmogram for IoT. International Conference on the Development of Biomedical Engineering in Vietnam. pp. 83–89. June 2016, Ho Chi Minh City, Vietnam.

49. Nguyen Gia T, Ben Dhaou, I, Ali M, Rahmani AM, Westerlund T, Liljeberg P, et al. Energy efficient fog-assisted IoT system for monitoring diabetic patients with cardiovascular disease. Future Gener Comput Syst. 2019; 93:198–211.

50. Bhat GM, Bhat NG. A novel IoT-based framework for blood glucose examination. Proceedings of the International Conference on Electrical, Electronics, Communication, Computer, and Optimization Techniques (ICE-ECCOT). 15–16 December 2017, Mysuru, India.

51. Istepanian RS. The potential of Internet of m-health things "m-IoT" for non-invasive glucose level sensing. Proceedings of the 2011 Annual International Conference of the IEEE Engineering in Medicine and Biology Society. March 2011, Boston, MA, USA.

52. Valenzuela F, Garcia A, Ruiz E, Vazquez M, Cortez J, Espinoza A. An IoT-based glucose monitoring algorithm to prevent diabetes complications. Appl Sci. 2020; 10(3):921.

53. Sunny S, Kumar SS. Optical based non-invasive glucometer with IoT. Proceedings of the 2018 International Conference on Power, Signals, Control and Computation (EPSCICON). 06-10 January 2018, Thrissur, India.

54. Alam MGR. CNN-based mood mining through IoT-based physiological sensors observation. Proceedings of the Korean Society of Information Sciences Academic Presentation. 2017; pp. 1301–1303.

55. Ahmad E. Meezaj: An interactive system for real-time mood measurement and reflection based on internet of things. Int J Adv Comput Sci Appl. 2020; 11:1–18.

56.   Pandey PS. Machine learning and IoT for prediction and detection of stress. Proceedings of the 2017 17th International Conference on Computational Science and its Applications (ICCSA); 03-06 July 2017, Trieste, Italy.

57.   Fu Y, Liu J. System design for wearable blood oxygen saturation and pulse measurement device. Procedia Manuf. 2015; 3:1187–1194.

58.   Agustine L. Heart rate monitoring device for arrhythmia using pulse oximeter sensor based on android. Proceedings of the 2018 International Conference on Computer Engineering, Network and Intelligent Multimedia (CENIM). 06–27 November 2018, Surabaya, Indonesia.

59   Von Chong A, Terosiet M, Histace A, Romain O. Towards a novel single-LED pulse oximeter based on a multispectral sensor for IoT applications. Microelectron J. 2019; 88:128–136.

60.   Larson EC. SpiroSmart: using a microphone to measure lung function on a mobile phone. Proceedings of the 2012ACM Conference on Ubiquitous Computing. 15 September 2012, New York, NY, USA.

61.   Li B, Dong Q, Downen RS, Tran N, Hunter Jackson J, Pillai D, et. al. A wearable IoT aldehyde sensor for pediatric asthma research and management. Sens Actuators B Chem. 2019; 287:584–594.

62.   Gurbeta L, Badnjevic A, Maksimovic M, Omanovic-Miklicanin E, Sejdic E. A telehealth system for automated diagnosis of asthma and chronic obstructive pulmonary disease. J Am Med Inform Assoc. 2018; 25(9):1213–1217.

63.   Gundu S. A novel IoT-based solution for monitoring and alerting bronchial asthma patients. Int J Res Eng, Sci Manag. 2020; 3(10):120–123.

64.   AL-Ja TG, Al-Hemiary EH. Internet of Things based cloud smart monitoring for asthma patients. Qalaai Zanist J. 2017; 2:359–364.

65.   Prasad AK. SMART asthma alert using IoT and predicting threshold values using decision tree classifier. Applications of Internet of @ings. Berlin, Germany: Springer; 2020. pp.141–150.

66.   Hui CY, Mckinstry B, Fulton O, Buchner M, Pinnock H. What features do patients and clinicians 'want' in the future Internet-Of-Things (IoT) systems for asthma: a mixed method study. Eur Respir J. 2020; 56.

67.   Shreyas A. IoT-enabled medicine bottle. Emerging Research in Computing, Information, Communication and Applications. Berlin, Germany: Springer; 2019. pp. 127–139.

68.   Bharadwaj SA. Enhancing healthcare using m-care box(monitoring non-compliance of medication. Proceedings of the 2017 International Conference on I-SMAC (IoT in Social, Mobile, Analytics and Cloud) (I-SMAC). 2017. 10–11 February 2017, Coimbatore, India.

69.   Medina J, Espinilla M, Garcia-Fernandez AL, Martinez L. Intelligent multi-dose medication controller for fever: from wearable devices to remote dispensers. Comput Electr Eng. 2018; 65:400–412.

70.   Chacko A, Hayajneh T. Security and privacy issues with IoT in healthcare. EAI Endorsed Trans Pervasive Health Technol. 2018; 4(14).

71.   Shah R, Chircu A. IoT and AI in healthcare: A systematic literature review. Issues Inf Syst. 2018; 19(3).

72. Zgheib R, Conchon E, Bastide R. Semantic middleware architectures for IoT healthcare applications. Enhanced Living Environments. Cham, Switzerland: Springer. 2019; pp. 263–294.
73. Jabbar S, Ullah F, Khalid S, Khan M, Han K. Semantic interoperability in heterogeneous IoT infrastructure for healthcare. Wirel Comm Mob Comput. 2017; 1:1–10.
74. Bhatt C, Dey N, Ashour AS, eds. Internet of Things and Big Data Technologies for Next Generation Healthcare. Springer: 2017.

Index